THE HASKINS SOCIETY JOURNAL

STUDIES IN MEDIEVAL HISTORY

The Charles Homer Haskins Society
Officers and Councillors for 2001

THE HASKINS SOCIETY JOURNAL

STUDIES IN MEDIEVAL HISTORY

EDITED BY STEPHEN MORILLO

Volume 10

2001

THE BOYDELL PRESS

First published 2002
The Boydell Press, Woodbridge

ISBN 0 85115 911 7

ISSN 0963–4959

The Boydell Press is an imprint of Boydell & Brewer Ltd
PO Box 9, Woodbridge, Suffolk IP12 3DF, UK
and of Boydell & Brewer Inc.
PO Box 41026, Rochester, NY 14604–4126, USA
website: www.boydell.co.uk

A catalogue record for this book is available
from the British Library

This publication is printed on acid-free paper

Printed in Great Britain by
Antony Rowe Ltd, Chippenham, Wiltshire

Contents

Illustrations

Editor's Note

This volume of the *Haskins Society Journal* includes papers read at the 19th Annual Conference of the Charles Homer Haskins Society at Cornell University in October 2000 and at other conferences in the year following the Haskins. The papers by Judith Green and Sir James Holt were featured papers at the Haskins Conference; the latter was the Warren Hollister Memorial Lecture. The papers by Shashi Jayakumar and Jennifer Paxton shared the 2000 Bethell Prize, which was judged by Janet Loengard.

This volume, my first as editor, appears on time, as will subsequent volumes based on 'submission years' starting roughly with each Haskins Conference. Subscribers will note that this volume, number 10, follows number 9 in order of publication but not in order of subscription year. Three volumes that come between number 9 and this one in terms of subscription year are in process, and will appear as quickly as possible around the regularly scheduled volumes; all volumes will be numbered sequentially. Apologies are again due to subscribers and above all to contributors to these late volumes; I hope this volume stands as partial assurance that work is now proceeding speedily on the backlog of late volumes. I would like to thank the members of the Haskins Board for assistance with the refereeing of submissions and Lynne Miles-Morillo for assistance with copy editing. I will also thank Richard Abels in advance for assuming the position of Assistant Editor to help with the late volumes.

The *Haskins Society Journal* is an international refereed journal, and its contents are not limited to papers read at the Society's own conference or at the sessions which it sponsors elsewhere. Papers on the history of England and its neighbors in the Central Middle Ages are welcome from anyone. Authors intending to submit are asked to write for guidelines and style sheets: contact Dr Stephen Morillo, Department of History, Wabash College, Crawfordsville, IN 47933, USA; email: morillos@wabash.edu. Information is also available at the Haskins Society website at www.haskins.cornell.edu.

Stephen Morillo, Editor

Abbreviations

A.H.R.	*American Historical Review*
A.N.S.	*Anglo-Norman Studies (formerly Proceedings of the Battle Conference on Anglo-Norman Studies)*
A.S.C.	Anglo-Saxon Chronicle; normally cited from *Two of the Saxon Chronicles Parallel*, ed. Charles Plummer (2 vols., Oxford, 1892–9), with year and MS
A.S.E.	*Anglo-Saxon England*
B.A.R.	British Archaeological Reports
Bk. of Fees	*Liber feodorum: The Book of Fees, commonly called Testa de Nevill* (3 vols., London, 1920–31)
B.L.	British Library, London
Bracton	*Bracton on the Laws and Customs of England*, ed. and trans. Samuel E. Thorne (4 vols., Cambridge, MA, 1968–77)
Bracton's Note Book	*Bracton's Note Book: A Collection of Cases decided in the King's Courts during the Reign of Henry the Third*, ed. F.W. Maitland (3 vols., London, 1887)
Cal. Chart. R.	*Calendar of the Charter Rolls, 1226–1516* (6 vols., London, 1903–27)
Cal. Docs. France, ed. Round	*Calendar of Documents preserved in France illustrative of the History of Great Britain and Ireland, I: A.D. 918–1206*, ed. J.H. Round (London, 1899)
Cal. Lib. R.	*Calendar of the Liberate Rolls preserved in the Public Record Office* (6 vols., H.M.S.O., 1917–64)
Cal. Pat.	*Calendar of the Patent Rolls preserved in the Public Record Office* (London, 1891 and in progress)
Camb. Hist. Jnl.	*Cambridge Historical Journal*
Close R.	*Close Rolls of the Reign of Henry III preserved in the Public Record Office* (14 vols., London, 1902–38)
Complete Peerage	*G.E. C[okayne], The Complete Peerage of England, Scotland, Ireland, Great Britain, and the United Kingdom, Extant, Extinct, and Dormant*, new edn. by V. Gibbs and others (12 vols. in 13, London, 1910–59)
Cur. Reg. R.	*Curia Regis Rolls preserved in the Public Record Office* (17 vols., in progress, London, 1922–91)

D.B.	*Domesday Book, seu liber censualis Wilhelmi primi regis Angliae*, [ed. Abraham Farley] (2 vols., London, 1783)
D.N.B.	*Dictionary of National Biography*, ed. Leslie Stephens and Stephen Lee
Eadmer, *H.N.*	Eadmer, *Historia Novorum*, ed. M. Rule (R.S., 81, London, 1884)
Ec.H.R.	*Economic History Review*
EETS	Early English Text Society
E.H.D.	*English Historical Documents, I: c. 500–1042*, ed. Dorothy Whitelock (2nd edn., London, 1979); *II: 1042–1189*, ed. David C. Douglas and George W. Greenaway (2nd edn., London, 1981); *III: 11891327, ed. Harry Rothwell* (London, 1975)
E.H.R.	*English Historical Review*
E.M.E.	*Early Medieval Europe*
E.Y.C.	*Early Yorkshire Charters*, ed. W. Farrer and C.T. Clay (13 vols.: vols. i–iii, Edinburgh, 1914–16; index to vols. i–iii, and vols. iv–xii, Yorkshire Archaeological Society Record Series., Extra ser., 1–10 [1935–65])
Gesta Stephani	*Gesta Stephani*, ed. K.R. Potter and revised R.H.C. Davis (Oxford, 1976)
Glanvill	*The Treatise on the Laws and Customs of the Realm of England commonly called Glanvill*, ed. and trans. G.D.G. Hall (London, 1965)
G.N.D., ed. van Houts	*The Gesta Normannum Ducum of William of Jumièges, Orderic Vitalis, and Robert of Torigni*, ed. and trans. Elisabeth M.C. van Houts (2 vols., Oxford, 19925)
Henry of Huntingdon, *Historia*	Henry, Archdeacon of Huntingdon, *Historia Anglorum: the History of the English People*, ed. and trans. Diana Greenway (Oxford, 1996)
Hist. Res.	*Historical Research* (formerly *Bulletin of the Institute of Historical Research*)
H.S.J.	*Haskins Society Journal*
J.M.H.	*Journal of Medieval History*
Jnl. Eccl. Hist.	*Journal of Ecclesiastical History*
John of Worcester, *Chronicle*	*The Chronicle of John of Worcester,* ed. J.R.H. Weaver (Oxford, 1908)
M.G.H.	Monumenta Germaniae Historica
MS./MSS.	Manuscript/Manuscripts
Orderic, *Eccl. Hist.*	*The Ecclesiastical History of Orderic Vitalis*, ed. Marjorie Chibnall (6 vols., Oxford, 1969–80)

P. & P.	*Past and Present*
P.B.A.	*Proceedings of the British Academy*
Pipe R.	*The Great Roll of the Pipe* (Pipe Roll Society), with regnal year
P.L.	*Patrologia latina cursus completus*, ed. J.-P. Migne (221 vols., Paris, 1844–64)
P.R.O.	Public Record Office, Kew, London
Rec. Com.	Record Commissioners
Recueil, ed. Fauroux	*Recueil des actes des ducs de Normandie de 911 à 1066*, ed. M. Fauroux (Caen, 1961)
Regesta	*Regesta regum Anglo-Normannorum, 1066–1154*, ed. H.W.C. Davis and others (4 vols., Oxford, 1913–69)
Rot. de Lib.	*Rotuli de liberate ac de misis et praestitis, regnante Johanne*, ed. T.D. Hardy (Rec. Com., 1844)
Rot. Hund.	*Rotuli hundredorum temp. Hen. III & Edw. I*, ed. W. Illingworth and J. Caley (2 vols., London, 1812–18)
Rot. Litt. Claus.	*Rotuli litterarum clausarum in turri Londinensi asservati, 1204–27*, ed. T.D. Hardy (2 vols., Rec. Com., 1833–44)
Rot. Litt. Pat.	*Rotuli litterarum patentium in Turri Londinensi asservati (1201–16)*, ed. T.D. Hardy (Rec. Com., 1835)
R.S.	Rolls Series
Sawyer, *Charters*	P.H. Sawyer, *Anglo-Saxon Charters: An Annotated List and Bibliography* (London, 1968), with charter number
s.a.	*sub anno/annis* [under the year/–s]
ser.	series
Settimane	*Settimane di Studio del Centro Italiano di Studi sull'Alto Medioevo*
Soc.	Society
Stubbs, *Charters*	*Select Charters and Other Illustrations of English Constitutional History from the Earliest Times to the Reign of Edward the First*, ed. William Stubbs (9th edn., revised H.W.C. Davis, Oxford, 1913)
s.v.	*sub verbo*
Symeon, *Opera*	*Symeonis monachi opera omnia*, ed. Thomas Arnold (R.S., 75, 2 vols., London, 1882–5)
T.R.H.S.	*Transactions of the Royal Historical Society*
Univ.	University
unpub.	unpublished
V.C.H.	*The Victoria History of the Counties of England* (in progress), with name of county

William of Malmesbury, *G.P.*	*Willelmi Malmesbiriensis monachi de gestis pontificum Anglorum libri quinque*, ed. N.E.S.A. Hamilton, R.S. 52 (London, 1870)
William of Malmesbury, *G.R.*	William of Malmesbury, *Gesta regum Anglorum*, ed. and trans. R.A.B. Mynors, R.M. Thomson, and M. Winterbottom (Oxford, 1998)
William of Malmesbury, *H.N.*	William of Malmesbury, *Historia novella*, ed. K.R. Potter (London, 1955)

1

The Piety and Patronage of Henry I[1]

Judith A. Green

When Robert of Torigny came to compose his obituary of Henry I, he gave the king credit for the generosity he showed to the church by founding religious houses and by pouring out money on building, not just in his own realms but abroad: he paid for a good deal of the church at Cluny, for the monastery of Saint-Martin-des-Champs at Paris, the domestic buildings of the monks of Tiron, the completion of the leper hospital at Chartres, the building of a road through the Alps for pilgrims, for the crusading orders (the Templars and Hospitallers), and for the rebuilding of the cathedral at Evreux, though this was admittedly in reparation for damage caused by his own army.[2] By contrast this chronicler, like others who wrote in the early twelfth century, said virtually nothing about the king's piety. This silence may be variously interpreted: that his piety was taken for granted; that its character aroused certain misgivings; or perhaps that the less that was written, the better.

Twentieth-century historians were not as reticent. Sir Richard Southern, with whom the history of the reign in modern times really began, believed that the king experienced two periods of spiritual crisis, the first after the death of his heir Prince William in the wreck of the White Ship, and the second between 1129 and 1131 when the prospects for the succession seemed unusually bleak. Southern suggested there was a natural alliance of interests between the king and the monastic houses. 'He could give them security; they could give him their prayers and their good opinion.' This was a king who in his last years 'was oppressed by the weight of his sins and the sense of hostility to his exactions. The flow of his monastic benefactions became a flood as the shadows lengthened . . . after his death, a monk of Bec saw him in a vision thrust into hell each morning and rescued by the prayers of the monks each evening.'[3] The image

---

[1] I should like to thank members of the Haskins Society Conference for the stimulating discussion which followed this paper, Mathieu Arnoux and Véronique Gazeau for their advice on the Norman church, and Ian Green, who examined the manuscript cited in note 3 below.

[2] Robert of Torigny, in *G.N.D.*, ed. van Houts, ii, 252.

[3] 'The Place of Henry I in English History', *P.B.A.*, 48 (1962), 155. The vision of the monk of Bec occurs in a composite manuscript, Cambridge University Library MS. Ff. i, 27, 217. This is a Parkerian Manuscript, 642 folio pages; of treatises of different periods; part one comprising the first eighteen items is no later than the thirteenth century; part two no earlier than the fourteenth century.

conjured up is congruent with the illustrations in the well-known illustrations inserted into the Worcester chronicle of the nightmares of Henry I.[4] Martin Brett evinced a certain scepticism about the first of these crises;[5] otherwise there has been little comment, though the subject is certainly important for a biographer. The first part of this paper therefore considers what may be said of the king's piety, before moving on to discuss the better-documented topic of his religious patronage.

Contemporaries make only chance allusions to Henry's piety. He is said to have approved of the feast of the Immaculate Conception, for instance, which was celebrated at Reading Abbey.[6] In 1118 he ordered his army not to fight on the feast of the Invention of the Holy Cross, though his order was disobeyed.[7] In 1113, on a visit to the abbey of Saint Evroul, he carried out an inspection of the monks according to Orderic Vitalis, who was probably present. Liking what he saw, he granted a charter to the abbey and was received into confraternity.[8] He was said to have been particularly attached to Abbot Boso of Bec, visiting the abbot frequently in his final illness and sitting at his bedside.[9] We know that he was present at the dedication of the abbey church at St Albans in 1115[10] and at similar services of dedication at Sées in 1126,[11] at Christ Church Canterbury, and at Rochester, both in 1130.[12] In 1124 he was present when the relics of St Romanus were exhibited at Rouen.[13] Toward the end of his life he probably visited Bury, perhaps as a penitent.[14] He may have touched for the king's evil,[15] and we know the name of one of his confessors, Adelulf, prior of Nostell and first bishop of Carlisle.[16]

There is, too, the account of the king's pious end, described in a letter by an eyewitness, Hugh, archbishop of Rouen: the king made his confession, received

[4] Oxford, Corpus Christi College MS. 157, 382–3.
[5] M. Brett, *The English Church under Henry I* (Oxford, 1975), 112 n. 4.
[6] *The Letters of Osbert of Clare*, ed. and trans. E.W. Williamson (Oxford, 1929), no. 7.
[7] Orderic, *Eccl. Hist.,* vi, 182.
[8] Orderic, *Eccl. Hist.,* vi, 174–6.
[9] Robert of Torigny, *G.N.D.*, ed. van Houts, ii, 254–5.
[10] *Regesta*, ii, no. 1102; *Gesta Abbatum Sancti Albani*, i, 71, in *Chronica Monasterii S. Albani*, ed. H.T. Riley (12 vols., R.S., 1865–76).
[11] Orderic, *Eccl. Hist.,* vi, 366.
[12] A.S.C. E 1130; Gervase of Canterbury, *Actus Pontificum: The Historical Works of Gervase of Canterbury*, ed. W. Stubbs (2 vols., R.S., 1879–80), i, 381–2.
[13] Rouen, Archives Départementales de la Seine Inférieure, G. 3666.
[14] John of Worcester, *Chronicle,* iii, 202; *Regesta*, ii, no. 1733.
[15] F. Barlow, *Edward the Confessor* (London, 1970), 270–71. William of Malmesbury wrote that the French said Edward the Confessor had touched for the king's evil (by which he understood leprosy) when he was a young man in Normandy, and that some claimed that the power was an hereditary royal prerogative, not the product of holiness: William of Malmesbury, *G.R.,* i, 406–8. Barlow suggested that this may have been a response to the comment by Guibert of Nogent that the English kings had not attempted to effect cures, unlike Philip I and Louis VI, *P.L.,* clvi, 616.
[16] Robert of Torigny, *Chronicle, Chronicles of the Reigns of Stephen, Henry II, Richard I*, ed. R. Howlett (4 vols., R.S., 1884–9), i, 123.

absolution, received the sacrament, and distributed alms.[17] A similar account appears in Orderic: the king confessed his sins first to his chaplains and then to the archbishop; he revoked sentences of forfeiture; he arranged for the payment of his servants, knights, and debtors; he instructed that his body was to be taken to Reading; he implored all to devote themselves to peace and protection of the poor, made his confession, received absolution, was anointed, and received the sacrament.[18] Now, there is nothing to say that the king's death did not take place in this way, but it is conspicuously the account of a 'good death' and closely parallels that of Louis VI described by Abbot Suger.[19] Nor are there any of the harrowing details of the (seemingly) gastric disorder that carried Henry off.

Finally, we must not forget the later twelfth-century life of the Somerset hermit, Wulfric of Haselbury, which however probably tells us more about the preoccupations of the hagiographer than about Henry I. Wulfric was falsely accused of hoarding the king's treasure; his accuser was inflicted with paralysis and only cured by Wulfric after the personal intervention of the king and queen.[20] The miracle showed the saint's power to punish a man of high social status and then his power to lift the punishment. On a later occasion Wulfric prophesied that if the king crossed to Normandy he would not return. The prophecy reached the king's ears and he checked its authorship. Although shaken, Henry did actually cross the Channel – and it was, of course, to be his last crossing.[21] Neither of these incidents was known to Henry of Huntingdon who inserted a short account of Wulfric in the *Historia Anglorum*.[22] Perhaps both did occur, but one may see how the first conformed to the idea of a saintly figure, able to punish his detractors, and the second to the saint's prophetic vision.

Up to this point, therefore, the comments that were made about Henry's piety suggest that it was conventional rather than exceptional: nothing is said about how often he attended mass. We do not know how he felt about ritual, but he evidently saw the wisdom of attending solemn dedication ceremonies, and he had a personal confessor. By comparing what contemporaries said about him with comments on his first wife, Queen Matilda, his father, and his brothers, we gain a sharper focus. Queen Matilda was a 'woman of exceptional holiness', who wore a hair shirt and went barefoot in Lent. She washed the feet of lepers, she loved sacred music, and she was generous to the church. She was buried at Westminster where 'her spirit showed by not insubstantial signs that it dwelt in Heaven'.[23] Her major project was the Augustinian priory of Holy Trinity, Aldgate, and, amongst others, a leper hospital at Saint Giles, Holborn, both just

---

17 William of Malmesbury, *H.N.*, 24–6.

18 Orderic, *Eccl. Hist.*, vi, 448.

19 Suger, *Vie de Louis VI le Gros*, ed. H. Waquet (Paris, 1929), 282–4.

20 John of Ford, *The Life of Wulfric of Haselbury*, ed. M. Bell (Somerset Record Society, 1933), 63–5.

21 *The Life of Wulfric of Haselbury*, 116–17.

22 The only miracle known to Henry was that of the cutting of the hauberk, Henry of Huntingdon, *Historia*, 696–7.

23 William of Malmesbury, *G.R.*, i, 754–8.

outside the city wall of London.[24] If the Conqueror's mark on the city had been the building of castles, especially the White Tower, and Rufus had built what was probably the largest stone hall in Europe at Westminster, then 'good Queen Maud' had added a church and a hospital.

The Anglo-Saxon Chronicler apostrophized William the Conqueror as 'gentle to the good men who loved God' and stern to everyone else, and he then continued by describing the king's foundation at Battle and the numbers of monks in the country before elaborating the sternness showed to others. William of Malmesbury rephrased the Anglo-Saxon Chronicler's verdict of 'gentle to the good men who loved God' as 'humble to the servants who loved God', and he continued that the Conqueror had been a practising Christian 'as far as a layman could be' who attended mass, vespers, and matins every day, a useful comment on what might be expected of a devout layman. The author went on to describe the Conqueror's generosity to the church, his advancement of Lanfranc, and the depositions of Mauger and Stigand from the archbishoprics of Rouen and Canterbury respectively.[25]

Little positive was said about Robert Curthose by early twelfth-century chroniclers based in England or Normandy who were writing with the benefit of hindsight after Robert's defeat in 1106. He was stigmatized as a duke who had failed in his duty to protect the church and the people of Normandy.[26] Worst of all, however, was the indictment of Rufus, especially by Eadmer: Rufus was an irreligious, profane, vainglorious man who did not believe in the power of saints and who was sceptical about ordeals and showed leniency to the Jews.[27] In each case the authors were painting stylized portraits, but a comparison of what is said in each case makes the silences about Henry eloquent. It would therefore seem reasonable to conclude that his attendance at divine service, unremarked, was unremarkable. The chroniclers did not praise his piety or ignore his concupiscence, but Henry did not attract the opprobrium of Rufus, either for the dissolute morals of his court or for fiscal exploitation of the church.

Was Henry so weighed down by a sense of sin and personal misfortune as to experience two spiritual crises, one following the wreck of the White Ship in 1120, the second between 1129 and 1131 when his daughter's marriage, and with it the chance of grandsons, fell apart? Southern's suggestion was made on the basis of royal writs and charters issued in favour of various churches and

[24] The best study of Matilda currently available is by Lois Huneycutt, '"*Proclaiming her dignity abroad*": The Literary and Artistic Patronage of Matilda of Scotland, Queen of England, 1100–1118', *The Cultural Patronage of Medieval Women*, ed. June Hall McCash (Athens, GA, 1996), 155–74.

[25] William of Malmesbury, *G.R.*, i, 492–500.

[26] This view was expressed most vehemently by Orderic, who portrayed Henry as the saviour of the church and people of Normandy from Robert: Orderic, *Eccl. Hist.*, iv, 114–15; vi, 62. It is found, too, in William of Malmesbury, *G.R.*, i, 700–6; for discussion see Judith A. Green, 'Robert Curthose Reassessed', *A.N.S.*, 22 (1999), 95–116.

[27] Eadmer, *H.N.*, 99–103; for discussion see E. Mason, 'William Rufus: Myth and Reality', *J.M.H.*, 3 (1977), 1–21.

churchmen on both sides of the Channel.[28] There are, however, at least three considerations that need to be borne in mind. The first is that there is likely to have been an upsurge in such grants for England after the king's return at the end of 1120 after an absence of over four years. There are clearly flurries of documentation at certain points in the reign. Secondly, it is not easy in general to distinguish between new grants (or specifically when these were made) and confirmations. Thirdly, it is often not easy to be certain about the authenticity of surviving texts.[29]

The restoration of the manor of Pytchley in Northamptonshire to Peterborough Abbey, for instance, turns out not to have been a new grant, but reflected the abbey's concern to recover the manor, which had been leased to the royal justice Geoffrey Ridel who had drowned in the White Ship.[30] A series of writs and charters for Westminster Abbey was issued in 1121 and 1122. The context here was the appointment in 1121 of a new abbot who sought to put his house in order and to recover lost lands and rights. Nevertheless the community seems to have taken the opportunity to win some recognition of a special relationship from the king.[31]

A third example is the grant of the valuable manor of King's Clere in Hampshire to Archbishop Geoffrey of Rouen, one of two or possibly three recorded grants of patronage.[32] The grant of King's Clere, which the editors of *Regesta Regum Anglo-Normannorum* assigned to 1121, may in fact have dated to 1115,

[28] 'Place of Henry I', 163-4.

[29] These two points are brought together in the case of a confirmation for the priory of Notre Dame du Pré (Bonne Nouvelle), just outside Rouen. Parts of Henry's corpse were buried there, and he is said to have built a hunting lodge where he preferred to stay rather than in the city, Robert of Torigny, in *G.N.D.*, ed. van Houts, ii, 252; Orderic, *Eccl. Hist.*, vi, 450; Stephen of Rouen, *Draco Normannicus, Chronicles of the Reigns of Stephen, Henry II and Richard I*, ed. Howlett, ii, 713. Yet the surviving text of Henry's confirmation, allegedly granted in 1122, 'the twenty-first year of his reign', is thought not to have been written in an early twelfth-century hand, and the names of two witnesses as well as the regnal year, are incompatible with a date of 1121. Henri Chanteux suggested that the text may have been based on a genuine surviving original revised in the late twelfth century, 'Recueil des actes de Henri Ier Beauclerc', unpublished thèse pour le diplôme paléographe, copy deposited in Paris, Ecole des Chartes, 1932, ii, 596–8. In addition to the (possibly) late twelfth-century text, two seventeenth-century copies were listed by Chanteux, Paris, Bibliothèque Nationale, MS. nouv. acq. latines, 1245, fols. 35, 37. I should like to thank M. le Directeur de l'Ecole des Chartes for permission to consult the thesis. There are problems of authenticity in the case of a charter of liberties for Holy Trinity, Aldgate which the king was said to have issued at this time, though again it would be surprising if the priory had not pressed for such a grant on the king's first return to England after the death of his wife: *Regesta*, ii, no. 1316; see further P. Chaplais, 'The Seals and Original Charters of Henry I', *E.H.R.*, 75 (1960), 260–75, at 275.

[30] For Peterborough's land at Pytchley in 1086, see *D.B.*, i, fol. 222; *The Peterborough Chronicle of Hugh Candidus*, ed. W.T. Mellows (Oxford, 1949), 88–9, 99.

[31] E. Mason, 'Westminster Abbey and the Monarchy between the reign of William I and John (1066–1216)', *Jnl. Eccl. Hist.*, 41 (1990), 199–216, at 209–10.

[32] For the manor of Bentworth see *Regesta*, ii, no. 1127. The lordship of Douvrend was apparently a restoration: *Regesta*, ii, no. 1234; Fauroux, nos. 10, 66, 67.

when the archbishop was in England.[33] Bishop Bernard of St David's, who witnessed the charter, was consecrated on 19 September 1115.[34] The archbishop witnessed a royal charter with the queen and Prince William, by which the king confirmed Bishop Bernard in his see.[35] Archbishop Geoffrey was head of the Norman church; he played a key part in Henry's rule in Normandy; he was an active diplomat and a keen advocate of reform of the clergy in Normandy, a cause dear to Henry's heart.[36] He had also probably been present after Christmas 1114 when the king had presented his heir to the Norman barons who had made oaths of allegiance to the prince.[37] Henry therefore had good reason to boost the archbishop's wealth around this time.

Henry probably did issue a foundation charter for Merton Priory in 1121, though again there are problems with the text as it stands.[38] The community had come into being several years earlier and had moved into its accommodation in 1117;[39] the timing of the royal charter was presumably another case where the canons pressed their case when the king returned to England. The king however was (somewhat reluctantly) persuaded to augment the original site at Merton given by Gilbert the sheriff, with a grant of the whole royal manor.[40] This act may have been associated with the king's sense of personal loss, for Queen Matilda was said to have taken a special interest in the nascent community, and to have taken Prince William there.[41]

Nostell and Carlisle were two communities for which the king did take important initiatives in 1121 and 1122, but these should be seen in the context of his concern with the north and his visit to Carlisle in 1122. There had been hermits living for some years on the Lacy honour of Pontefract near Nostell when a decision was taken to convert the community into an Augustinian priory. Archbishop Thurstan was involved when he was finally allowed to enter his archdiocese in 1121; the first prior was Adelulf, Henry's confessor, and the plan evidently was that Nostell was to become an important focus for the

[33] *Regesta*, ii, no. 1289.
[34] Eadmer, *H.N.*, 235–6; *Councils and Synods with other Documents relating to the English Church*, I, pt ii, *1066–1154*, ed. D. Whitelock, M. Brett, and C.N.L. Brooke (Oxford, 1981), 709–10.
[35] *Regesta*, ii, no. 1091.
[36] For Archbishop Geoffrey, see David S. Spear, 'Geoffrey Brito, Archbishop of Rouen (1111–28)', *H.S.J.*, 2 (1990), 123–37; *Des clercs au service de la réforme: études et documents sur les chanoines réguliers de la province de Rouen*, sous la direction de M. Arnoux, Bibliotheca Victorina, xi (Paris, 2000), 54–5.
[37] A.S.C. E 1115; Henry of Huntingdon, *Historia*, 460.
[38] *Regesta*, ii, no. 1301; J. H. Round, *Geoffrey de Mandeville* (London, 1892), 433-4 for the comment that although the names on the witness list were consistent with the date, 'all else is fatally bad'.
[39] M.L. Colker, 'Latin Texts concerning Gilbert, founder of Merton Priory', *Studia Monastica,* 12 (1970), 241–71, at 250, 252.
[40] 'Latin Texts', 254–6.
[41] 'Latin Texts', 252.

regeneration of religious life in the north.[42] At Carlisle a man named Walter the priest was in charge of the local churches and, probably in 1122 when Henry visited Carlisle and strengthened the castle there, the first steps were taken to use the endowments of these churches for a new Augustinian priory.[43] At Carlisle as at Sées, as Mathieu Arnoux has pointed out, an Augustinian priory was to be the format for a cathedral chapter, in each case on the frontiers of Henry's realms.[44]

The foundation of Reading Abbey was therefore Henry's major new initiative in 1121. There can be no doubt about Henry's grief at the loss of his heir, whose body had no grave, and, as Pauline Stafford has recently reminded us, his hopes for a fruitful second marriage spurred him on to action.[45] The project may already have been in view, however.[46] Henry had probably already been funding the costs of building the great abbey church at Cluny.[47] There may have been a scheme to take over the Cluniac priory of Montacute founded either by Robert, count of Mortain or his son William, whom Henry had disinherited and imprisoned.[48] Notwithstanding any earlier plans, Henry now decided to go for a new foundation. He had been generous to the Augustinians and to newer communities such as the Savigniacs and the Tironensians, but he had not as yet made a grand gesture of his own. One was surely on the cards, however. His father had founded Saint Stephen's Caen and Battle Abbey, and his mother Holy Trinity at Caen, and Henry was generous to all of these.[49]

---

[42] D. Nicholl, *Thurstan, Archbishop of York (1111–40)* (York, 1964), 127–37.

[43] J.C. Dickinson, 'The Origins of Carlisle Cathedral', *Transactions of the Cumberland and Westmorland Antiquarian and Archaeological Society,* 45 (1946), 134–43; *Regesta,* ii, no. 1491 (where a date of 1127 is suggested); Nicholl, *Thurstan,* 140–41.

[44] *Des clercs au service de la réforme,* 39–55.

[45] P. Stafford, 'Cherchez la femme: Queens, Queens' Lands and Nunneries: Missing Links in the foundation of Reading Abbey', *History,* 85 (2000), 1–27.

[46] *Reading Abbey Cartularies,* ed. B. R. Kemp, Camden Society, 4th ser. xxxi, xxxiii, (2 vols., 1986–7), i, 14.

[47] Henry was later remembered as one of the chief patrons, as Abbot Peter the Venerable recalled, *The Letters of Peter the Venerable,* ed. G. Constable (Cambridge, MA, 1967), no. 89.

[48] D. Knowles, C.N.L. Brooke, and V. London, *Heads of Religious Houses in England and Wales, 940–1216* (Cambridge, 1972), 121; C.N.L. Brooke, 'Kings and Princes as Patrons of Monasteries', *Il Monachesimo e lo riforma ecclesiastica (1049–1122), Settimana di studio,* 4th Passo della Mendola, 1968. *Miscellanea del Centro di studi medioevali,* vi (Milan, 1971), 125–44, at 127.

[49] Henry's principal gift to St Stephen's, in 1101 or 1102, was the manor of Burton Bradstock, given in return for the regalia which his father had deposited in the abbey: *Regesta,* ii, no. 601. Subsequently there followed a stream of documents mainly confirming grants: nos. 764, 1184, 1188, 1215, 1341, 1352, 1575, 1593, 1600–1, 1672, 1702, 1907, 1926–7; for Battle there are some forty-one texts listed (not all authentic), and in the *Chronicle of Battle Abbey* the king was remembered as a patron, see *The Chronicle of Battle Abbey,* ed. and trans. Eleanor Searle (Oxford, 1980), 108, 118, 122–4. Holy Trinity received the munificent gift of Tilshead. This gift occurred may have occurred earlier in the reign than indicated by the editors of *Regesta,* ii, nos. 1692, 1928. For the suggestion that it may have been given in exchange for land which Henry had decided to give to Bernard de Balliol, see *Charters and Custumals of the Abbey of Holy Trinity, Caen,* ed. M. Chibnall, Records of Social and Economic History, new ser. v (British Academy, 1982), xxvi–xxviii.

Henry conceived a church planned on a large scale, probably envisaged from the first as his own final resting place, with a community organised along lines acceptable to reformed thinking. Its endowment with the lands of three religious houses, Reading, Cholsey, and Leominster, which either had decayed or could be thus represented, was an act of restitution. In all this there were undoubtedly motives of grief, penance (what have I done wrong to deserve this?), and passionate hope for the birth of a new heir. Yet we should be careful not to associate the foundation of Reading too closely with the idea of a spiritual crisis in the sense of a crisis of belief or a retreat from the world. What is after all remarkable about Henry's actions from Christmas 1120 is how quickly he was back in business. His marriage, probably already negotiated, was hastened on: the wedding took place only a few weeks after the shipwreck. The king kept himself busy dealing with matters of state, and he made expeditions to Wales and to the north to restore royal authority after a long absence.

The second period of crisis Henry was alleged to have experienced was in 1130 and 1131, and was accompanied by gifts to Fontevraud and Cluny. Henry's generosity, especially to the Cluniacs, went far beyond recorded gifts of land and revenue. There were three overlapping considerations: first, to ensure that the Angevin alliance worked; secondly, the king's attachment to the Cluniacs and, thirdly, to ensure that both Pope Innocent II and Louis VI remained allies. The king could afford to be generous and almost certainly was thinking about his latter days; generosity was not necessarily the outcome of crisis so much as a symbol of Henry's power and magnanimity.

The abbey of Fontevraud in Anjou had come into being as a community of men and women under the charismatic leadership of Robert of Arbrissel.[50] It soon developed into a house for women, especially women of aristocratic birth, and it had been particularly favoured by the counts of Anjou. Count Fulk had been a persistent enemy of Henry I, and Henry's plan to neutralize that enmity through the marriage of Prince William to Fulk's daughter Matilda had been scuppered by William's death. Matilda had eventually returned from England to Anjou without the lands, towns and castles promised on marriage, much to her father's annoyance. The envoys he had sent to England in 1123 had returned empty-handed.[51] Fulk in anger had been persuaded to bestow another daughter, Sybil, on William Clito, Henry's nephew, a match which had been successfully scotched at Rome for falling within the prohibited degrees.[52]

Henry's revival of the project of an alliance, this time between his widowed daughter Matilda and the count's son Geoffrey would, from Henry's perspective, neutralize the threat of a coalition between the Angevins, Louis VI, and William Clito, and it also chimed with Fulk's plan to leave France and travel to

---

[50] Jean-Marc Bienvenu, *L'Etonnant fondateur de Fontevraud Robert d'Arbrissel* (Paris, 1981).
[51] A.S.C. E 1123.
[52] The legate John of Crema was thought to have been instrumental here. See S. Burton Hicks, 'The Anglo-Papal Bargain of 1125: The Legatine Mission of John of Crema', *Albion,* 8 (1976), 301–10.

the Holy Land to marry the daughter of the king of Jerusalem who had no sons to succeed him. The marriage took time to negotiate, because Henry was obviously concerned to ensure that Anjou would pass safely to Fulk's son Geoffrey, but in May 1128 Fulk took the cross, the wedding took place in June, and Fulk left for Jerusalem. A generous gift by Henry to Fontevraud was thus an act of piety; it may have been implicitly restitution for Matilda of Anjou's dowry; and it was a sign of commitment to the Angevin alliance. The first gift (a generous one hundred pounds each year from the mint at Rouen, thirty marks from the farm of London, and twenty from the farm of Winchester) was probably made soon after the marriage; a charter was drawn up and a version taken to the empress in Anjou.[53] The grant may not have been activated before the marriage collapsed, however, and the empress returned to Normandy.

Henry was as generous to the Templars as he was to Fontevraud.[54] In 1128 the master of the Templars, Hugh de Payens, returned to France, probably in the company of an embassy from Baldwin, king of Jerusalem to drum up supplies of men and money.[55] He was well received by Henry's nephew Theobald, count of Blois,[56] and by William Clito.[57] Hugh was present when Count Fulk took the cross and probably also at the wedding of Geoffrey and Matilda two weeks later.[58] Henry now made gifts to Hugh and allowed him to cross from Normandy to England on a fundraising drive.[59] Again we can see a mixture of motives here: Fulk's departure; the urgent needs of the Templars; and probably Henry's belated recognition, as the brother of a hero of the first crusade, that he ought to make some kind of gesture.

Henry's gifts to Fontevraud and the Templars were, however, outclassed by the continuing favour he showed towards Cluny, which reached a crescendo in the late 1120s and early 1130s. Building at Cluny was still proceeding: work on the third abbey church had been set back by a collapse in the nave in 1125, and it was finally dedicated in September 1130 by Pope Innocent II.[60] Underwriting building costs was only one aspect of Henry's generosity. In 1123 he had nominated a Cluniac monk to the great abbey of Mont-Saint-Michel.[61] Three years

---

53 *Regesta*, ii, nos. 1580–81.
54 At some point Henry made a gift of Villedieu to the Hospitallers: *G.N.D.*, ed. van Houts, ii, 256–7. This was Villedieu-les-Poêles: M. Miguet, *Templiers et Hospitaliers en Normandie: comité des travaux historiques et scientifiques* (Paris, 1995), 230–35.
55 Orderic, *Eccl. Hist.*, vi, 390–93; see M. Barber, *The New Knighthood: A History of the Order of the Temple* (Cambridge, 1994), chapter 1.
56 Barber, *New Knighthood*, 13.
57 *Cartulaire générale de l'ordre du Temple 1119–1150: recueil des chartes et des bulles relatives à l'ordre du Temple* (Paris, 1913), no. 7.
58 Barber, *New Knighthood*, 14.
59 A.S.C. E 1128.
60 Orderic, *Eccl. Hist.*, vi, 418–20.
61 Dom Laporte, 'Les séries abbatiales et priorales du Mont-Saint-Michel', *Millénaire monastique du Mont-Saint-Michel*, i (Paris, 1966), 274. Thanks to Dr V. Gazeau for this reference.

later his nephew Henry of Blois was put in charge of Glastonbury,[62] and in the following year he promised Peterborough Abbey to the enterprising Henry of Poitou, already abbot of Saint Jean d'Angély.[63] Finally, late in 1129 or early in 1130, the abbot of Reading, Hugh of Amiens, moved to the archbishopric of Rouen.[64]

In February 1130 a disputed papal election took place: a minority of cardinals, chiefly from northern Europe, jumped the gun and elected Gregorio Papareschi, who took the name Innocent II.[65] The majority of cardinals subsequently elected Peter Pierleoni, who took the name Anacletus II. Anacletus and his supporters held Rome, and so Innocent II travelled north. He was warmly received at Cluny whilst diplomatic negotiations with the kings of France and England and the emperor Lothar were set in motion.

How would Henry react to these events? William the Conqueror had stood aloof from the struggle between Gregory VII and the antipope Clement III; Rufus had delayed recognizing Urban II until 1095, when in return for recognition he extracted the concession that papal legates would never be sent to England. Times had changed, however, and it was unlikely that Henry would be able to delay recognizing one pope or the other for very long. Moreover, as his own affairs were so precariously balanced, he needed support, or at least no outright opposition, from the successful pope. Geoffrey and Matilda were related to the same degree as William Clito and Sybil, whose marriage had been annulled at Rome. The last thing Henry needed at a time when his daughter's marriage had broken down was the possibility that the bridegroom might seek an escape. It was reported that Geoffrey was planning to make a pilgrimage to Compostela and that Henry was angry.[66]

---

[62] John of Worcester, *Chronicle,* iii, 188. It is a moot point whether Henry was ever formally elected abbot. See D. Knowles, *The Monastic Order in England* (2nd edn., Cambridge, 1963), 282. It may have been at this time that the king made a grant to Marcigny, as his charter was witnessed by Henry as abbot of Glastonbury and Andrew de Baudemont, Theobald's seneschal: *Regesta,* ii, no. 1599a.

[63] A.S.C. E 1127–32; C. Clark, ' "This ecclesiastical adventurer": Henry of Saint-Jean d'Angély', *E.H.R.* lxxxiv (1969), 548–60.

[64] Hugh was still at Rome in May 1129, *Papsturkunden in England,* ed. W. Holtzmann, Abhandlung der Gesellschaft der Wissenschaften in Göttingen, Phil. - Hist. Klasse, Dritte Folge xxv, xiv–xv, xxxii, (1952), no. 21, as cited by Thomas G. Waldman, 'Hugh of Amiens, Archbishop of Rouen (1130–64)', *H.S.J.,* 2 (1990), 139–53, at 141. The pope wished to keep Hugh at the curia, but on hearing this the king threatened to withdraw the gifts he had made to Reading Abbey. In June the pope wrote to Henry that he was sending Hugh back to Reading, which suggests that his election to Rouen had not yet taken place, *Papsturkunden in England,* iii, no. 22 cited by Waldman, 141. For the date of his election see P. Hébert, 'Un Archevêque de Rouen au XIIe siècle: Hugues III d'Amiens, 1130–64', *Revue des Questions Historiques,* 44 (1898), 325–71, at 330n.

[65] I.S. Robinson, *The Papacy, 1073–1198* (Cambridge, 1990), 69–76.

[66] Hildebert of Lavardin, archbishop of Tours, *Letters, P.L.,* clxxi, cols. 131–3.

Of the two popes, Innocent II was the better prospect for Henry.[67] As one of the negotiators of the compromise over investitures reached with the emperor in 1122, Innocent was unlikely to want to overturn the settlement, whereas Anacletus, who had taken an uncompromising line, might have chosen to do so.[68] At a council at Etampes in May 1130 Innocent had been recognized by a council of the French church.[69] St Bernard also threw his weight behind Innocent,[70] as did Abbot Peter the Venerable.[71] Peter visited England 'after Easter' in 1130,[72] and the question of the schism must surely have been discussed with the king, though his visit would have had other objectives, such as soliciting further gifts for building work at Cluny, and the state of the Cluniac houses in England. Henry crossed to Normandy probably during the first week of September, and by this time he had probably decided to recognize Innocent.[73]

By January 1131 Innocent was at Chartres. Here he met Henry, who prostrated himself before the pope and presented him with gifts.[74] By this time evidently the prospects of restoring Matilda to her husband were improving, and the pope confirmed a new and still more generous grant made by Henry to Fontevraud.[75] There would have been little point in such a charter if there was no future in the marriage, because the partners were irreconcilable or because the pope was going to dissolve it.

By May the pope arrived at Rouen where a great company assembled, including the archbishops of Tarragona and Rouen, the bishops of Chartres, Lisieux, and Sées, abbots Suger, Bernard, and Peter the Venerable. Henry was there, as was his daughter, and on this occasion the king assigned one hundred marks' revenue from England each year to Cluny; both he and his daughter added their signs to the document.[76] The timing and the scale of Henry's generosity thus cannot be dissociated from the criss-crossing of his concerns with the position of Innocent II and the diplomacy of Peter the Venerable. 'Spiritual crisis' may thus

---

67 Henry's decision was by no means a foregone conclusion. William of Malmesbury included a letter by one of Anacletus's supporters, denouncing the election of Innocent II, in his *Historia Novella*, 14–18. Whilst the fact that the author recognized the letter to have been too favourable to Anacletus, the fact that it was included may be read as an indication that English ecclesiastics were by no means certain about the issue.

68 J.N.D. Kelly, *The Oxford Dictionary of Popes* (Oxford, 1986), 167–70.

69 *Recueil des actes de Louis VI, roi de France (1108–37)*, publié sous la direction de Robert-Henri Bautier par Jean Dufour (4 vols., Paris 1992–4), ii, no. 291; iii, 215.

70 Ernaldi, 'S. Bernardi Abbatis Vita', Bk II c. I, 4 *P.L.*, clxxxv, col. 271. St Bernard wrote to Archbishop Hildebert of Tours to persuade him to support Innocent, *Letters*, ed. J. Leclercq, H.M. Rochais, C.H. Talbot (Rome, 1957–77), no. 124, no. 127 in the translation of B.S. James (Stroud edn., 1998).

71 'Vita Petri Venerabilis', *P.L.*, clxxxix, col. 20.

72 A.S.C. E 1130.

73 Henry of Huntingdon, *Historia*, 486–7 and n.; by 8 September, however, Henry was at Bec in the company of the newly elected archbishop of Rouen: Robert of Torigny, *Chronicles . . . Stephen, Henry II, Richard I*, iv, 117.

74 Orderic, *Eccl. Hist.*, vi, 420.

75 *Regesta*, ii, no. 1687.

76 *Regesta*, ii, no. 1691.

not quite capture the bundle of motives behind Henry's gifts in 1130 and 1131, though it is obviously reasonable to assume that in his last years he *was* deeply concerned about his past life and his prospects of salvation.

The story that he made a pilgrimage to Bury after a miraculous escape from shipwreck occurs only in the Worcester chronicler's annals covering the last years of Henry's life.[77] These included the famous account of Henry's nightmares. They were written up as a group and, as I have argued elsewhere, were designed to heighten the reader's awareness about the need for repentance and the dire events which were to follow Henry's death.[78] Henry may have visited Bury in 1131 or 1132, though there is no corroboration of the claim that he made a pilgrimage.

What then were the principal characteristics of his religious patronage taken as a whole? This is a topic about which much could be said, regarding the nature of the communities, the balance as between established churches and new foundations, and the balance between England and Normandy.[79] All I can hope to do here is to make a few points, which I discuss in more detail in a forthcoming biography. The first is about the kinds of communities patronized. Henry showed himself to be consistently loyal to the houses favoured by his parents, to the two abbeys at Caen, to Bec, and to Battle. This was not surprising in itself, for it demonstrated filial piety, but so far as the three Norman houses are concerned there is also the very important political point that his gifts were legitimate, before and after 1106. After 1106, when many in Normandy would have regarded him as a usurper, his duty to make gifts to communities founded by his parents could not be disputed. He may also, as Véronique Gazeau has suggested recently, have been trying to outdo his brother Duke Robert who had also made gifts to the abbeys at Caen and to Bec.[80]

Henry was attached above all to the Cluniacs. Here again he followed a precedent set by his father who had tried unsuccessfully to secure Cluniac monks for Battle.[81] His sister Adela became a nun at Cluniac Marcigny-sur-Loire,[82] and his nephew Henry became a monk at Cluny.[83] Henry I became a notable benefactor of the Augustinians, as is well known, being credited with the foundation

[77] John of Worcester, *Chronicle,* iii, 202.
[78] 'History, Prophecy, and Henry I', unpublished paper delivered at the International Medieval Congress at Leeds, July 2000.
[79] For a review, see E. Hallam, 'Aspects of the Monastic Patronage of the English and French Royal Houses, c. 1130–1270', Ph.D. thesis, London University, 1970, chapter 2.
[80] 'Henry I and the Norman Benedictine Abbots', unpublished paper, delivered at the International Medieval Congress at Leeds, July 2000. Dr Gazeau proposes to discuss further the relationship between Henry and the Norman abbots in a forthcoming book.
[81] F. Barlow, 'William I's Relations with Cluny', *Jnl. Eccl. Hist.,* 32 (1981), 131–41; B. Golding, 'The Coming of the Cluniacs', *A.N.S.,* 3 (1980), 65–77.
[82] Hugh the Chanter, 154.
[83] William of Newburgh, *Historia Rerum Anglicarum, Chronicles ... Stephen, Henry II and Richard I,* i, 31.

of at least five houses in England, Cirencester,[84] Dunstable,[85] Carlisle,[86] Wellow by Grimsby,[87] and St Denys at Portswood near Southampton,[88] as well as his role in the refoundation of several others,[89] and in Normandy, too, he played a crucial role in promoting Augustinian foundations, most notably the regularization of the cathedral chapter at Sées, which has already been mentioned.[90]

Secondly, he was responsive to new trends, to Savigny, Tiron, Fontevraud, to the crusading orders and, late in life, to the Cistercians. His grant of exemption from toll for the food, clothing, and other necessities of the monks of Pontigny was possibly made in May in 1131 when he met St Bernard at Rouen.[91] Subsequently he showed favour to the fledgling community at Rievaulx in Yorkshire.[92] He also had a hand in the foundation of several hospitals on both sides of the Channel, though it is not always easy to sort out exactly where the king's role started and where it ended.[93] Many hospitals were being founded to cater for the growing problem of the sick, and lepers in particular, in medieval towns. Queen Matilda had led the way in the foundation of leper hospitals in England with

---

[84] For Cirencester, where the endowment was essentially that previously held by Regenbald the chancellor (of William the Conqueror), see *The Cartulary of Cirencester Abbey Gloucestershire*, ed. C.D. Ross (3 vols., London, 1964–77), i, xix–xxii.

[85] *Regesta*, ii, nos. 1826–7.

[86] See above, n. 43.

[87] *Regesta*, ii, no. 1737.

[88] *Regesta*, ii, nos. 1507–8; *The Cartulary of the Priory of St Denys near Southampton*, ed. E.O. Blake, Southampton Record Series, xxiv, xxv (2 vols., 1981), ii, appendix 1, nos. 1–2.

[89] Viz. Merton and Nostell, see above, nn. 38, 42. Leading members of Henry's court endowed Augustinian houses, and Henry granted charters to several. The classic study is that by J.C. Dickinson, *The Origins of the Austin Canons and their Introduction into England* (London, 1950).

[90] The indispensable work is that directed by Mathieu Arnoux, *Des clercs au service de la réforme*, see 120, 142–4, 215–20 for a careful analysis of Henry's involvement at Sées, Sainte Barbe-sur-Auge, and Notre-Dame du Val. For a detailed study of Notre-Dame du Val see M. Arnoux, 'Actes de l'abbaye Notre-Dame-du-Val', *Deux Abbayes de Basse-Normandie: Notre-Dame du Val et le Val Richer (XIIe–XIIIe siècles), Le Pays Bas-Normand*, nos. 237–8, 2000, 5–65. I should like to thank Prof Arnoux for helpful discussions about Henry and the houses of canons regular in Normandy.

[91] *Le premier cartulaire de l'abbaye Cistercienne de Pontigny (XIIe–XIIIe siècles)* (Paris, 1981), no. 3.

[92] *Regesta*, ii, nos. 1720, 1740–41, 1961. Henry also rescued the abbey of Mortemer, which adopted the Cistercian way of life a few years after its foundation, see below, n. 112.

[93] England: St Bartholomew's, Oxford, St John's, Cirencester, Holy Innocents', Lincoln, plus encouragement to Eudo *dapifer*'s foundation at Colchester: *V.C.H.*, *Oxfordshire*, ii, 157; *Gloucestershire*, ii, 122; *Lincolnshire*, ii, 230; *Essex*, ii, 184. E. J. Kealey, *Medieval Medicus: A Social History of Anglo-Norman Medicine* (Baltimore and London, 1981), appendix 2 lists these, and adds St Mary's, Newcastle. This last seems, however, to be mistaken, and the hospital was probably founded in the mid-twelfth century: D. Knowles and R. Neville Hancock, *Medieval Religious Houses in England and Wales* (2nd edn., London, 1971), 378. Normandy: La Madeleine d'Orbec, Falaise, Mont-aux-Malades Rouen, see Arnoux, *Des clercs au service de la réforme*, 119–22; M. Arnoux, 'Aux origines d'une léproserie: la pancarte de la Madeleine d'Orbec (1107–35)', *Mélanges Michel Nortier, Cahiers Léopold Delisle,* xliv (1995), 209–22.

Saint Giles, Holborn.[94] In Normandy Henry had a part in the foundation of Mont-aux-Malades outside Rouen.[95] He also made a gift to the Grand Beaulieu at Chartres, a house patronized by his sister Adela.[96]

A third point is about the balance between Henry's generosity toward established churches and toward new foundations. Wealthy and established churches were not likely in general to receive large new grants of land; nevertheless it is possible to see how some churchmen and churches were treated with more generosity than others, making every allowance for the uneven survival of documentation. In England Henry was conspicuously generous to Abingdon Abbey in the time of Abbot Faritius, one of his principal physicians. The community accordingly grew and prospered.[97] Bishop Roger of Salisbury, the king's chief minister, was able to use his position to secure grants of lands and privileges as he built up the number of prebends at Salisbury. These included the grant of a seven-day fair, tithes from the New Forest and all the forests in his diocese, as well as a grant of Malmesbury Abbey, whose abbot was deposed in 1118.[98] Roger's nephew Alexander was also particularly favoured in the later years of the reign. He stepped into his predecessor's role as local justiciar;[99] he built a castle at Newark on Trent and was given permission to assign a third of the knights owed in royal castleguard at Lincoln;[100] and he was granted the Eastgate in the city of Lincoln.[101] It seems that the king was deliberately strengthening the bishop's influence, apparently with a view to counterbalancing the power of the two most powerful local lay lords in the closing years of the reign, Ranulf, earl of Chester and his brother William de Roumare.[102] Once again, it is hard to dissociate Henry's actions from his concerns about the succession.

However, such generosity was not widely distributed amongst the cathedrals and monasteries of England. Bishop Ranulf Flambard was restored to Durham after his reconciliation with the king, and he worked hard to recover lands and

---

[94] *Monasticon*, vi, ii, 635–6: charter of Henry II confirming a grant of 60 shillings a year given by his grandmother for the hospital of St Giles.

[95] A grant by Henry of 40 shillings (Rouennais) to Mont-aux-Malades was referred to in a confirmation by Duke Geoffrey: *Regesta*, iii, no. 730.

[96] For Le Grand Beaulieu, François-Olivier Tonati, *Maladie et société au moyen age: la lèpre, les lépreux et les léproseries dans la province ecclésiastique de Sens jusqu'au milieu du XIVe siècle* (Bruxelles, 1988), 258, 430, 484; *Cartulaire de la léproserie du Grand-Beaulieu*, ed. R. Merlet and M. Jusselin (Chartres, 1909), no. 1; *Regesta*, ii, no. 1917. This grant was confirmed by Innocent II in 1131.

[97] See *Chronicon Monasterii de Abingdon*, ed. J. Stevenson (2 vols., R.S., 1858), ii, 49, 248, 289; Knowles, *Monastic Order*, 181n. No fewer than eighty-eight texts in favour of Abingdon are listed in *Regesta*, ii, of which the great majority were issued during the period when Faritius was abbot.

[98] E.J. Kealey, *Roger of Salisbury, Viceroy of England* (Berkeley, 1972), 99–101.

[99] *Regesta*, iii, no. 490.

[100] *Regesta*, ii, nos. 1770, 1773, 1791.

[101] *Regesta*, ii, no. 1784.

[102] For their ambitions in the county in the following reign see P. Dalton, 'Aiming at the Impossible: Earl Ranulf II and Lincolnshire in the Reign of King Stephen', *The Earldom of Chester and Its Charters*, Chester Archaeological Society, 71 (1991), 109–34.

rights he had lost during the period of his disgrace, but he never totally succeeded.[103] Carlisle and Teviotdale ceased to be in his care,[104] and the manors of Northallerton, Welton, and Howden were not apparently recovered until 1116.[105] The same pattern was true for established monasteries in England. A few received favours, but others only confirmations, freedom from tolls, or grants of markets or fairs – which in some cases were again probably confirmations rather than new grants.

Finally, when the balance of patronage as between England and Normandy is compared, some interesting points about the latter emerge. The first is the selective nature of Henry's patronage in the duchy. As far as the bishoprics are concerned, Evreux was treated favourably: Henry had burned down the cathedral in 1119 and had promised its bishop that he would make amends.[106] Lisieux, rather surprisingly perhaps given that Bishop John was Henry's chief minister in Normandy, did not receive any exceptional marks of favour; likewise Bayeux, where the cathedral had been burned in the fighting in 1105,[107] and the western bishoprics of Coutances and Avranches. Henry showed more interest in Sées, where the see had suffered in the time of Robert de Bellême, and although Bishop Serlo returned to Normandy from exile in 1105, we do not know how far recovery had progressed. Orderic, who would have been able to tell us, repeats nothing but praise of a man he admired.[108] Serlo was succeeded in 1124 by John, the nephew of Bishop John of Lisieux, and it was only then that the see was reorganized and the cathedral rebuilt.

Henry's dealings with the Norman abbeys deserve more space than may be accorded here, but if his written acts are considered as a group, some significant trends emerge. First, Henry was liberal with letters of protection, exemptions from toll and passage, and confirmations of grants made by others. He was also prepared to intervene to protect the English interests of Norman religious houses.[109] Secondly, he made gifts to houses patronized by his parents. Thirdly, he was very selective about making gifts of land in Normandy to Norman houses, and there seems to have been a certain reluctance to take new initiatives. There are exceptions, though again there are usually special circumstances. First, there is the abbey of Montebourg, which had probably been founded by his father. The role of protector seems to have passed to Henry's friend Richard

---

103 H.S. Offler, 'Ranulf Flambard as bishop of Durham', *Durham University Journal,* 64, new ser. 33 (1971–2), 14–25.
104 Offler, 'Ranulf Flambard as bishop of Durham', 17.
105 *Regesta,* ii, no. 1124.
106 Robert of Torigny in *G.N.D.,* ed. van Houts, ii, 256–7 and n.
107 Orderic, *Eccl. Hist.,* vi, 78.
108 Orderic, *Eccl. Hist.,* vi, 336–40.
109 Judith A. Green, 'L'abbaye de Fécamp et les rois anglo-normands', paper delivered at Colloque Volpiano, Fécamp, June 2001.

de Redvers in the 1090s and then to have been resumed by Henry after 1100.[110] Secondly, he was an important patron of Savigny, strategically situated on the very frontier of Normandy.[111] Thirdly, not long before his death he rescued the struggling community at Mortemer, which had been founded by Robert de Chandos and his wife, and he offered an alternative site.[112] Yet he clearly did not lash out with gifts from the ducal demesne, underlining the commitment he had made when he took Normandy from his brother Robert, that he would protect the church and restore lands and rights lost since the death of his father.

Henry's life spanned an era of great change within the church, and whilst retaining a traditional approach to his rights he also responded positively to the new kinds of communities which were springing up. Was he – to an exceptional degree – riddled with a sense of spiritual crisis in his later years? I have suggested here that the gifts he made, particularly in 1130 and 1131, were made with one eye on the future of his dynasty (was he literally to be the end of his line?) and one on the wider diplomatic context. His contemporaries, King David, and Louis VI, were both generous patrons of the church in their different ways; in that sense, what was unusual about Henry was the scale of his giving. That was a reflection of his wealth and munificence, as well as his more directly spiritual concerns.

---

[110] This subject has been investigated by M.L. Neuwirth, 'L'abbaye de Montebourg', thèse de Maîtrise, Université de Caen. I should like to thank Dr V. Gazeau for kindly drawing my attention to this work, and to M. Neuwirth for kindly sending me a copy of his research in advance of publication.

[111] This subject needs further investigation. See meanwhile B. Poulle, 'Savigny and England', *England and Normandy in the Middle Ages*, ed. D. Bates and A. Curry (Hambledon, 1994), 159–68.

[112] See P.F. Gallagher, 'The monastery of Mortemer-en-Lyons in the Twelfth Century – Its History and Cartulary', Ph.D. thesis, University of Notre Dame (1970), chapter 1. The foundation history of the abbey may be found in A. du Monstier, *Neustria Pia* (Rouen, 1663), 768–78, and, more accessibly, in J. Bouvet, 'Le Récit de la Fondation de Mortemer', *Collectanea Ordinis Cisterciensium Reformatorum*, 22 (1960), 149–68.

2

The Denis Bethell Prize Essay

Some Reflections on the 'Foreign Policies' of Edgar 'the Peaceable'

Shashi Jayakumar

Like his son, Æthelred 'the Unready', King Edgar (959–975) took time to earn his byname. The earliest reference to his being called 'Peaceable' is found in the work of the twelfth-century monk John of Worcester, who consistently calls him 'Eadgarus Pacificus'.[1] To the monks Edgar was of course the ruler who had sponsored the monastic reform along Benedictine lines. In addition, he presided over a halcyon period of peace before the Danish invasions of the late tenth century. What happened in Edgar's reign in terms of purely political events was thus felt to be of secondary importance compared to his patronage of the religious revival. Even if such men had wanted to write a secular history of the times it would have been difficult: the paucity of contemporary sources for the 960s and 970s was then as it is now a near-insurmountable obstacle. Hence the commonly accepted view of Edgar runs something like this: since the *Chronicle* and other sources are relatively bare, nothing of great importance apart from monastic reform could have occurred during his reign. Sir Frank Stenton himself argued that 'it is a sign of Edgar's competence as a ruler that his reign is singularly devoid of recorded incident'.[2]

It is certainly true that Edgar's reign had within a generation of his death taken on something of the quality of a golden age. By the early eleventh century, Archbishop Wulfstan II of York had begun to compare the troubled reign of Æthelred 'the Unready' with the tranquil times of his father. He did so in his

[1] *The Chronicle of John of Worcester*, ii, ed. R.R. Darlington and P. McGurk (Oxford, 1995); see for example s.a. 964, 967, 968, 969, 972, 973, and 975. My thanks go to Patrick Wormald, Lesley Abrams, Umej Bhatia, James Campbell, George Garnett, Simon Keynes, and Jinty Nelson for reading versions of this article and making valuable comments (not to mention saving me from some grisly errors!). I have also greatly benefited from discussions with Ann Williams and Gareth Mann, who took the time to read the portion of my D.Phil from which this article is distilled. Finally, I am deeply grateful to the members of the Haskins Society for showing me many kindnesses during my stay at Cornell; not least among them were Richard Abels, Robin Fleming, Paul Hyams, Chris Lewis, and Stephen Morillo.
[2] F.M. Stenton, *Anglo-Saxon England* (3rd edn., Oxford, 1971), 368.

Sermon of the Wolf to the English, but also more subtly in Æthelred's later law codes as well as Cnut's, for which he was responsible.[3] These borrow extensively from Edgar's codes, and we know from the *Chronicle* that when Cnut met the English councillors at Oxford in 1018 there was a mutual undertaking to keep to Edgar's law.[4] These are the real beginnings of how Edgar's reign came to be seen as a byword for peace and prosperity. Conversely, the authoritarian side to Edgar and the measures he took to enforce the peace have received comparatively little attention. Many years ago Dorothy Whitelock pointed to the fact that Edgar had issued what was in effect a personal edict of unprecedented savagery in order to suppress thievery. This involved the mutilation of the culprit and the amputation of his limbs, followed by the abandonment of his body to wild animals.[5] It might also be added that Edgar was willing to use or at least condone severe measures against those who stood against him, or who were not willing to fall in line with his policies. After 975, a characteristic complaint of landowners seeking to recover the estates they had sold to the ecclesiastical reformers was that they had not particularly wanted to part with their lands, but had been forced to, and been afflicted with 'violence and pillage'.[6] Finally, the *Chronicle's* sparse entries for the 960s also provide tantalizing glimpses into this world where order was maintained by personal rule with an iron fist. In 969 we learn that Edgar ordered the island of Thanet to be ravaged.[7] Additional information on this incident comes from another source: Roger of Wendover, whose work, the *Flores Historiarium* (*c*. 1235) used sources which in many cases have not otherwise come down to us. Edgar, he says, did this as he was 'moved to exceeding rage' when the islanders despoiled some merchants from York of their property. It is not without reason that in his assessment of Edgar, Roger notes how the king 'kept the rebellious under severe correction'.[8]

---

[3]   D. Whitelock, ed., *Sermo Lupi Ad Anglos* (Exeter, 1976), 56. The Edgar reference is in MS. 'E' (Bodleian, MS. Hatton 113) and it is probably Wulfstan's own addition. For Wulfstan and the laws, see D. Whitelock, 'Wulfstan and the Laws of Cnut', *E.H.R.*, 63 (1948), 433–52, and *idem*, 'Wulfstan's authorship of Cnut's Laws', *E.H.R.*, 70 (1955), 72–85.

[4]   'Wulfstan and the Laws of Cnut', 433–44.

[5]   D. Whitelock, 'Wulfstan Cantor and Anglo-Saxon Law', in *Nordica et Anglica: Studies in Honor of Stefán Einarsson*, ed. A.H. Orrick (The Hague, 1968), 83–92. The evidence depends ultimately on the testimony of Lantfred, a member of the community at Winchester, who *c*. 975 wrote an account of the translation of the relics of St Swithin. For the translation and commentary (relying on Prof Lapidge's forthcoming edition), see P. Wormald, *The Making of English Law: King Alfred to the Twelfth Century* (Oxford, 1999), 125–6 (hereafter *MEL*).

[6]   Such complaints are relatively common in the portion of the *Liber Eliensis* known as the *Libellus Æthelwoldi*, which in its original form was probably a vernacular land register compiled by the Ely monks in the closing years of the tenth century. See A.G. Kennedy, 'Law and Litigation in the *Libellus Æthelwoldi episcopi*', *A.S.E.*, 24 (1995), 131–83; I am grateful to Prof Keynes for allowing me to use the forthcoming edition of the *Libellus* which he and Dr Kennedy have in hand.

[7]   *A.S.C.* 'D', s.a. 969.

[8]   *Matthæi Parisiensis monachi Sancti Albani Chronica Majora*, ed. H.R. Luard, i (R.S., 1872), 466.

Perhaps this did not fit in well with John of Worcester's idealized image of Edgar, for he ignores not only Edgar's ravaging of Thanet but also another incident which took place in 966, when a certain Thored ravaged Westmorland. This may or may not have been done at Edgar's behest. [9] John's silence is made all the more interesting by the fact that the version of the *Chronicle* he used was very close to the 'D' text – it is this exemplar that records both attacks. John records everything else of note to be found in 'D's account of the 960s. The likelihood is that he deliberately chose to leave out these two incidents, in effect reworking the reign of Edgar, and omitting what was felt to be irrelevant in order to fit the popular conception that was current in his own day. He was not entirely successful in this: we learn from the list of virtues he attributed to the king that Edgar *Pacificus* was 'strong in arms' and 'warlike', 'royally defending the rights of his kingdom with military power'.[10] The apparent contradiction is explained by the fact that John is at this point heavily reliant on Byrhtferth's *Life* of Oswald, which exists as a Worcester manuscript. This is what Byrhtferth had to say about Edgar:

the warlike king Edgar, strong through sceptres and diadems, and regally protecting by the power of war the laws of the kingdom, overcame the proud necks of all of his enemies at his feet – not only the princes and tyrants of the islands but also the kings of many peoples feared him; hearing of his prudence, they were overpowered by fear and also terror.

He established himself as befits a king, munificent by his generosity, as is fitting. The kings of the surrounding peoples magnificently praised him for his generous gifts, and seeing that he had the anger of a ferocious lion against his enemies, the neighbouring kings and *principes* became very scared of him.[11]

Byrhtferth's martial image was modified slightly – and not altogether successfully – by John of Worcester, who attempted to illustrate how Edgar's might made fighting unnecessary. This was nonetheless a powerful idea, and one that would have seemed especially resonant in the troubled first decades of the eleventh century. It is this theme which has become inextricably intertwined with the famous gathering at Chester in 973, where six, or according to some sources eight kings submitted to Edgar.[12] The 'D' rescension of the *Chronicle* has in its annal for 959 an alliterative panegyric for Edgar which makes what is

9 For the various Thoreds in this period see *MEL*, 191–4. For comment see F.M. Stenton, 'Pre-Conquest Westmorland', in *Preparatory to Anglo-Saxon England*, ed. D.M. Stenton (Oxford, 1970), 214–23, at 218–19. Stenton's suggestion that this was essentially an act of private violence is seemingly borne out by Gaimar's statement that Thored lost his life as a result of his actions: Gaimar, *L'Estoire des Engleis*, ed. A. Bell (Oxford, 1960) ll.3579–82. However this may equally have been mere embroidery on Gaimar's part.

10 John of Worcester, *Chronicle*, ii, s.a. 959. See R.R. Darlington and P. McGurk, 'The "Chronicon ex Chronicis" of "Florence" of Worcester and its use of sources for English History before 1066', *A.N.S.*, 5 (1982), 184–96, at 191–2.

11 Byrhtferth, *Vita Oswaldi*, in *Historians of the Church of York and its Archbishops*, ed. J. Raine (3 vols., R.S., 1871–94), i, 399–475, at 425, 435 (my translation).

12 Stenton, *Anglo-Saxon England*, 368–70.

probably a reference to the same event when it states that 'kings and earls will-
ingly submitted to him and were subjected to whatever he wished ... And
without battle he brought under his sway all that he wished'.[13] The author of this
panegyric was probably Archbishop Wulfstan II, writing soon after the turn of
the millennium. In writing this, Wulfstan was strongly influenced by Ælfric's
'Judges', which also emphasized the peaceful submission of foreign potentates
in similar language.[14] It is this image which won out over competing ones, such
as that which can be glimpsed not only in Byrhtferth, but also in the 'C'
rescension of the *Chronicle*, which alludes more than once to the martial aspects
of Edgar's rule. The 'C' version preserves two unique poems in its annals for
974 and 975, which deal respectively with his 'imperial' coronation and his
death. These poems were probably written at Abingdon not long after Edgar's
death. [15] The first poem states that Edgar was 'bold in battle' which can hardly
be a topos. And in fact there is no reason to suppose that it is. References in the
Welsh sources show us that raids into Wales continued to occur, as they had
done under previous kings. The *Annales Cambriae* record how in 967 'the
English laid waste the kingdom of the sons of Idwal' (i.e. Gwynedd) and the
Brut y Tywysogyon states that this expedition was led by Ælfhere, the ealdorman
of Mercia.[16] Interestingly, 'C', perhaps the version of the *Chronicle* whose
annals were being written closest to the events in question, makes no mention at
all of the Chester gathering, and was much more interested in the details of his
Bath coronation just prior to this. The submission is however central to the
'northern' rescensions 'D' and 'E' whose annals for Edgar's reign have other
items of northern interest, and which state that Edgar continued on from Bath
and went to Chester, where six kings 'all gave him pledges that they would be
his allies on sea and on land'.[17] There may thus be reasons for suspecting that

[13] *A.S.C.* 'D', s.a. 959.

[14] D. Whitelock et al., *The Anglo-Saxon Chronicle: A Revised Translation* (London, 1961); 'D',
s.a. 959 and n.10. For Ælfric's 'Judges', see *E.H.D.*, i, 928.

[15] *The Anglo-Saxon Chronicle: A Collaborative Edition. 10: The Abingdon Chronicle A.D. 956–
1066.* ed. P.W. Conner (Cambridge, 1996), lxxii–lxxiii; and also *The Anglo-Saxon Chronicle ... 5:
MS C*, ed. K. O'Brien O'Keeffe (Cambridge, 2001), 82–3. Conner (if I understand his argument
correctly) suggests that original poems are contemporary with the events they describe, but given
that the 973 poem refers to events according to what 'I have heard tell' and 'what the documents
say' this seems impossible and a slightly later date seems preferable.

[16] *Annales Cambriae*, ed. J. Williams Ab Ithel (London, 1860), 19; *Brut Y Tywysogion*, ed. Ab
Ithel (London, 1860), 25 and 29. Note that the ruler of Gwynedd, Hywel ap Ieuaf, was killed by
the English in 985 – according to the *Brut*, 'through the treachery of the Saxons' (*Brut Y
Tywysogion*, p. 29). See also the entry in the *Brut y Twysogion*, s.a. 977 which records the devasta-
tion of the 'grove of Celynog the Great by Howel, son of Ieuaf, and the Saxons'. Ælfhere is said
by the same source to have acted in another incident in concert with Hywel ap Ieuaf against Einion
ap Owain the ruler of Brycheiniog, in 983. There is incidentally another late but possibly trust-
worthy reference to Edgar personally leading an expedition into Wales, found in the twelfth-
century *Life* of St Illtyd. See G.H. Doble, *Lives of the Welsh Saints*, ed. D.S. Evans (Cardiff,
1971), 117.

[17] *A.S.C.*, 'D' and 'E', s.a. 972 (for 973).

the image of Edgar *Pacificus* was carefully cultivated by the Worcester/York nexus via Ælfric and Wulfstan.[18]

I shall deal with the Chester 'submission' further below, but would like at this point to highlight part of the 959 panegyric where Wulfstan diverges from Ælfric and says something specifically new – perhaps the only criticism of Edgar in any pre-Conquest source. Wulfstan says that Edgar

did one ill-deed too greatly: he loved evil foreign customs and brought too firmly heathen manners within this land, and attracted hither foreigners and enticed harmful people to this country.[19]

This is well-known, but it needs to be put in context. The archbishop was writing in the dark days of Æthelred's reign, during the course of the Danish invasions. For him to say something like this about his hero can only mean one thing – he was making an important political statement relevant to his contemporaries. It was in looking back to Edgar's reign that he saw things begin to go wrong.

A recent discussion of Edgar has suggested that this criticism should be linked with certain provisions in the law code IV Edgar, a possibility which needs to be investigated further.[20] This remarkable code was probably promulgated in the last years of Edgar's reign. It appears to have been aimed at the Danelaw and part of Mercia, and the ealdormen who held authority in these areas were tasked to ensure the dissemination of the code throughout their spheres of authority.[21] The traditional view of this code is that many concessions are made to the Danelaw, including the right to decide upon their own laws in most matters:

It is my will that there should be in force among the Danes such good laws as they best decide on, and I have ever allowed them this and will allow it as long as my life lasts, because of your loyalty, which you have always shown in me . . .

I will be a very gracious lord to you as long as my life lasts, and I am very well pleased with you all, because you are so zealous about the maintenance of the peace . . .[22]

Just why does Edgar, who brooked no opposition in other respects, appear to be conceding so much now to the Danelaw? For part of the answer we need to go back to the period 957–9, when Edgar was king of the Mercians and

---

18 For the later tradition of historical writing at Worcester, see M. Brett, 'John of Worcester and his Contemporaries', in *The Writing of History in the Middle Ages: Essays presented to Richard William Southern*, ed. R.H.C. Davis and J.M. Wallace-Hadrill (Oxford, 1981), 101–26.

19 *A.S.C.*, 'D', s.a. 959.

20 S. Miller, 'Edgar', in *The Blackwell Encyclopaedia of Anglo-Saxon England,* ed. M. Lapidge et al. (Oxford, 1999), 158–9.

21 For discussion (especially concerning the date of the code, which is disputed), see *MEL*, 317–20.

22 IV Eg 12 and 16. *Die Gesetze der Angelsachen*, ed. F. Liebermann (3 vols., Halle, 1903–16), i, 212–14. See also *The Laws of the Kings of England from Edmund to Henry I*, ed. and trans. A.J. Robertson (Cambridge, 1925), 37 and 39.

Northumbrians. As long ago as 1976 Neils Lund argued that Edgar had been set up by a group of Danelaw magnates in opposition to Edgar's brother Eadwig, because they were eager to preserve their local autonomy.[23] Drawing on the evidence of IV Edgar, he also says that 'the legal autonomy which Edgar allowed [the Danelaw] in return for their loyalty is virtually equivalent to domestic self-government and it reduced the practical implications of West Saxon rule to the least possible minimum. From the point of view of the unification of England this was a set-back.'[24] And he adds that Æthelred considered it an urgent task to claw back this control over the north that had been lost, which is one reason why he found it so difficult to fight off the Danes when his own provinces were so restive.

It is true that one of Edgar's diplomas from 958 is from the York archive, attested by a number of Northumbrian magnates.[25] In addition, in IV Edgar the king does declare himself pleased with the loyalty of the Danelaw, and the code is marked by the use of Scandinavian vocabulary.[26] Perhaps there was something of a *quid pro quo* with regard to the earlier support of the Danelaw nobility for Edgar's royal claims. However, some caution is required here as there is no evidence that Edgar was actually set up as king by these men in 957. What *is* likely is that the attendance of these men at his fledgeling court, while sporadic, was a tremendous boost in terms of credibility to the young king and his supporters, who seem mainly to have been key members of the West Saxon aristocracy opposed to Eadwig.[27] A second point is that we should not be so quick to see IV Edgar as marking a 'setback' in terms of national unity. Felix Liebermann ingeniously suggested that the key clauses in the code show Edgar as the first king definitively to draw the Danes *within* the orbit of the West Saxon house in terms of lawmaking.[28] Liebermann was certainly correct in his contention that the Danelaw was not far from Edgar's legislative eye. It is worth noting however that some of the key aspects of IV Edgar are by no means unique. II Edmund, which among other things is concerned with regulating the feud, is a case in point. Most importantly, the homiletic tone in II Em 5 where the king in the first person declares himself pleased with the loyalty of those addressed and states the necessity of their maintaining the public peace has distinct echoes in IV Eg 16, where Edgar declares his satisfaction with his subjects

[23] N. Lund, 'King Edgar and the Danelaw', *Medieval Scandinavia*, 9 (1976), 181–95. A similar approach to the vital clauses in IV Edgar may be found in Stenton, 'The Danes in England', *in Preparatory to Anglo-Saxon England*, 136–65, at 163–4.
[24] 'King Edgar and the Danelaw', 195.
[25] Sawyer, *Charters*, no. 679. Subsequent references to charters will take the prefix 'S' followed by the number assigned to them in Sawyer's edition.
[26] *MEL*, 319.
[27] See B. Yorke, 'Æthelwold and the Politics of the Tenth Century', in Yorke (ed.), *Bishop Æthelwold: His Career and Influence* (Woodbridge, 1998), 65–88, at 75–9. The other charters in which the northern *duces* make an appearance during the division of the kingdom are S 674 (958, from the Peterborough archive), S 677 (958, Wells) and S 681 (959, Peterborough).
[28] *Gesetze*, iii, 141.

in very similar terms.[29] Although in IV Edgar the king allows the Danes to observe their own customs and states that 'I have always granted you such a concession', one has to wonder whether Edgar was doing much more than renewing certain practices that had been current at least since the time of his father – practices subject to royal acquiescence. This impression is reinforced at clause 2a when he insists on his 'royal prerogatives' just as his father had held them, and furthermore states that he is to hold them 'in every borough and in every county I possess'. No mention is made of any exception for the Danelaw. Rather than allowing the Danelaw to go its own way, Edgar simply seems to have been permitting the continuance of certain customs (mainly involving tithe and theft) in which the Danelaw had always had a certain amount of latitude.[30]

IV Eg is to be found in B.L., Cotton Nero E.i, which survives as loose leaves of what was originally a Worcester compilation put together in the 990s.[31] II Em is only found in manuscripts of later (twelfth-century) date, and in the relevant manuscripts they also appear together with the 'Laws of Edward and Guthrum' ('Edward-Guthrum'), which was shown by Whitelock to have been written by Archbishop Wulfstan II.[32] If there is a connecting thread in all this, it is Wulfstan. The archbishop was one of Æthelred's key officials in the Danelaw, as well as being responsible for some of Æthelred's law. In addition, he was instrumental in the preservation of older codes – witness the survival of IV Eg in Worcester manuscripts.[33] Wulfstan was to become steeped in the Anglo-Saxon legal tradition, and was thus probably familiar with the content of IV Eg and by implication its ramifications. Some of Wulfstan's own views on the Danelaw may be gleaned from 'Edward-Guthrum' and other related texts. In 'Edward– Guthrum', Wulfstan is clearly preoccupied with the security of the church and clergymen in the Danelaw. But in addition, he makes certain distinctions between fines for some offences to be paid in English districts, and the *lahslits* due in Danish areas.[34] In the text known as *Norðleoda Laga*, Wulfstan similarly distinguishes between the wergilds in place between different classes of people in the north of England. Wulfstan was thus conversant with the realities that recognized the legal distinctiveness of the Danelaw, and saw that there were

---

[29] *Gesetze*, i, 214.

[30] In support of this view, one should also consider the potential significance of the 'Alfred– Guthrum Appendix', to be found in the 'London' version of the *Quadripartitus*. It has been suggested that this was tacked on to the Alfred–Guthrum treaty by a mid-tenth-century compiler, intent on rectifying a loophole in Edward the Elder's laws that left certain judicial measures to be decided according to the 'peace-documents' of what were then unconquered territories. When the appendix was written, the king (possibly Edgar) may have been trying 'to extend the ramifications of English law northwards, as he made his power felt'. *MEL*, 379–80; see also *Gesetze*, i, 394 and iii, 233.

[31] *MEL*, 182–5.

[32] D. Whitelock, 'Wulfstan and the so-called Laws of Edward and Guthrum', *E.H.R.*, 51 (1941), 1–21; see also *MEL*, 389–91. For the text see *Gesetze*, i, 128ff. (and iii, 86–9 for commentary, now superseded by Whitelock).

[33] Corpus Christi College Cambridge, MSS. 265 and London, B.L., Cotton MS. Nero E.i.

[34] Edward–Guthrum III.2 (*Gesetze*, i, 130).

customs prevalent there that had no application further south. This is clearly illustrated (for example) in VI Atr 37 (which Wulfstan certainly drafted) which recognizes the different modes of clearing oneself of plotting against the king: 'he shall do so by means of the most solemn oath or by the triple ordeal in districts under English law, and in those under Danish law in accordance with their constitution'. This is in fact the earliest reference in the law codes to the Danelaw, or 'Dena lage'.[35] In his later texts Wulfstan talks about the 'North English Law' to which offenders are subject.[36] A corollary to all this is that *Wulfstan would have balked at very little that he saw in IV Eg*. The references to the continuance of Danish law in the Scandinavian areas were something that the archbishop provided for in his own writings. Indeed in the prologue to 'Edward–Guthrum', Wulfstan is anxious to give the impression that this fundamental difference stemmed from long-established custom.[37]

The point of this rather lengthy excursus is that while Wulfstan's criticism of Edgar in the *Chronicle* is enormously significant, it must be more than an inference from the type of reading that one might otherwise be tempted to give to IV Eg. If Edgar was indeed allowing the Danelaw more autonomy, one would not expect the type of criticism that Wulfstan actually makes. Wulfstan is blaming Edgar for the *inclusiveness* of his policies and (it seems) for allowing more Danes into his realm.[38]

For Wulfstan's real grievance it is necessary to turn away from IV Eg and ask why he would have made this remarks at a time when the country was being swamped by Danish armies. If he did not have in mind the Scandinavians who had settled in areas of the Danelaw, then one should consider the possibility that he was thinking of relative newcomers. He does after all refer to 'heathen customs' in the *Chronicle* panegyric. This was a point that was elaborated by William of Malmesbury. He says Edgar was so famous that

foreigners in crowds, Saxons, Flemings, even Danes, visited this country and became Edgar's friends; and their arrival had a very bad effect on its inhabitants, who learnt from the Saxons unalloyed ferocity, from the Flemings a spineless physical effeminacy, and

---

[35] Robertson, *Laws*, 103. See also *MEL*, 330–45, Whitelock, *Sermo Lupi*, 23, and her 'Wulfstan at York', in *Franciplegius: Medieval and Linguistic studies in Honor of Francis Peabody Magoun*, ed. J.B. Bessinger Jr and R.P. Creed (NY, 1965), 214–31 at 224–5.

[36] *Grið* 13–14 and 1–6 (*Gesetze*, i, 470–71).

[37] *MEL*, 380–91.

[38] It has been suggested that the 'Danes' mentioned in IV Eg were transients and later arrivals, whose presence in England was never as permanent as the earlier settlers. S. Reynolds, 'What Do We Mean by "Anglo-Saxon" and "Anglo-Saxons"?', *Journal of British Studies,* 24 (1985), 395–414, at 409; see also D.M. Hadley, ' "And they proceeded to plough and to support themselves": the Scandinavian settlement of England', *A.N.S.,* 19 (1996), 69–96, at 85. It is difficult to accept these arguments, at least in the context of IV Eg. When the Danes are mentioned in the code, they clearly stand for a people, and as such are contrasted to 'the English', or to 'the Britons' (IV Eg 2a). In addition, the fact that the code is to be distributed under the aegis of the three ealdorman with authority in the Danelaw is an indication that the people of these regions must be the 'Danes' referred to elsewhere in the text (IV Eg 15).

from the Danes a love of drinking, though previously they had been immune from such failings and had maintained their own standards naturally and simply without coveting those of others . . .[39]

It has usually been thought that William was simply embroidering on the *Chronicle*. However this is still interesting in that he explicitly says what Wulfstan leads us to suspect: namely, there was an influx of Danes into the kingdom as a result of Edgar's reputed cosmopolitanism.

What kind of links do we know there to have existed with Scandinavia in the tenth century? King Æthelstan had been in friendly contact with Harold Fairhair, the unifier of Norway, and had fostered his son Hakon, who was to become the first Christian king in that country.[40] William of Malmesbury records how two Norwegians named Helgrim and Osfrid were dispatched by Harold to Æthelstan, bearing rich gifts.[41] There is no evidence for similar missions carried out in Edgar's reign, but modern scholarship has demonstrated that England played a major role in the Christianization of parts of Scandinavia.[42] It has also been shown that a proportion of Edgar's moneyers bore Scandinavian names – both Norse and Danish. In particular, the proportion of Scandinavian moneyers involved in the production of his last, and most famous type (the 'Reform' issue after 973) was equal to that of English moneyers.[43] One area where Scandinavian moneyers plied their trade in great numbers (though not to the exclusion of English ones) was Chester, an area where their activity was, as Metcalf puts it, of 'an astonishing scale' in the tenth century.[44]

The extant sources make it clear that Scandinavian merchants and moneyers were present in England in the tenth century. Missionaries probably travelled the other way. There is a fourth important group – mercenaries, or more accurately, stipendiary fighting men. Some of the critical evidence for this lies in a

---

[39] William of Malmesbury, *G.R.*, i, 241.

[40] Stenton, *Anglo-Saxon England*, 348–9. For the history of Scandinavia at this time, see G. Jones, *A History of the Vikings* (Oxford, 1973), 59ff.

[41] William of Malmesbury, *G.R.*, i, 217.

[42] Essential is L. Abrams, 'The Anglo-Saxons and the Christianization of Scandinavia', *A.S.E.*, 24 (1995), 213–50, at 219ff.; see also P. Sawyer, 'Ethelred II, Olaf Trygvason, and the conversion of Norway', in *Anglo-Scandinavian England: Norse-English Relations in the Period before the Conquest*, ed. J.D. Niles and M. Amodio (Boston and London, 1989), 17–24, at 21; F. Birkeli, 'The Earliest Missionary Activities from England to Norway', *Nottingham Medieval Studies*, 15 (1971), pp. 27–37; and C.J.A. Oppermann, *The English Missionaries in Sweden and Finland* (London, 1937), 58ff.

[43] See V. Smart, 'Scandinavians, Celts, and Germans in Anglo-Saxon England: the evidence of moneyers' names', in *Anglo-Saxon Monetary History*, ed. M.A.S. Blackburn (Leicester, 1986), 171–84, at 178; O. von Feilitzen and C. Blunt, 'Personal names on the coinage of Edgar', in *England before the Conquest: Studies in Primary Sources presented to Dorothy Whitelock*, ed. P. Clemoes and K. Hughes (Cambridge, 1971), 183–214, at 208.

[44] D.M. Metcalf, 'The monetary history of England in the tenth century viewed in the perspective of the eleventh century', in Blackburn (ed.), *Anglo-Saxon Monetary History*, 133–57, at 144.

comparatively neglected source for late Anglo-Saxon history, the post-Conquest compilation ascribed to John of Wallingford. It has been known for some time that 'John' does at several points preserve information surviving nowhere else that ought to be taken seriously, but only recently has this been applied within the context of reconstructing tenth-century political history.[45] One passage bears directly on the issue of Danish immigration and the uses it was put to:

[Æthelred's] reign was marked by dangers and calamities which came upon him by reason of the perfect liberty of access granted to the Danes by his predecessors . . . the Danes had increased in the land ever since the time of king Ethelstan, who had held them in high favour; and they now possessed the best cities in the island. Indeed, as all the kings of the West Angles made use of them in their attacks on the provinces of their neighbours, a law had been passed that every house that was able should support one Dane, and there might always be a sufficient force to serve in the royal campaigns. Thus did the Danes increase by degrees, till they oppressed the people of the land . . .[46]

He then explains that their practice of combing their hair every day, bathing every Saturday and changing their garments often led the Danes to be infinitely more attractive to local noblewomen then native Englishmen. When Æthelred at last found their insolence too much to handle he allowed the English to deal with them as they saw fit. This led to the events of St Brice's day in 1002 when according to the *Chronicle* 'all the Danish men who were in England' were killed because Æthelred feared treachery on their part.[47]

Not all of this should be accepted as it stands. No trace of the law described by John remains. However, it is significant that Æthelstan is singled out. Besides his links discussed above with Norway, there is also a tradition recorded by the famous scald Egil Skallagrimson that Æthelstan had Norsemen in his pay fighting with his army at the Battle of Brunanburh.[48] Perhaps this is what John of Wallingford meant when he said that Æthelstan had held the 'Danes' in high regard. But if Æthelstan did employ Scandinavians in a military capacity, he

---

[45] *The Chronicle attributed to John of Wallingford*, ed. R. Vaughan, Camden Miscellany, xxi, Camden Society, 3rd ser., xc (London, 1958), 1–74 [translation in *The Church Historians of England*, ed. and trans. J. Stevenson, vol. 2 part II (London, 1854), 523–64.] For recent examples of the use of this source in modern scholarship, see S.D.Keynes, 'The Additions in Old English', in J.J.G. Alexander and N. Barker, *The York Gospels* (London, 1986), 87 and n. 35. Until a thorough investigation into John's sources can be made, the best general guide is still Vaughan's introduction at ix–xv.

[46] John of Wallingford, *Chronicle*, 60 (trans. Stevenson, 558).

[47] *A.S.C.*, 'C', s.a. 1002. John states that the day of the massacre was planned for a Saturday to take advantage of the fact that the Danes would be unprepared on that day; oddly enough, St Brice's Day in 1002 did indeed fall on a Saturday. John of Wallingford, *Chronicle*, 60 n. 1.

[48] *Egil's Saga*, in *Early Sources of Scottish History, A.D. 500 to 1286*, ed. A.O. Anderson (2 vols., Stamford, 1990), i, 410ff.; see also A. Campbell, *Skaldic Verse and Anglo-Saxon History* (London, 1971), pp. 5–7. Campbell is sceptical about using the description of the battle at 'Vin Moor' in *Egil's Saga* as evidence for Brunanburh, but admits the possibility that Æthelstan might have had Norse allies with him.

would not have been the first West Saxon king to do so. Asser, King Alfred's biographer, states that Alfred had many 'pagani' in his service.[49]

There were many groups of Scandinavians in the late ninth and tenth centuries which should be distinguished from those who had already settled in England. Some should essentially be seen as stipendiaries. Professor Keynes has noted a reference in the *Chronicle* entry for 917 to 'vikings' fighting with the Danes in East Anglia in a context which differentiates them from the Danes already established in England, and which implies that they were pirates.[50] There was nothing that prevented the same men from assuming multiple identities and from time to time being traders or merchants, but one must not overlook the fact that many were chiefly interested in fighting for money. As Patrick Wormald has remarked of such men 'they were probably bad, and certainly dangerous to know'.[51] And it should not be assumed that they offered their services just to the West Saxon kings.[52] A letter from a tenth-century Canterbury letter-book written by an English ecclesiastic to Arnulf, count of Flanders (possibly to be dated to Edgar's reign) refers to 'Danis vestris', and the fact that these Danes, presumably in Arnulf's service, had made off with a certain woman.[53]

For the present though we are concerned with the use of such men by the English kings. As a lead in to this, I would like to turn to the fleet. There is relatively plentiful evidence for the existence of the fleet under Æthelred, and this has been discussed in depth by modern commentators.[54] But was it ever exclusively 'English'? Late in the ninth century, King Alfred had used Frisians to man his ships.[55] There is also a reference by the scald Ottar the Black (who took service with Cnut) to Frisians fighting on the English side during Æthelred's reign.[56] Æthelred can also be shown to have had Scandinavian retainers with ships under their command. The *Chronicle* entry for 1001 tells us of a certain

---

49 *Asser's Life of King Alfred together with the Annals of St Neots*, ed. W.H. Stevenson (Oxford, 1904), 60: 'Franci autem multi, Frisones, Galli, pagani, Britones, et Scotti, Armorici sponte se suo dominio subdiderant'. Professor Nelson suggests to me that 'dominio' was meant in the sense of 'military household'.

50 *A.S.C* 'A', s.a. 917; S.D. Keynes, 'Vikings', in *The Blackwell Encyclopaedia of Anglo-Saxon England*, 460–61. Prof Keynes sees these men as 'hired killers'.

51 P. Wormald, 'Viking Studies: Whence and Whither', in *The Vikings*, ed. R.T. Farrell (London, 1982), 128–56, at 148.

52 See N. Lund, 'Allies of God or Man? The Viking Expansion in a European Perspective', *Viator*, 20 (1989), 45–59, at 47.

53 *Memorials of St Dunstan*, ed. W. Stubbs (R.S., 1874), p. 362.

54 See especially N. Hooper, 'Some Observations on the Navy in Late Anglo-Saxon England', in *Studies in Medieval History Presented to R. Allen Brown*, ed. C. Harper-Bill, C.J. Holdsworth, and J.L. Nelson (Woodbridge, 1989), 203–14; C.W. Hollister, *Anglo-Saxon Military Institutions* (Oxford, 1962), 103–26, and R. Abels, *Lordship and Military Obligation in Anglo-Saxon England* (California, 1988).

55 *A.S.C* 'A', s.a. 896.

56 *Knútsdrápa*, in *English and Norse Documents relating to the reign of Æthelred the Unready*, ed.and trans. M. Ashdown (Cambridge, 1930), 139.

Pallig, who together with his ships deserted Æthelred and joined with the Danish forces. This man, a brother-in-law of King Swein, was apparently killed together with his family – on the massacre of St Brice's Day.[57]

Domesday Book shows us that some of the men associated with the fleet in the eleventh century have Scandinavian connections. To take just two examples: A certain Worcester landowner suggestively named Thorkell is named by Domesday Book as 'King Edward's steersman'. Another steersman named Eadric, from Norfolk, is interestingly said to have been exiled to Denmark after 1066.[58] These links can be traced back further in time. In Æthelred's reign, some of the key terms in Anglo-Saxon naval terminology are words which have their origins from across the North Sea. Scandinavian loan words in Middle English are well attested, but in Old English the number is far less; the earliest and most numerous appear to be concentrations of either military or naval terms.[59] For example, the enigmatic *lithsmen* who appear in the eleventh century *Chronicle* entries, frequently in a naval context, derive from *lið*, which is a Scandinavian word for 'ship'. According to Neils Lund they were also loosely knit gangs of warriors (or naval fighting men) in Scandinavia. [60] One could go on. The term *scegth*, used in the *Chronicle* entry for 1008, is a Scandinavian one which seems originally have meant 'longship'.[61] And *Butscarls* ('boatmen'), may also ulti- mately have its origins in the Scandinavian word for a warship.[62]

The evidence with regard to the fleet suggests that Æthelred may have been attempting to revive practices that had been current under his predecessors. In particular, shipsokes are thought to have had their origins in Edgar's reign. [63] There is also a reference in Æthelred's Fifth Code to the fleet being ready every

---

[57] William of Malmesbury, *G.R.*, i, 301; *A.S.C* 'A', s.a. 1001. The other obvious example of Viking stipendiaries in the fleet is of course Thorkell the Tall and his fleet of forty-five ships, which came over to Æthelred's side in 1012. *A.S.C* 'C', s.a. 1012, 1013.

[58] D.B. i 174 (the Worcester Thorkell). A second steersman's name *could* be Scandinavian ('Ulfheah'), but equally it might simply be a variant on 'Wulfheah' (D.B. i 217v). For the exiled Eadric, see D.B. i 200. For this man see *V.C.H. Norfolk*, ii, 122 and A. Williams, *The English and the Norman Conquest* (Woodbridge, 1995), 19 and 35. He is not to be confused with Eadric 'the Steersman', from the Worcester diocese who presumably was part of the Worcester shipsoke. D.B. i 173v; *The English and the Norman Conquest*, 93 n. 114.

[59] The crucial discussion is that of A. Wollmann, 'Scandinavian Loan Words in Old English', in *The Origins and Development of Emigrant Languages: Proceedings from the 2nd Rasmus Rask Colloquium*, ed. H.F. Nielsen and L. Schøsler (Rask Supp. vol. 6/Nowelle Supp. col.17, Odense, 1996).

[60] XXX. Lund, 'The Armies of Swein Forkbeard and Cnut: *leding* or *lið*?', *A.S.E.*, 15 (1986), 105–18, at 106. For the *lithsmen* see also Hooper, 'Some Observations', 205–6. The relevant *Chronicle* entries are: 'E', s.a. 1036, s.a. 1047, 1052 *bis*; and 'C', s.a.1055, 1066.

[61] See D. Whitelock, *Anglo-Saxon Wills*, (Cambridge, 1930), 137. Whitelock points out that the word derives from the old Icelandic *skeið*, and also notes how the 'F' manuscript of the *Chronicle* translates *secgþ* as 'magnam navem'. See also Hooper, 'Some Observations', 212–13.

[62] Hooper, 'Some Observations', 206–7; see also P. Vinogradoff, *English Society in the Eleventh Century* (Oxford, 1908), 20–21. Also useful is the discussion of M.K. Lawson, *Cnut: The Danes in England in the Early Eleventh Century* (London, 1993), 177–84.

[63] See especially Hooper, 'Some Observations'.

year after Easter, and this finds an echo in John of Worcester's famous description of how Edgar's fleet numbered 3600 ships, with the king every year after Easter dividing it equally to patrol the western, eastern, and northern coasts of Britain. In this way the realm was kept free 'contra externos'. [64] Much of this is later accretion, but it is possible that John, drawing on the Worcester tradition, knew something about Edgar's fleet.[65] The size of the fleet however has obviously been distorted through time. What is clear though is that Edgar's navy was a formidable one. The 'D' version of the *Chronicle* for 975 says in a slightly sinister fashion that there was no 'fleet so proud nor host so strong that it got itself prey in England as long as the noble king held the throne'.[66] Even in the 960s and 970s the fleet cannot simply have been engaged in symbolic perambulations around the Island, for it is impossible for Edgar to have been unfamiliar with the Vikings. Maccus Haraldson, descended from the Limerick Norse, had by the 970s had established a kingdom on the Isle of Man, and with his brother Guthfrith was conducting regular raids into north-west Wales.[67]

How did Edgar view these men? Prof Whitelock once drew attention to the fact that some charters of the late 960s warn of the impending end of the world, and suggested that this was be linked to the renewed activity on the part of the Vikings. [68] She seems to have later changed her mind, but there is a charter of Edward the Martyr dated 977 granting a coastal estate in Cornwall to the ealdorman Æthelweard, which omits to mention the usual duty of bridgework placed upon the beneficiary, instead insisting upon 'maritime guard' 'vigiliis marinis'.[69] Exactly what was meant by this is uncertain, but it was probably one measure aimed at curbing the activities of the Vikings whom we know to have been in the neighbourhood. There are thus reasons for believing that some Vikings were already on the prowl from the 960s and 970s, but were perhaps kept at bay by Edgar. Indeed, the only noteworthy reference to Edgar that I have been able to find in the Scandinavian sources seems to hint at an appreciation of his might, with Ottar the Black referring to Cnut having 'smote the race of Edgar'.[70]

There is the possibility though that relations were symbiotic. Others have tentatively suggested that some of the 'harmful people' present in England in the

---

[64] John of Worcester, *Chronicle*, ii, s.a. 975.

[65] It is also noteworthy that John of Worcester made no mention of the Worcester tradition that Edgar had conquered the Dublin from the Norse king, a story that was certainly doing the rounds by the time he was writing. *Memorials of St Dunstan*, 422–3.

[66] *A.S.C* 'D', s.a. 975.

[67] See G.V.C. Young, *The History of the Isle of Man under the Vikings: Now through a Glass Darkly* (Isle of Man, 1981), 32ff.; E. Callow, *From King Orry to Queen Victoria* (London, 1899); A. Moore, *A History of the Isle of Man* (2 vols., London, 1900), i, 82ff.

[68] *E.H.D.*, i, 345 (1st edn.) first drew attention to this feature of Edgar's charters. These remarks are not in the second edition of *E.H.D.* See also J.L .Nelson, 'Inauguration Rituals', in her *Politics and Ritual in Early Medieval Europe* (London, 1986) 283–308, at 302.

[69] S 832. See *E.H.D.*, i, (2nd edn.), 566–7.

[70] *Knútsdrápa* (as above) 138; though see the similar reference to Edmund at 139.

tenth century were Scandinavians used by the West Saxons kings to man the fleet, but the suggestion has never received detailed consideration.[71] In indirect support of this is the fact that from the period 970–1050 there was an outflow of silver from England towards the north. For this period there are over fifty thousand English coins in Scandinavian hoards.[72] Some of this was certainly the result of trade, and Æthelred's reign saw the Danes carrying off plunder and tribute-money. However, matters are not so certain for the rest of this period. It is instructive that the age structure of some hoards suggests that at least part of the eleven thousand pounds levelled in 1041 by Harthacnut to pay the fleet found its way into Scandinavia.[73] One could also usefully look ahead to Edward the Confessor, who was also a king criticized for bringing unwanted foreigners into the realm. After 1051, when the Confessor's fleet was disbanded, the number of English coins in Scandinavian hoards decreases dramatically.[74] All this is not coincidence. It must be an indication as to just how many Scandinavians served in the fleet in the eleventh century – indeed, it has been suggested that their predominance within the fleet had something to do with the Confessor's decision to pay off his ships.[75] Going back to the opposite end of the spectrum, numismatists tell us that the beginnings of the outflow of silver lie in the 970s, best illustrated by a group of Scandinavian and Manx hoard-finds in which Edgar's pre-reform type is the predominant issue.[76] It has also been suggested that the reform type first reached Scandinavia, especially Gotland, in the mid-970s.[77] This was before the first Viking raids in England were known to

[71] P. Sawyer, *From Roman Britain to Norman England* (London, 1978), 127; Hooper, 'Some Observations', 204.
[72] The hoard evidence is discussed in D. Metcalf, 'The Monetary history of England in the tenth century viewed in the perspective of the eleventh century', in *Anglo-Saxon Monetary History*, 133–57, at 134–5 and Sawyer, 'Anglo-Scandinavian Trade', in *idem*, 185–99, at 194–5.
[73] J. Gillingham, 'Chronicles and Coins as Evidence for Levels of Tribute and Taxation in Late Tenth- and Early Eleventh-Century England', *E.H.R.*, 105 (1990), 939–50, at 946–7; but see also M.K. Lawson, 'Danegeld and Heregeld once More', *idem*, 951–61.
[74] Sawyer, 'Anglo-Scandinavian Trade', p.195.
[75] It is an open question as to the extent to which Edward the Confessor's fleet was manned by Scandinavians. P. Sawyer in some incidental remarks suggests that it was essentially a 'Scandinavian fleet'. See his 'Anglo-Scandinavian trade in the Viking Age and after', in Blackburn (ed.), *Anglo-Saxon Monetary History*, 185–99, at p. 195. See also P. Nightingale, 'The Origin of the Court of Husting and Danish Influence on London's Development into a Capital City', *E.H.R.*, 102 (1987), 559–79, at 569–70; where it is suggested that Edward's fear of a coup on the part of the Scandinavian naval force led his decision to disband the fleet.
[76] See C.E. Blunt, 'A New Parcel from the Douglas, I.O.M., 1894 Hoard (?)', *British Numismatic Journal*, 35 (1966), 7–11; M. Dolley, 'Some Preliminary Observations on Three Manx Coin-Hoards Appearing to End with Pennies of Eadgar', *Numismatic Circular* (1975), 146, 190–2; and H.E. Pagan, 'The 1894 Ballaquayle Hoard: Five Further Parcels of Coins of Æthelstan-Eadgar', *British Numismatic Journal*, 1 (1980), 12–19. For the Scandinavian hoards see above, at n. 72.
[77] See M. Blackburn and K. Jonsson, 'The Anglo-Saxon and Anglo-Norman element of north European coin finds', *Viking Age Coinage in the Northern Lands*, ed. M. Blackburn and D.M. Meltcalf, (Oxford, *BAR International Series*, I 22 (i), 1981), 147–256, especially at 153–65 and 184.

have begun, so it is unlikely that these finds primarily represent plunder. These finds are I think an indicator as to the Scandinavianization of the navy in the 960s and 970s.

To what extent can Edgar be shown to have been involved in the type of dealings with the Vikings that might have facilitated such arrangements? The key figure here is Maccus Haraldson, king of Man, who was one of those who attended the famous gathering at Chester in 973, where, according to the English sources, they all submitted to Edgar. Much of the life of Maccus is shrouded in the obscurity of oral tradition and the sagas. One oft-repeated Manx tradition, not written down until a very late stage, has it that 'King Maccus was deprived of the crown of Man for refusing to do homage to Edgar, who afterwards not only restored him to the throne, but made him admiral of a great fleet with which he swept the seas of the Danes and the Norwegians.'[78] This cannot, of course be accepted, but one may be reasonably certain that there was *something* going on at Man during this time. Edgar's coins are the latest issues found in the three major Manx hoards found from around this period, the most famous being the Ballaquayle Hoard, unearthed at Man in 1894. Their concealment is a good indicator of political activity – or turmoil.[79] One study of these hoards has suggested that the finds reflect Edgar's largesse to Maccus at Chester in 973 and it is to this meeting that we must now turn.

I do not intend to provide a comprehensive treatment of the issues or protagonists – this has been done elsewhere.[80] But the gathering itself, when shorn of the propaganda that cocoons it, can still be examined to see if it provides any corroboration for the idea of co-operation between Edgar and Maccus. Chester did of course conjure up shades of the Roman imperial past and would have been an ideal setting for the type of submission that later writers thought had taken place. Thus Ælfric, writing in the 990s, could state that

all the kings who were in this island, Cumbrians and Scots, came to Edgar, once eight kings on one day, and they all submitted to Edgar's direction. [81]

Ælfric uses the word for homage [*gebugon*] – it is this aspect of the meeting which came to be emphasized by later writers.[82] If John of Worcester is to be

---

[78] See Young, *The History of the Isle of Man*, 34. See also H.A. Bullock, *The History of the Isle of Man* (London,1816), 5–6.

[79] Young, *History of the Isle of Man*, 34. See Blunt, 'A New Parcel', and M. Dolley, 'Some Preliminary Observations', 190–92. Dolley also suggests that the concealment of the hoards because 'some cataclysm struck the Irish sea Vikings at the end of the 970s'. This is also the proposal of Wilson, who suggests that the hoarding took place at the time of Earl Sigurd's attack on Man *c.* 982. D.M. Wilson, *The Viking Age in the Isle of Man* (Odense, 1974), 39–40.

[80] Stenton, *Anglo-Saxon England*, 368–71. I am also extremely grateful to Ann Williams for allowing me to see her forthcoming paper, 'An Outing on the Dee: King Edgar at Chester, A.D. 973'.

[81] Ælfric, *Life of St Swithin*, in *E.H.D.*, i, 927; see *Ælfric's Lives of the Saints*, ed. W.W. Skeat (4 vols., EETS, 1881–1900), i, 468.

[82] See W.H. Stevenson, 'The Great Commendation to King Edgar in 973', *E.H.R.*, 13 (1898), 71–7.

believed they then rowed him on the River Dee, with Edgar acting as cox. But really there is no reason why this story should be believed. What we need to consider is that the various rulers must have come to Chester with their individual (and differing) agendas, and some certainly would not have been negotiating from a position of weakness. Edgar's dealings with Kenneth, king of the Scots (for example) have in our available accounts really much more the quality of negotiations between near-equals than anything else. After all, it was around this time that he ceded Lothian to Kenneth.[83] Later historians made this a grant in return for homage done to Edgar.[84] The attempts of the Norman kings to bring Scotland within their orbit may well have been a factor that led the twelfth- and thirteenth-century historians to treat the Chester meeting as they did, showing Scotland as a client to the house of Wessex. Kenneth's career, and aggression towards the English, shows him to have been anything but that.[85]

It could also legitimately be asked why the eight kings did not meet Edgar at Bath, where Edgar received his 'imperial' coronation. The possibility is that they would not.[86] As Alfred Smyth notes, the meeting at Chester took place 'on the middle ground at the most important port on the Irish Sea', and it would thus have been convenient not only for the island Vikings, but also for the northern Welsh princes, and for the kings of Strathclyde and Scotland.[87] Chester may well have represented a neutral venue away from the heart of Edgar's power in the south-east, looking out to the Irish Sea, where the attendee kings could meet on terms that approached something like equality. Doubtless there were out-

---

[83] There are three accounts of the event. The earliest version is contained in the tract called *De primo Saxonum adventu*, which was probably compiled in Northumbria between 1122 and 1128. Two other versions (not entirely independent of the first) are found in the *Flores historiarum* of Roger of Wendover (*c.* 1235) and another work from St Albans, the *Chronicle* of John of Wallingford (*c.* 1240). Though there are important differences between the accounts, it seems likely that they were ultimately drawing upon the same lost northern source. See M.O. Anderson, 'Lothian and the Early Scottish Kings', *Scottish Historical Review,* 39 (1960), 98–112, and B. Meehan, 'The siege of Durham, the battle of Carham and the cession of Lothian', *ibid*, 55 (1976), pp. 1–19, at 4–5 and 17.

[84] John of Wallingford, *Chronicle*, 54–5. The legendary story related by William of Malmesbury concerning Edgar's meeting with Kenneth, and Kenneth's humiliation, seems to owe something to this tradition as well. William of Malmesbury, *G.R.*, 255–7.

[85] A.P. Smyth, *Warlords and Holy Men: Scotland, AD 800–1000* (London, 1984), 224–9. See 229 for a discussion of Kenneth's raid on Stainmore *c.* 971.

[86] The forged S 808, which was concocted at Christ Church to reinforce their claim to Sandwich, has seven of the eight kings present, witnessing Edgar's grant of Sandwich to Christ Church. The charter is said to have been drawn up 'on the feast of Pentecost, at Bath'.

[87] In particular it would have been an especially convenient stopping-off point for Maccus, who can be shown to have been raiding Ireland at almost the same time. *The Annals of the Four Masters* records a raid by Maccus 'along with the Lawmen of the islands' on Inishcathy in 972. However the chronology at this point is confused – both 972 and 974 have been put forward as the actual date (*Early Sources of Scottish History*, i, 479; Moore, *A History of the Isle of Man*, i, 92–3). In view of Maccus's own activities and those of all the eight 'kings', it might be added that getting them all together at Chester was a quite spectacular administrative feat. How many months in advance would the invitations have had to be sent?

standing issues to be resolved amongst themselves as well, not least in the meeting between the princes of Gwynedd and their tormentor, Maccus. Smyth rightly draws attention to the type of gatherings in Ireland known as *ríg-dál*, a 'royal conference' or 'parliament of kings', and suggests that this was the type of parley that took place at Chester.[88]

The 'D' and 'E' texts of the *Chronicle* tend to support the above interpretation ('C', it will be remembered, has no interest in the affair at all). They simply note that these rulers made a truce or agreement with Edgar (*trywsodon*), agreeing to be his 'efenwyrhton' in land and sea. 'Efenwyrhton' literally means 'equal-workers' but 'allies' is the usual rendering.[89] However, it is also in these relatively early accounts that the seeds for the idea of 'submission' were sown, for they say that the eight rulers gave Edgar *pledges* that they would be his equal-workers. The truth is that early medieval diplomacy could often be represented by each side to show some sort of subordination for propagandistic purposes. To simply assume that later writers would cloak such meetings with the language of homage is itself misleading, as there can be no doubt that such overtones could be present contemporaneously, on the ground itself. The parameters for this type of obfuscation were set by the Carolingians: Prof Reuter notes how in 798 Alfonso II of Asturias sent Charlemagne important trophies following the capture of Lisbon. The imperial court seized on these gifts as tribute, although Alfonso did not see it that way.[90] It is thus likely that on the ground itself in 973 there were individual negotiations and gift-givings (which can be dimly glimpsed in the number of Manx hoards from the 970s) and also counter-gifts which could very quickly be interpreted as tribute.[91] The atmosphere one must envisage is one of ceremony and ritual that was honorific to both sides.

There is no doubt that Edgar and his advisers chose at once, or at least very quickly, to present 973 in a certain light: in his Fourth Law Code, Edgar makes a reference to certain provisions applying 'to all who inhabit these islands', and this might reflect his claim to influence over Man and the Isles. [92] All this is reflected in the 'imperial theme' that becomes prominent in Edgar's last years,

---

88 Smyth, *Warlords and Holy Men*, 228.

89 *An Anglo-Saxon Dictionary Based on the Manuscript Collections of the Late Joseph Bosworth*, ed. T.N. Toller (Oxford, 1973), 241, where 'fellow worker' or 'co-operator' is suggested.

90 T. Reuter, 'Plunder and Tribute in the Carolingian Empire', *T.R.H.S.*, 5th ser., 35 (1985), 75–94, at 85–6.

91 'Plunder and Tribute', 87, see also P. Grierson, 'Commerce in the Dark Ages: A Critique of the Evidence', *T.R.H.S.*, 5th ser., 9 (1959), 137. Grierson remarks, 'tribute consists of placing other people morally in one's debt, for a counter-gift – or services in lieu of one – is necessary if the recipient is to retain his self-respect'. See M. Mauss, *Essai sur le don* (1935), trans. I. Cunnison, *The Gift: Forms and Functions of Exchange in Archaic Societies* (London, 1969).

92 There is a late charter of Edgar which has the royal style 'Eadgarus tocius Albionis basileus necne maritimorum seu insulanorum meorum subjectione regum circum habitancium' (S 796/B 1301). The date, 974, is instructive, and is to my mind a reflection of the king and his circle reading a great deal into their deal-making with Maccus. The charter however may not be wholly authentic.

above all in his charter styles.[93] This has been fully dealt with elsewhere.[94] What
should be noted is that while such themes irradiate the meeting at Chester, they
serve to obscure the motivations of the other attendees – and our understanding
of them. It also makes it doubly difficult to discover the precise nature of
Edgar's dealings with the Vikings. Fortunately, there are other sources which
provide some tantalizing clues. We have seen how Byrhtferth of Ramsey
describes how Edgar held sway over the 'princes of the islands'. Is this simply a
biblical flourish? There was also at least one other attendee at Chester with a
Scandinavian name, and he appears in later accounts as either 'Siferth' (John of
Worcester), or 'Giferth' (William of Malmesbury).[95] There was a king named
Siferth who was a contemporary of Edgar: his suicide and burial at Wimborne
are recorded in the 'A' rescension of the *Chronicle* for 962. Whitelock suggested that he should be placed in the Isles.[96] Nothing else is known of this man,
and at any rate he certainly cannot have been at Chester in 973. There are two
more likely candidates. One is Guthfrith Haraldson, the brother of Maccus, who
was eventually to succeed him when Maccus was killed in 977. His presence at
Chester would not have been unusual, for two other attendees were also in the
company of the men they were to replace: Hywel ap Idwal who came with his
uncle Iago of Gwynedd, and Malcolm of Strathclyde along with his father
Dufnal.[97] There is, however, an equally tempting possibility. John of Wallingford, like Byrhtferth, also employs the plural when dealing with the Island

[93] See for example S 775 from 970 (B 1259) where Edgar is styled 'imperator augustus'.

[94] There is a huge literature on this. See in general John, *Orbis Britanniae*, 52ff., E.E. Stengel,
'Imperator und Imperium bei den Angelsachsen', in *idem, Abhandlungen und Untersuchungen zur
Geschichte des Kaisergedankens im Mittelalter* (Cologne, 1965), 287–338; R. Drögereit, 'Kaiseridee
und Kaisertitel bei den Angelsachsen', in *Zeitschrift der Savigny-Stiftung für Rechsgeschichte*,
Germ. Abt. 69 (1952), 24–73 at 24ff. (for a summary of his argument see H. Loyn, 'The Imperial
Style of the Tenth-Century Anglo-Saxon Kings', *History*, 40 (1955), 111–15); R. Deshman,
Christus rex et magi reges: Kingship and Christology in Ottonian and Anglo-Saxon Art,
Frümittelalterliche Studien (1976), pp. 367–405, and Nelson, 'Inauguration Rituals', pp. 297–304.
The 'imperial' consecration of 973 is discussed by A. Jones, 'The Significance of the Regal Con-
secration of Edgar in 973', *Jnl. Eccl. Hist.*, 33 (1982), 375–90.

[95] John of Worcester, *Chronicle*, s.a. 973, William of Malmesbury, *G.R.*, i, p. 239. Both John of
Worcester and William of Malmesbury seem to have been relying on a common stock of
Worcester material: *G.R*, ii, 133; see in general Brett, 'John of Worcester and his Contemporaries',
113–17. Ann Williams suggests to me that the original source read 'Siferth', to be later modified
by William of Malmesbury or his own source. This might seem to support to second identification
I make above, but in this there can be no certainty.

[96] *A.S.C.* 'A', s.a. 962 (where he is called 'king'). Nothing is known of Siferth. Williams suggest
that as he was buried at Wimbourne, 'he was presumably a hanger-on of the West Saxon court,
perhaps one who had sought refuge there' ('An Outing on the Dee', forthcoming). He may or may
not be the same Siferth who attests a charter of 955 in the company of Welsh *reguli. Anglo-Saxon
Charters*, ed. A.J. Robertson (Cambridge, 1956), xxx.

[97] For these men, see Stenton, *Anglo-Saxon England*, 369–70. In my view the latest editors of
William of Malmesbury's work dispense with this possibility rather too freely, overlooking the
fact that Maccus and Guthfrith were brothers and placing too much trust on the forged S 808.
(*G.R.*, ii, 132–3). The editors also identify Hywel ap Idwal with Hywel the Great, King of Wales
942–50, but the two were of course different men.

princes. He states that besides Maccus, 'various kings of the Orcades' did homage to Edgar.[98] Presumably he means the Orkneys and this is significant, for we know that Sigurd 'the Fat', Earl of Orkney, was active in the area. He was to attack Man in 980. According to a late source, the *Flóamanna Saga*, this was at the behest of Earl Hakon of Norway, because Man had neglected tribute for three years. Sigurd may well have been the Siferth said to have been at Chester. He only seems to have become Earl in 976/7, but like Malcolm, son of Dufnal he may already have been exercising some authority under his father, Hlodve, Earl of Orkney.[99]

The mechanics of the Chester meeting provide just one possible context for the use of Scandinavian hirelings whom I suspect Edgar depended on, but it deserves attention because men like Sigurd, Maccus, and Guthfrith are known to have had powerful war-fleets.[100] Edgar had dealings with at least one of them. It cannot be proved that Maccus (or any of these men) took service in Edgar's fleet, still less that he became Edgar's 'admiral'. But it remains a tempting possibility that in the 973 meeting, the issue of stipendiaries to serve in Edgar's navy was on the agenda. [101] One could also look to the parallel with Eric Bloodaxe, who used the Scottish isles as a base, and one from which warriors could be recruited.[102] In a wider context, Edgar would not have been doing anything that was specifically new: he would simply have been falling in line with the continental, Byzantine, and Russian rulers who made use of Vikings as fighting men.[103]

*   *   *

It will be readily admitted that there are questions which cannot be answered with certainty. There is no evidence that the type of arrangements sketched above, informal or otherwise, persisted into Æthelred's reign. The *Chronicle*

---

98 John of Wallingford, *Chronicle*, 55.

99 *Early Sources of Scottish History*, i, 481; for the attack against Godfrey, see 500, 502. Nelson states 'two sea-kings of the western and northern isles' attended the Chester meeting ('Inauguration Rituals', 302). Certainly she had Maccus in mind as ruler of the Western Isles, but I am unclear as to whom she meant as the second 'sea-king'.

100 See *Early Sources of Scottish History*, i, 497, 500, 528; Young; *History of the Isle of Man*, 37.

101 Æthelweard the Chronicler has an intriguing reference to how in the years after Brunanburh, 'there was peace everywhere . . . no fleet has remained here, having advanced against these shores, except under treaty with the English'. *Chronicon*, ed. A. Campbell (London, 1962), 54. Is it possible that he was referring to the type of arrangements made between Edgar and the Vikings? Alternatively, he may have had in mind the treaties that Æthelred concluded with the invading armies. Æthelweard was himself a key player in the negotiations which lead to the 994 peace with Olaf Trygvason (*A.S.C.* 'C', s.a. 994). Note that the passage in Æthelweard's work is similar to one found in Ælfric's *Life of Swithin*: 'his [Edgar's] kingdom continued ever at peace so that no fleet was ever heard of except of our people who held the land'. *E.H.D.*, i, 927. For Æthelweard's links with Ælfric, see the introduction to the *Chronicon*, xiv–xv.

102 See A.P. Smyth, *Scandinavian York and Dublin* (2 vols., New Jersey and Dublin, 1979), ii, 174–5. Late Irish tradition records Eric's title as 'king of the Scottish Isles' (176).

103 Lund, 'Allies of God or Man?', 45–52.

entry for 992 which notes how Æthelred ordered 'that the ships that were of any use should be assembled at London' would seem to suggest a system which had been running down. Perhaps Edgar's Scandinavians were paid off at his death; this would certainly be one reason that could account for the rise in the number of English coins within Scandinavian hoards from the 970s. However, there is no need to suppose that all these men went home. For one thing is clear: by Æthelred's time there were a lot of *very* recent Scandinavian arrivals in the country – men whom we should not necessarily group with the Danish raiders of the 990s. Æthelred himself complains in his foundation charter for St Frideswide's, Oxford (with reference to the massacre of St Brice's Day), that they had sprouted up 'like cockles amongst the wheat'.[104] We do not know how many there were, or how they got there. But Æthelred's desire to be rid of them during the Danish invasions might be readily understandable if, as John of Wallingford suggests, they were professional fighting men.[105]

A Dane coming from across the North Sea would have seen much to attract him to Edgar's England, besides employment. [106] Areas of the country were already settled in by their compatriots.[107] The oral and written culture of England was marked by Scandinavian influence – an important facilitator of acculturation. The ethos of the warrior nobility was one that could readily appreciate the type of sagas and heroic literature that was undoubtedly being disseminated even then.[108] Although the Brunanburh poem (for example) was certainly composed by an Englishman, it has links with Scandinavian eulogistic poetry,

---

[104] The charter to St Frideswide's is S 909. See A. Williams, '"Cockles Amongst the Wheat": Danes and English in the Western Midlands in the First Half of the Eleventh Century', *Midland History*, 11 (1986), 1–22, at 1. Williams says 'it is worth mentioning that the beginnings of the influx predate the reigns of Swein and his son.'

[105] It is an interesting question as to when we are to date the beginnings of the rise in Danish numbers in major towns in England outside of the Danelaw. For the Danish presence in London, see Nightingale, 'The Origin of the Court of Husting'. The *Winchester Annals* actually blame Edgar for allowing Danish emigrants into the cities of the realm, but this is a late source and the passage may not be independent of William of Malmesbury's description of English virtue corrupted by Scandinavian drinking habits. *Annales Monastici*, ed. H.R. Luard (R.S., London, 1865), ii, 12–13. For a discussion of the work, attributed to Richard of Devizes, see xii–xiv.

[106] For a treatment of the main issues, see G. Fellows-Jensen, 'The Vikings in England: a review', *A.S.E.*, 4 (1975), 181–206; Loyn, *The Vikings in Britain*, pp. 113-ff.; a more recent discussion is in Hadley, 'And they Proceeded to Plough and to Support themselves', 69–96.

[107] Gunnlaug Serpent's-Tongue famously said that 'at that time [Ethelred's] there was the same speech in England as in Norway and Denmark, but the speech in England was changed when William the Bastard won the land.' *English and Norse Documents*, ed. Ashdown, 191. He was writing in the thirteenth century and was certainly exaggerating, but still not too far from the mark: see P.H. Sawyer, *Kings and Vikings* (London, 1987), pp. 102–3; and Lyon, *The Vikings in Britain*, pp. 114ff. In his account of the invasions during Æthelred's reign, John of Wallingford states that 'the inhabitants of this province [York] had for a long time before this had much intercourse with the Danes, and intermarried with them, and become like them in speech.' John of Wallingford, *Chronicle*, 61 (trans. Stevenson, 560).

[108] For insights to the ethos of this class, P. Wormald, 'Bede, *Beowulf* and the conversion of the Anglo-Saxon Aristocracy', in *Bede and Anglo-Saxon England,* ed. R.T. Farrell (Oxford, 1978), 32–95 is essential.

and is a good indicator as to the extent to which the contemporary English audience had a scaldic tooth.[109] Interestingly, the poetic eulogy of Edgar in the 'C' version of the *Chronicle* recalls something of this past. It is said there that Edgar was not only 'bold in battle', but more significantly that he was known as a 'dispenser of treasure to warriors'.[110] This was how Edgar was remembered after his death by some, and a reminder that there is far more to him than meets the eye.

[109] See J.D. Niles, 'Skaldic Technique in Brunanburh', in *Anglo-Scandinavian England*, pp. 69–78, and J. Harris, 'Brunanburh 12b–13a and some Skaldic passages', in *Magister Regis: Studies in Honour of Robert Earl Kaske,* ed. A. Groos et al. (New York, 1986), 1–8. Harris claims that Egil learnt his rhyming metre in England and 'certainly composed verse for Æthelstan', and seems to imply some connection between Egil and the authorship of the poem. But it is inconceivable that he was responsible for the Old English original, which has no reference to Norse involvement in Æthelstan's cause.

[110] *A.S.C.* 'C' s.a. 975.

3

Religious Life in Eleventh-Century Salerno: The Church of Santa Lucia in Balnearia

Valerie Ramseyer

A priest and abbot named Raidolfus built a church dedicated to Santa Lucia sometime before January of 1047 on some land he owned in Balnearia, a small village located midway on the road from Salerno to Nocera. (See Map 2) In January of 1047 Raidolfus gave the church the land on which it was built and then oversaw the donation of additional lands by his brother Sesamus, an aunt and three cousins, and members of two other families and two clerics, all referred to as 'parentes'. Shortly thereafter the same group of people leased out some lands to the church's priests in exchange for a payment (*cens*) three times a year. Raidolfus, who served as Santa Lucia's abbot, appointed priests to serve in the church in 1047 and again in 1058. In 1050 the archbishop of Salerno issued a *charta libertatis*, declaring the church of Santa Lucia free from archiepiscopal control. In 1053 Raidolfus leased out some of the church's land to his brother Sesamus in exchange for part of the produce and ten years later the same Sesamus donated to the church some lands which he had recently purchased. One of Raidolfus's sons, Peter, sold one-third of the church in 1068 to a cleric named Maraldus, while another son of Raidolfus, John, donated two parts of the foundation in 1092 to the church of San Nicola in Gallocanta near Vietri, which in turn was absorbed by the Abbey of the Holy Trinity of Cava in the early twelfth century. After this the church of Santa Lucia all but disappears from the documents.[1]

---

[1] Most of the information we have on the church of Santa Lucia comes from a single charter found in the Cava archives: XV, 60, with a copy XV, 61. Parchment charters at Cava are organized into two sections, based on an ancient division made by Abbot Vittorino Manso (1588–92), which was revised by later archivists such as Agostino Venereo (d. 1638) and Salvatore Di Blasi (1778–88): the 'Armario Magno', which contains what Manso saw as the more important documents of the monastery, and the 'Archae'. Charters from the Armario Magno are identified by a capital letter, followed by an Arabic numeral, with approximately 40–50 documents per letter. Charters in the Archae are identified by a Roman numeral followed by an Arabic one, with 120 documents per Archae. In this article, I will identify all charters using the system established by the Cava archivists. Editions of the charters are available up through 1080 in *Codex Diplomaticus Cavensis*, I–VIII, ed. M. Morcaldi et al. (Milan/Naples, 1873–93) and IX–X, ed. S. Leone and G. Vitolo (Badia di Cava, 1984–90). An edition of charters relating to the church of San Nicola of Gallocanta from the ninth to the twelfth centuries has also been published. Paolo

The village of Balnearia was located in the heart of the Lombard Principality of Salerno, an autonomous kingdom in Southern Italy ruled by princes between 849 and 1077.[2] The Principality of Salerno included a large stretch of territory that extended south from the Amalfi coast through the plain of Paestum and the rolling hills of Cilento to the gulf of Policastro and inland from the Irno river valley down along the Picentino mountains to the plain of Eboli and from there through the Alburni mountains into the Valley of Diano and the Tanagro River Valley. (See Maps 2–3) The Lombard princes of Salerno, who had split from the Principality of Benevento during a succession crisis in 849, reached the apex of their power during the reign of Guaimarius IV (1027–52), who claimed authority not only over the Principality of Salerno, but also over the coastal cities of Amalfi and Sorrento, the county of Capua, and large parts of Calabria and Apulia.[3] Guaimarius IV's power was more illusory than real, however, and the Norman leader Robert Guiscard would conquer the Principality soon after, during the reign of Guaimarius IV's son and successor Gisolf II (1052–77). Nonetheless, the capital of the new Norman Duchy of Apulia remained Salerno and the new Norman regime sought to disrupt life in the area as little as possible.

Cherubini, *Le Pergamene di S. Nicola di Gallucanta (secc. IX–XII)* (Salerno, 1990). For edited charters, I will indicate the numbers assigned to them in the *Codex Diplomaticus Cavensis* (hereafter CDC) in addition to their archival identification. An edition of the 1092 charter (XV, 60) can be found in Cherubini, *Le Pergamene*, 288–90, no. 115.

In addition to the act that took place in 1092, the charter also mentions and then briefly summarizes six earlier charters which were shown at the time the 1092 act was written down. This is a common practice in Salerno, seen in charters dating back to the ninth century. Of the six charters mentioned in the 1092 charter, three of the originals still survive in the abbey of Cava's archives: the 1050 emancipation charter (A, 32; CDC VII, 1146; Cherubini, *Le Pergamene*, 181–3, no. 67), the 1053 sharecropping agreement (X, 63; CDC VII, 1183; Cherubini, *Le Pergamene*, 187–9, no. 71) and the 1063 land sale (XI, 98; CDC VIII, 1346; Cherubini, *Le Pergamene*, 211–13, no. 84). Two other charters not mentioned in the 1092 document likewise relate to Santa Lucia and its founders: a 1047 charter in which the founders of Santa Lucia leased out lands to priests appointed in the church in exchange for a payment three times a year and a 1068 charter in which Raidolfus's son Peter sold his one-third of Santa Lucia to Maraldus. The 1068 charter also mentions a division of lands and possessions in Balnearia between Raidolfus's two sons Peter and, presumably, John, although the charter is corrupt and only Peter's name can be read. IX, 81 (CDC VII, 1073; Cherubini, *Le Pergamene*, 175–78, no. 64); XII, 65 (CDC IX, 56).

[2] For a political narrative of the Lombards in southern Italy, see Ferdinando Hirsch, *Il Ducato di Benevento* and Michelangelo Schipa, *Storia del Principato Longobardo di Salerno* both in *La Longobardia meridionale*, ed. Nicola Acocella (Rome, 1968); Vera von Falkenhausen, 'I Longobardi meridionali', in *Storia d'Italia: Il Mezzogiorno dai Bizantini a Federico II*, ed. Giuseppe Galasso (Turin, 1983), iii, 249–364; Stefano Gaspari, *I Duchi Longobardi, Studi Storici dell'Istituto Storico Italiano per il Medio Evo*, 102 (Rome, 1978); Nicola Cilento, *Le origini della signoria capuana nella Longobardia minore, Studi Storici dell'Istituto Storico per il Medio Evo*, 69–70 (Rome, 1966); Huguette Taviani-Carozzi, *La Principauté Lombarde de Salerne (IXe–XIe): Pouvoir et Société en Italie Lombarde Méridionale* (Rome, 1991); and in English Barbara Kreutz, *Before the Normans: Southern Italy in the Ninth and Tenth Centuries* (Philadelphia, 1991) and chapter 1 of G.A. Loud, *The Age of Robert Guiscard: Southern Italy and the Norman Conquest* (Harlow, 2000).

[3] Between 1043 and 1047 Guaimarius IV signed his documents as 'prince of Salerno and Capua, duke of Amalfi and Sorrento, and duke of Calabria and Apulia.'

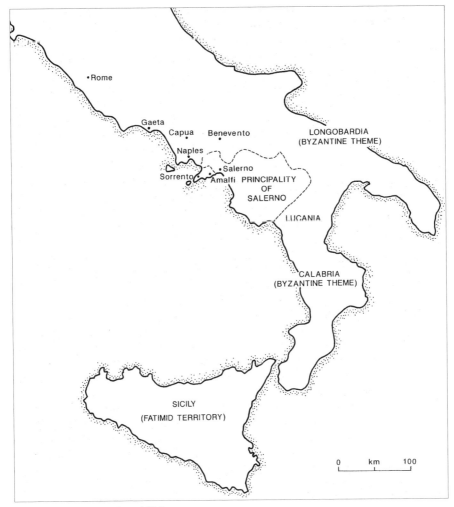

Map 1: Southern Italy c. 1000.

The Principality of Salerno remained a wealthy and prosperous region in the late eleventh and twelfth centuries.[4]

The Abbey of the Holy Trinity of Cava (Metiliano) was founded in the early part of the eleventh century by a nobleman from Salerno named Alferius.

4 On the Norman conquest of southern Italy, see Ferdinand Chalandon, *Histoire de la domination normande en Italie méridionale et en Sicile* (Paris, 1907); Lothar von Heinemann, *Geschichte der Normannen in Unteritalien und Sizilien* (Leipzig, 1894; repr., Aalen, 1969); Ernesto Pontieri, *I normanni nell'Italia meridionale* (Naples, 1948); Salvatore Tramontana, *Mezzogiorno normanno e svevo* (Messina, 1972); Salvatore Tramontana, 'La monarchia normanna e sveva', in *Storia d'Italia: Il Mezzogiorno dai Bizantini a Federico II*, ed. Giuseppe Galasso (Turin, 1983), iii, 437–810; Huguette Taviani-Carozzi, *La Terreur du Monde: Robert Guiscard et la conquête normande en Italie* (Paris, 1996); Richard Bünemann, *Robert Guiskard 1015–1085. Eine Normanner erobert Süditalien* (Cologne, 1997); Donald Matthew, *The Norman Kingdom of Sicily* (Cambridge, 1992); Loud, *Age of Robert Gusicard*.

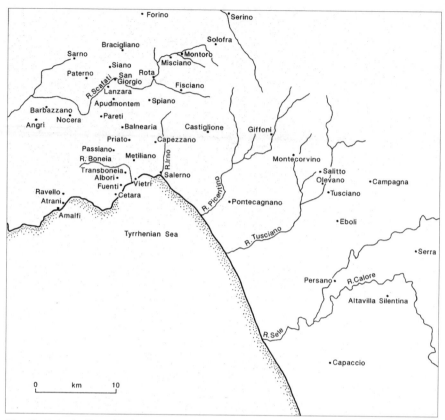

Map 2: Principality of Salerno (northern regions).

Alferius had spent time in two Benedictine monasteries in the north, San
Michele della Chiusa in northern Italy and the abbey of Cluny in France, before
he built the small monastery dedicated to the Holy Trinity in the mountains
above Salerno.[5] Over the course of the eleventh and twelfth centuries, the abbey
of Cava grew rapidly in size, taking over large areas of land and absorbing
numerous religious houses. By the twelfth century, it had become the largest
ecclesiastical foundation in the province, wealthier and more powerful than the
cathedral church of Salerno. Today the abbey is home to an important archive
that includes numerous manuscripts and charters related not only to the abbey of

---

[5] On the history of the abbey of Cava, see Paul Guillaume, *Essaie historique sur l'abbaye de
Cava* (Cava dei Tirreni, 1877); Carmine Carlone, *Le origini e la costituzione patrimoniale della
Badia di Cava (1025–1124)* (Tesi di laurea, University of Salerno, 1971–2); G.A. Loud, 'The
Abbey of Cava, its Property and Benefactors in the Norman Era', *A.N.S.*, 10 (1986), 143–77;
Taviani-Carozzi, *La Principauté*.

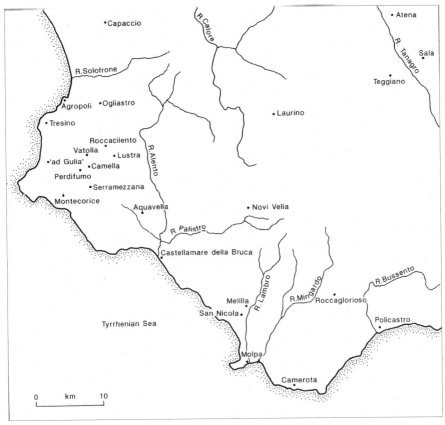

Map 3: Principality of Salerno (southern regions).

Cava itself but also to its dependent houses, including the church of Santa Lucia.[6]

Most of the information we have on Santa Lucia and its founders comes from a single charter found at the abbey of Cava dated September 1092. Although our knowledge of the church is limited, Santa Lucia nonetheless provides a good illustration of the many small family and community foundations that dominated the ecclesiastical landscape of the Principality of Salerno between the ninth and eleventh centuries: the church was founded by a small group of people who were linked by family and community ties, it was administered by the

6   For a history and description of the archives at Cava, see Giovanni Vitolo, 'L'Archivio della Badia della SS. Trinità di Cava', in *Guida alla Storia de Salerno e della sua provincia*, ed. Alfonse Leone and Giovanni Vitolo (Salerno, 1982), iii, 894–99; Imma Ascione, 'L'Archivio', in *La Badia di Cava*, ed. Giuseppe Fienzo and Franco Strazzullo (Cava dei Tirreni, 1990), ii, 185–222; and Taviani-Carozzi, *La Principauté*, xxv–xxxiii.

founders themselves and was free of episcopal authority, and it served the religious needs of the surrounding community, following local traditions and practices. This article proposes to examine religious life in eleventh-century Salerno using the example of Santa Lucia to discuss the following four issues: the nature of family and community houses, the careers of priests and clerics, the authority of the archbishop of Salerno over ecclesiastical organization, and the relationship between Greek and Latin foundations.

Over one hundred small religious foundations appear in charters found at the abbey of Cava dated 800–1100. Although few documents describe the actual foundation of religious houses, the Cava archives do contain some twenty-seven charters in which church owners, both lay and ecclesiastical, appointed clergy-men to serve in their houses as well as nine emancipation charters issued by the bishops of Salerno and Paestum to church founders.[7] Like Santa Lucia, the vast majority of these foundations were small religious houses built by untitled individuals of modest means who appear only a few times in the documents.

Most religious houses in early medieval Salerno were founded by groups of people rather than individuals. Like the founders of Santa Lucia, they would pool their resources together in order to provide the necessary financial support to build the church and provide for a priest. In general they were either members of the same family or residents of a small community who formed a consortium specifically for the purpose of building and then overseeing a religious house.[8] The founders of Santa Lucia were relatives, referred to as 'parentes' in a 1047 document, and the group formed a legal unit specifically for the purpose of building and overseeing the new church.[9]

---

[7] Information in this section comes from a study of the following charters that either describe the foundation or emancipation of a church or document the appointment of a priest or abbot to head a foundation: A, 2 (CDC I, 87); I, 113 (CDC I, 119); II, 24 (CDC I, 150); II, 43 (CDC I, 169); A, 7 (CDC I, 179); II, 101 (CDC II, 231); II, 111 (CDC II, 241); A, 10 (CDC II, 263); III, 14 (CDC II, 265); III, 16 (CDC II, 267); III, 25 (CDC II, 276); III, 44 (CDC II, 297); III, 69 (CDC II, 323); III, 120 (CDC II, 376); IV, 6 (CDC II, 382); IV 12 and 13 (CDC II, 388 and 389); A, 14 (CDC II, 412); A, 22 (CDC VI, 896) with date corrected by Maria Galante, *La Datazione dei documenti del Codex Diplomaticus Cavensis* (Salerno, 1980), 55, no. 34; A, 23 (CDC VI, 898) with date corrected by Galante, *La Datazione*, 57–8, no. 36; V, 81 (CDC IV, 582); V, 112 (CDC IV, 614); VI, 84 (CDC IV, 707); XX, 114; VI, 115 (CDC V, 738); VII, 14 (CDC V, 757); A, 19 (CDC V, 764); VII, 68 (CDC V, 812); VIII, 39 (CDC VI, 910); VIII, 116 (CDC VI, 990); IX, 24 (CDC VI, 1016); IX, 59 (CDC VI, 1052); IX, 78 (CDC VII, 1070); IX, 85 (CDC VII, 1077); A, 30 (CDC VII, 1086); IX, 102 (CDC VII, 1096) with date corrected by Galante, *La Datazione*, 119–20, no. 94; X, 6 (CDC VII, 1121); XI, 15 (CDC VII, 1131); A, 32 (CDC VII, 1146); X, 55 (CDC VII, 1174); X, 58 (CDC VII, 1178); A, 35 (CDC VII, 1194); X, 83 (CDC VII, 1205); X, 97 (CDC VII, 1220); XI, 9 (CDC VIII, 1252); XI, 14 (CDC VIII, 1258); XI, 26 (CDC VIII, 1270); XI, 97 (CDC VIII, 1345); XII, 22 (CDC IX, 1); XII, 48 (CDC IX, 32); XIII, 62 (CDC X, 98).

[8] The word 'consortium' rarely appears in documents, although people are regularly referred to as 'consortes'. For groups of people referred to as 'consortes' who built and administered ecclesi-astical foundations, see II, 101 (CDC II, 231) and VII, 14 (CDC V, 757).

[9] IX, 81 (CDC VII, 1073).

Owners needed no special permission from the archbishop or the prince in order to build their churches. Likewise the management of religious houses was carried out autonomously by the owners and clergy. The owners themselves were required to find a priest or abbot to serve as rector, while the administration and upkeep of the foundations was the duty of the rectors appointed. Like the abbot of Santa Lucia, the rectors personally administered all the lands and property belonging to their churches. They were also allowed to keep all donations and tithes given to the church, with the understanding that they would use the revenues for the benefit of the religious house.[10]

The founders of religious houses came from a wide variety of social and economic backgrounds and were usually members of the laity, not the clergy. Documents suggest that founding a house was simply a matter of having enough land and wealth to construct and then outfit a church with the necessary books, garments, and ornaments and enough resources to sustain one or more clergymen. Thus the ability to found ecclesiastical foundations in early medieval Salerno was opened to a large spectrum of people, and was not reserved for members of the noble class or the clergy.

In charters the owners and clerics were instructed to run their churches according to tradition and local custom. Usually the clerics were instructed to officiate as was right for peasant priests ('sicut decet sacerdos billanos') or as was fitting for a peasant or rural church ('sicut meruerit ecclesia villana/ecclesie foras civitate').[11] However, one charter specifically stated that the new priest of a church in Tresino (Lucania) would officiate day and night according to the custom of the place ('sicut ipso locum meruerit et consuetudo ibi fuit').[12] Another investiture charter told the new rector of the church of San Matteo and San Tomaso in Salerno to officiate as was right for a church of its type ('sicut decet ecclesia que similis est de illa').[13] Finally the new priest installed in the church of San Giovanni of Vietri in 1067 was to officiate as was fitting for a peasant church of a similar size ('sicut meruerit ecclesie villane que similem possessionem habet').[14] Clearly local custom and the neighboring population exerted a powerful force over the priests and clerics.

The sphere of influence of most family and community churches was limited, only extending to a small area nearby the church, and family and consortium members played important roles in both administering and supporting the houses. In the case of Santa Lucia, the man who actually built the church, Raidolfus, served as abbot for at least the first ten years, in addition to appointing other priests to officiate in the church. Moreover, Raidolfus's brother

---

[10] A, 32 (CDC VII, 1146).
[11] III, 69 (CDC II, 323); IV, 12 (CDC II, 388); V, 81 (CDC IV, 582); VII, 14 (CDC IV, 757); VII, 68 (CDC V, 812); VIII, 39 (CDC VI, 910); IX, 24 (CDC VI, 1016); IX, 59 (CDC VI, 1052); IX, 78 (CDC VII, 1070); IX, 85 (CDC VII, 1077); IX, 102 (CDC VII, 1096); X, 6 (CDC VII, 1121); X, 83 (CDC VII, 1205); X, 97 (CDC VII, 1220); XI, 9 (CDC VIII, 1252).
[12] VIII, 116 (CDC VI, 990).
[13] XI, 15 (CDC VII, 1131).
[14] XII, 48 (CDC IX, 32).

Sesamus donated lands to the church in 1047 and again in 1063.[15] Sesamus also leased lands belonging to the church in 1053, promising to improve the lands by planting fruit trees and vines.[16] During the first eight years, Sesamus would pay only the *terraticum* on grain output, after which he would also give the church one-half of the wine production as well as the *palmenticum* for use of the wine press. In addition Sesamus agreed to transport the wine himself to the rector's house, a requirement found in only a few agricultural contracts. Sesamus, a landowner himself, clearly was not forced to do so because of poverty or low social status. The service most likely was seen as a pious act meant to help support the church and its clergy. Thus the economic and religious needs of Santa Lucia were taken care of almost exclusively by the members of the founder's family.

The owners of religious houses could sell, trade, or donate their foundations freely, again without permission from the archbishop or prince, and normal inheritance practices applied to the houses as well. Religious foundations built by a family or consortium that survived beyond one generation were generally divided between heirs of the original founders. The division of religious houses was a common practice in Salerno, and for houses that survived beyond two generations, the list of owners could become quite large. Although our information on the ownership patterns of Santa Lucia is incomplete, we do know that part of the church was inherited by two sons of Raidolfus, Peter and John.[17]

Religious houses in early medieval Salerno were often ephemeral, surviving one, two, or perhaps three generations, basically as long as the family or consortium remained an interested party. Although Santa Lucia did survive into the twelfth century as a dependency of the abbey of Cava, the sons of Raidolfus were clearly not interested in administering the house themselves. In 1068 Peter, along with his wife Alferada and with the permission of his father Raidolfus, sold his one-third of the church of Santa Lucia to a cleric Maraldus son of Amatus, a priest and cardinal in the cathedral church of Salerno.[18] Then in 1092 John donated two parts of the church to San Nicola in Gallocanta.[19] Thus the two brothers began alienating their portions of Santa Lucia even before their father's death, and if Cava had not taken over management of Santa Lucia, the church could very well have disappeared soon after the death of the original founder, Raidolfus.[20]

---

[15] XV, 60; XI, 98 (CDC VIII, 1346).

[16] X, 63 (CDC VII, 1183).

[17] XII, 65 (CDC IX, 56); XV, 60.

[18] XII, 65 (CDC IX, 56).

[19] XV, 60.

[20] Our information on Santa Lucia in the twelfth century comes from two brief mentions in charters dated 1117 that refer to lands bordering the church of Santa Lucia and claim that the church belonged to Cava. XX, 75; XX, 80. Interestingly, Santa Lucia is not mentioned in the papal bulls issued in 1100 and 1149 confirming Cava's dependencies, even though San Nicola of Gallocanta is listed, as is one of San Nicola's dependencies, Sant'Andrea of Albori. C, 21; D, 26.

Raidolfus is referred to in the documents as both a priest and abbot, reflecting the overlap of the lifestyles and duties of monks and secular clerics in early medieval Salerno. Although the documents for Santa Lucia consistently refer to the foundation as a church (*ecclesia*), other religious houses are alternately called monasteries and churches in the charters.[21] Abbots are found officiating in churches that clearly exercised pastoral duties and many foundations contained both priests and monks.[22] San Nicola of Gallocanta, for example, was headed by an abbot who performed all the duties of a priest, and its community included clerics and monks.[23] Likewise other ecclesiastical foundations in early medieval Salerno combined the functions of monastery and church and many clerics are found who, like Raidolfus, blended the roles of secular and regular clergy.

Documents also suggest that the line between the laity and clergy was not pronounced in early medieval Salerno. Like Raidolfus, priests married, held private property, and appear in the documents in all capacities without any legal limitations or privileges.[24] Moreover, priests and clerics did not fill any specific political or administrative functions in the region. Notaries and judges tended to be from the laity; disputes and trials in Salerno were conducted in the prince's palace in front of lay judges and gastalds.[25] Thus ecclesiastics did not exercise unique legal functions or monopolize administrative offices which required education and literacy. Moreover, lay participation in the ecclesiastical system of Salerno remained strong throughout the medieval period: the majority of the religious houses in the area were founded by members of the laity who then appointed the priest and clerics to officiate in them. Although certain religious functions priests alone could exercise, the laity were extremely active in the religious life of their communities. Religious worship and organization in the early medieval period was a joint endeavor between the laity and clergy.

[21] The princely foundation San Massimo in Salerno, for example, is generally referred to as a church, but on at least three occasions it was called either a monastery or a chapel. I, 111 (CDC I, 116); A, 5 (CDC I, 117); II, 76 (CDC I, 206).

[22] San Massimo, Santa Maria de Domna, the palace chapel of San Pietro, Santa Maria in Nocera, Sant'Adiutore in Nocera, Santa Sofia in Salerno, Sant'Angelo in Capaccio, and San Nicola of Gallocanta were all headed by abbots exercising pastoral duties.

[23] XI, 26 (CDC VIII, 1270); XII, 22 (CDC IX, 1); XVIII, 111; XIX, 5; XII, 80 and 81 (CDC IX, 82). The investiture charter from 1058 clearly stated that the abbot Theophilus was to perform the divine office daily ('peraget cotidie divinum officium').

[24] In the tenth and eleventh centuries, priests, clerics, and even monks, acting as individuals or as part of a family group and not *pro parte* of an ecclesiastical foundation, bought or sold land over thirty times. Likewise they leased out approximately thirty pieces of lands and appeared as tenants over forty times. Clerics were also involved in land divisions and property disputes. See V, 112 (CDC IV, 614); VI, 93 (CDC V, 716); VII, 52 (CDC V, 796); XII, 65 (CDC IX, 56); III, 3 (CDC II, 253); IV, 38 (CDC II, 415); VI, 1 (CDC IV, 623).

[25] In the city of Salerno itself, only one example of an ecclesiastical notary is documented before the late eleventh century. Taviani-Carozzi, *La Principauté*, 542–3.

Like many priests, Raidolfus had a son, John, who himself became a cleric.[26] In fact, the priesthood in early medieval Salerno seems almost hereditary at times: the documents contain many examples of sons of priests who likewise entered the clergy, and in one case a father and son even served together in a church.[27] Interestingly, although Raidolfus's son John did choose to become a cleric, he did not become abbot of Santa Lucia or serve in the church.

In his emancipation charter issued in 1050, John, the archbishop of Salerno conceded to Raidolfus and his heirs complete authority over the church of Santa Lucia, declaring that the church would always remain free and secure from the archbishop's power.[28] The archbishop specifically stated he would not interfere in any aspect of the church's administration: Raidolfus and his heirs had the right to appoint priests and clerics and to keep all taxes and services owed to the church. The archbishop, however, did retain the right to reconsecrate contaminated altars, and he also received a yearly fee (*censum*) of wax from Raidolfus and his heirs on the feast day of Santa Lucia.

Only seven such emancipation charters (*chartae libertatis*) issued by the bishops and archbishops of Salerno survive in the abbey of Cava's archives for the period 800 to 1130.[29] In one way this makes sense since the Cava archives house few documents relating to the cathedral church. However, the archiepiscopal archives in Salerno contain only one such document, a seventeenth-century copy of a document dated to 1005.[30] Since the archiepiscopal archives were organized at a later date, and, in fact, contain few documents from before the twelfth century, it is possible that more such emancipation charters were redacted but then lost. Thus it is difficult to know how often this type of document was actually issued to new foundations in the medieval period. However, given the large number of ecclesiastical foundations found in documents dated between 800 and 1100, it seems safe to assume that the majority of small foundations clearly did not receive any special privileges from the bishops or archbishops.

A study of all the documents relating to the cathedral church of Salerno between the ninth and mid-eleventh centuries shows that the bishop, who became

---

[26] In the 1092 charter, John is referred to as 'Iohannes clericus filius quodam Raidolfusi presbiteri et abbatis'. XV, 60.

[27] X, 55 (CDC VII, 1174).

[28] A, 32 (CDC VII, 1146).

[29] A, 2 (CDC I, 87) issued in 882 to San Massimo; A, 10 (CDC I, 263) issued in 970 to San Matteo and San Tomaso; A, 14 (CDC II, 412) issued in 989 to Santa Maria de Domno; A, 23 (CDC VI, 898) issued in 1005 to Santa Maria in Vietri, with date corrected by Galante, *La Datazione*, 57–8, no. 36; V, 112 (CDC IV, 614) issued in 1009 to San Nicola in Tostaccio; A, 32 (CDC VII, 1146) issued in 1050 to Santa Lucia; B, 2 (CDC IX, 103) issued in 1071 to San Nicola in Salerno. Also a 996 document for San Nicola of Gallocanta mentions a *charta libertatis* issued by the bishop of Salerno to Marino, the founder, in 981, although the original does not survive. IV, 115 (CDC III, 494).

[30] An edition of the charter is found in Maria Galante, 'La documentazione vescovile Salernitana: aspetti e problemi', in *Scrittura e produzione documentaria nel Mezzogiorno Longobardo: Atti del Convegno internazionale di studio, Badia di Cava, 3–5 October 1990*, ed. Giovanni Vitolo and Francesco Mottola (Salerno, 1991), 251–3.

an archbishop sometime in the late tenth century, exercised little authority, direct or indirect, over the ecclesiastical system of the Principality of Salerno.[31] Although the bishops and archbishops occupied a special place in the religious life of the city of Salerno itself, and played important political roles at times as well, they rarely participated in the construction or maintenance of religious houses, either in the city of Salerno or outside. Investiture charters clearly show that the founders of religious houses, along with the priests and abbots they appointed, administered their foundations autonomously. Even within the city of Salerno itself, the archbishop gave the Church of Santa Maria de Domno many rights usually reserved for the cathedral church, including the authority to baptize, found other churches, and bury the dead.[32] Moreover, the cathedral church of Salerno possessed little wealth in comparison to its counterparts in the north.[33]

Bishops and archbishops did not appoint priests and clerics in other churches, except for the ones directly dependent on the cathedral church. Nor did they require the church owners to seek episcopal permission or approval when installing new abbots and priests. Moreover, in the *chartae libertatis* that they issued, bishops and archbishops claimed no power over investitures.[34] They also do not appear to have taken an active role in the training or education of priests or clerics. The Principality of Salerno seems to have had a sort of apprenticeship program whereby clerics served alongside priests for some years before being appointed to head their own religious house.

---

[31] No papal privilege survives for the elevation of Salerno to the status of metropolitan. Nonetheless two 983 documents still refer to the head of the Salerno church as bishop, while a 989 papal privilege from Pope John XV to Amatus calls him an archbishop, demonstrating that the elevation took place sometime between 983 and 989. See III, 96 (CDC II, 352) and III, 99 (CDC II, 355) for the 983 documents and Kehr *Italia Pontificia*, viii, 340 and 346, no. 11 for the 989 papal privilege. For more information on episcopal authority and 'private' churches in both Lombard southern Italy generally and in the Principality of Salerno specifically, see H. E. Feine, 'Studien zum langobardisch-italienischen Eigenkirchenrecht', *Zeitschrift der Savigny-Stiftung für Rechtsgeschichte*, 30 (1941), 1–95; 31, pp. 1–105; Bruno Ruggiero, 'Per una storia della pieve rurale', *Studi medievali*, 16 (1975), 583–626. Reprinted in *Potere, istituzioni, chiese locali: Aspetti e motivi del Mezzogiorno medievale dai Longobardi agli Angioini* (Bologna, 1977), 59–87; C. D. Fonseca, 'Aspetti Istituzionali dell'Organizzazione Ecclesiastica Meridionale dal VI al IX Secolo', in *Dalla prima alla seconda distruzione: Momenti e aspetti della storia cassinese (secc. VI–IX): Convegno internazionale di studio sul Medioevo meridionale, Cassino-Montecassino, 27–31 May 1984* (Montecassino, 1987). Reprinted in *Particolarismo Istituzionale e Organizzazione Ecclesiastica del Mezzogiorno Medievale* (Galatina, 1987), 3–20; Giovanni Vitolo, 'Vescovi e Diocesi', in *Storia del Mezzogiorno*, ed. Giuseppe Galasso (Naples, 1990), iii, 73–151.

[32] A, 14 (CDC II, 412).

[33] At least three times bishops in the tenth century were compelled to grant religious houses to laymen to restore and administer due to poverty. II, 43 (CDC I, 169); A, 6 (CDC I, 170); II, 297 (CDC III, 44). Moreover, few agricultural contracts were issued by the bishops and archbishops in the tenth and eleventh centuries, despite the fact that other religious houses issued many such contracts.

[34] A, 2 (CDC I, 87); A, 10 (CDC I, 263); A, 14 (CDC II, 412); A, 23 (CDC VI, 898); V, 112 (CDC IV, 614).

The bishop of Salerno in the early medieval period neither headed a territorial diocesan system nor controlled a system of parish churches.[35] Moreover, there is no evidence that he attempted to regulate religious practices or create a hierarchical ecclesiastical system, as Merovingian and Carolingian bishops did. Evidence survives for only three councils held in southern Lombard territories, all dating from the second half of the ninth century, and although these councils did push for territorial organization and religious standardization, they do not appear to have had much effect on religious life in Salerno. The canons of all three councils exist in singles copies, two of which are found at Montecassino and one of which is located in the British Library, and there is no indication that the bishops of Salerno participated in any of these councils.[36] Clearly the bishop of Salerno did not play a central role in the religious life or religious organization of his diocese.

Beginning in the mid-eleventh century, the archbishop of Salerno began to assert more authority over the churches and clergy of his diocese with the support of the papacy and princes of Salerno, and the *charta libertatis* for Santa Lucia shows the increasing power and prestige of the archbishop of Salerno in the eleventh century.[37] Although the owners of the church administered the foundation autonomously, appointed the clergy themselves, and kept all the donations and incomes for the church's own use, the archbishop reserved the right to make the priests, monks, and clerics in the church appear before him whenever he wished in order to examine and judge them ('potestatem . . . ad nos illos venire facere et illos requirere et iudicare illos'). In addition, Archbishop John prohibited Raidolfus from appointing clergymen from outside the diocese without the archbishop's permission. Emancipation charters from the ninth and tenth centuries make no such demands.[38]

Other documents from the second half of the eleventh century likewise show the archbishop of Salerno attempting to increase his power over the clergy and ecclesiastical foundations in his diocese. Papal privileges from the second half of the eleventh century clearly stated that archbishops alone had the right to appoint and ordain clerics and abbots in their diocese and even declared that all ecclesiastical foundations in the diocese of Salerno, along with their revenues, rightly pertained to the archbishop.[39] Likewise the Lombard princes of Salerno

[35] Ruggiero, 'Per una storia'; Vitolo, 'Vescovi e Diocesi'.
[36] D. Germain Morin, 'Un concile inédit dans l'Italie méridionale à la fin du IXe siècle', *Révue Benedictine*, 17 (1900), 143–51. A. Amelli, 'Synodus Orietana', and 'Acta Synodi Ecclesiae', *Spicilegium Casinense* (Montecassino, 1888), i, 377–81, and 388–93.
[37] A, 32 (CDC VII, 1146).
[38] See, for example, the emancipation charters for San Massimo, San Matteo and San Tomaso, and Santa Maria de Domno. A, 2 (CDC I, 87); A, 10 (CDC I, 263); A, 14 (CDC II, 412).
[39] See in particular the 1058 privilege issued by Stephen IX, the 1067 bull of Alexander II, and the 1092 document issued by Pope Urban II during a dispute between Archbishop Alfanus II and Duke Roger Borsa. Julius von Pflugk-Harttung, *Acta Pontificium Romanorum Inedita* (Stuttgart, 1881–86), ii, 82–4, no. 116; Ferdinando Ughelli, *Italia Sacra* (Venice, 1717–22), vii, 382–3; C, 40 and Pflugk-Harttung, *Acta Pontificium*, ii, 149–50, no. 184.

declared all priests, deacons, subdeacons, and clerics in the diocese to be under the judicial power of the archbishop.[40] Even more importantly, the archbishops of Salerno, beginning with the tenure of Archbishop Alfanus I (1058–85), began to create a hierarchical and centrally controlled metropolitan made up of bishops and archpresbyters, with the archbishop himself sitting at the top. As shown in the *charta libertatis* for Santa Lucia, the archbishops also began to insist on the right to monitor and supervise all clerics in their diocese, rather than allowing church owners full and complete authority over the clergy they appointed. Unfortunately, the archbishops would only prove partially successful in their quest to take control of the ecclesiastical system in the Principality of Salerno.[41]

In 1092 Raidolfus's son John donated his portion of Santa Lucia to San Nicola of Gallocanta, a religious house located outside of Salerno near the village of Vietri. The church of San Nicola of Gallocanta had been built sometime between December of 979 and September of 981 by a smith named Marinus.[42] It was purchased by Count Adelbertus in 996, after which it remained in the possession of Adelbertus and his descendents for over one hundred years.[43] Over the course of the eleventh century, San Nicola became a prominent landholder in the region, thanks mainly to donations made by Adelbertus's heirs not only in the village of Vietri but also in Priato, Albori, Salitto, Bosanola, and Balenearia.[44] A document from the eleventh century also mentioned a dependent church, Sant'Andrea in Albori.[45] In addition, San Nicola was well furnished and possessed a variety of movable wealth, including books, robes, chalices, crosses, icons, candelabras, and animals.[46] Between 1087 and 1118, the church of San Nicola was donated piecemeal to the abbey of Cava by its owners, and presumably the church of Santa Lucia became a possession of Cava during this time as well.[47]

---

[40] See the privileges issued by Princes Guaimarius III and IV in 1023, by Prince Guaimarius IV in 1032, and by Prince Gisolf II in 1058. Ludovico Antonio Muratori, *Antiquitates Italicae Medii Aevi* (Milan, 1738–42), i, 187–8 and 189–92.

[41] For more information on the reorganization of Salerno's metropolitan and the expansion of archiepiscopal power, see Valerie Ramseyer, 'Ecclesiastical Reorganization in the Principality of Salerno in the Late Lombard and Early Norman Period', *Anglo-Norman Studies*, xvii (Woodbridge, 1995), 206–12.

[42] For more information on the church of San Nicola of Gallocanta, see the Introduction to Cherubini, *Le Pergamene di S. Nicola di Gallucanta* and Giovanni Vitolo, 'La Latinizzazione dei Monasteri Italo-Greci del Mezzogiorno Medievale: L'Esempio di S. Nicola di Gallocanta Presso Salerno', *Benedictina*, 19 (1982), 437–60. Reprinted in *Minima Cavensis: Studi in margine al IX volume del Codex Diplomaticus Cavensis*, ed. Simeone Leone and Giovanni Vitolo (Salerno, 1983), 75–90.

[43] IV, 115 (CDC III, 494).

[44] V, 35 (CDC IV, 534); IX, 83 (CDC VI, 1075); XII, 37 and 38 (CDC IX, 19); XIV, 116; XV, 72; XVI, 70.

[45] XII, 27 (CDC IX, 9).

[46] XI, 14 (CDC VIII, 1258); XI, 26 (CDC VIII, 1270); XII, 22 (CDC IX, 1).

[47] XIV, 78; XIX, 31; XIX, 52; XIX, 90; E, 37; XX, 54; XX, 59.

The priests appointed to officiate in San Nicola were all required to follow Greek practices or, more precisely, to perform the office of God as was right for a Greek priest ('peragat officium Dei sicut decet presbiteris greci').[48] San Nicola was not the only Greek foundation in the Principality of Salerno, and Greek churches and monasteries were, in fact, found in all regions of southern Italy in the Middle Ages.[49] Greek foundations in Salerno co-existed peacefully with neighboring Latin churches and monasteries, and no evidence points to friction between them. Even after the Norman conquest not only did old Greek foundations continue to exist, but new ones were founded, sometimes even with the patronage of Norman rulers.

The origins of Greek-speaking Christian communities in southern Italy is

---

[48] XII, 22 (CDC IX, 1). Also see XI, 14 (CDC VIII, 1258); XI, 26 (CDC VIII, 1270); XVIII, 111.
[49] The bibliography on Greek foundations and the 'hellenization' and then 'latinization' of southern Italy and Sicily is long. The important works include François Lenormant, *La Grande-Grèce: Paysages et histoire* (Paris, 1881–4), ii; Pierre Batiffol, *L'abbaye di Rossano: Contribution à l'Histoire de la Vaticane* (Paris, 1891); Kirsopp Lake, 'The Greek Monasteries in South Italy', *Journal of Theological Studies*, 4 (1903), 345–68, 517–42; 5 (1904), 22–41; Alberto Vaccari, *La Grecia nell'Italia meridionale: Studi letterari e bibliografia*, Orientalia Christiana, xiii (Rome, 1925); Lynn White Jr, *Latin Monasticism in Norman Sicily* (Cambridge, 1938); Peter Charanis, 'On the question of the Hellenization of Siciliy and Southern Italy during the Middle Ages', *A.H.R.*, 52 (1946), 74–86; Mario Scaduto, *Il Monachesimo Basiliano nella Sicilia Medievale* (Rome, 1947; repr. 1982); Léon-Robert Ménager, 'La 'byzantinisation' religieuse de l'Italie méridionale (IXe–XIIe siècles) et la politique monastique des Normands d'Italie', *Revue d'Histoire Ecclésiastique*, 53 (1958), 747–74; Biagio Cappelli, 'I Basiliani nel Cilento Superiore', *Bollettino della Badia Greca di Grottaferrata*, 16 (1962), 9–21; Biagio Cappelli, *Il monaschesimo basiliano ai confini calabro-lucani* (Naples, 1963); Silvano Borsari, *Il Monachesimo Bizantino nella Sicilia e nell'Italia Meridionale Prenormanni* (Naples, 1963); Agostino Pertusi, 'Aspetti Organizzativi e Culturali dell'Ambiente monacale greco dell'Italia meridionale', and André Guillou, 'Il monachesimo greco in Italia meridionale e in Sicilia nel medioevo', in *L'eremitismo in Occidente nei secoli XI e XI: Atti della seconda Settimana internazionale di studio, Mendola, 30 August– 6 September 1962* (Milan, 1965), 382–426 and 355–426; André Guillou, *Aspetti della civiltà bizantina in Italia: Società e cultura* (Bari, 1976); Dieter Girgensohn, 'Dall'Episcopato Greco all'Episcopato Latino nell'Italia Merionale', and Peter Herde, 'Il Papato e la chiesa greca nell'Italia meridionale dall'XI al XIII secolo', in *Chiesa Greca in Italia dall'VIII al XVI secolo: Atti del Convegno storico interecclesiale, Bari, 30 April–4 May 1969* (Padova, 1972–3), ii, 25–43 and 213–55. Walther Holtzmann, 'Papsttum, Normannen und griechische Kirche', *Miscellanea Bibliothecae Hertzianae* (Munich, 1961), 69–79; Enrico Morini, 'Eremo e cenobio nel monachesimo greco dell'Italia meridionale nei secoli IX e X', *Rivista di storia della Chiesa in Italia*, 31 (1977), 354–90; Vera von Falkenhausen, 'I monasteri greci dell'Italia meridionale e della Sicilia dopo l'avvento dei Normanni: continuità e mutamenti', in *Il passaggio dal domino bizantino allo stato normanno nell'Italia meridionale: Atti del II Convegno internazionale di studi sulla Civiltà rupestre medioevale nel Mezzogiorno d'Italia, Taranto-Mottola, 31 October–4 November 1973* (Taranto, 1977), and 'Patrimonio e politica patrimoniale dei monasteri greci nella Sicilia normanno-sveva', in *Basilio di Cesarea: la sua età e il Basilianesimo in Sicilia: Atti del Congresso Internazionale, Messina, 3–6 December 1979* (Messina, 1983), 777–90; Vitolo, 'La Latinizzazione dei Monasteri Italo-Greci'; and in English Loud, *The Age of Robert Guiscard*, 54–9.

a topic that has generated much debate.[50] Epigraphical evidence demonstrates that Christians in Sicily used the Greek language from the earliest days of Christianity.[51] Christianity, in fact, was introduced to the island mostly by Greek-speaking easterners.[52] Nonetheless, epigraphical evidence suggests that in certain areas of southern Italy, such as Calabria, Greek replaced Latin as the main liturgical language sometime in the early Middle Ages.[53] Likewise in other areas of southern Italy, Greek-speaking clerics established religious houses in the early medieval period, although without radically changing the religious environment. In the city of Salerno, at least three houses contained Greek-speaking clerics, while two Greek foundations were established in and around Vietri and in southern regions numerous Greek houses and Greek clerics could be found.[54]

Even more difficult is defining the precise difference between Latin and Greek Christianity in southern Italy. Historians generally identify Greek foundations based on linguistic evidence: if liturgical books, inscriptions, charters, or even signatures were written in Greek, then the church or monastery is characterized as 'Greek'. Yet the question arises of how these foundations and their clerics differed from their Latin counterparts. Was language the only distinguishing characteristic, or did liturgy, practices, and hierarchy likewise set them off?

In the Principality of Salerno, Greek foundations were never under the direct control of the patriarch of Constantinople. Not only distance but also the political environment prevented the Greek-speaking clerics in the region from being

---

50 See, in particular, Lenormant, *La Grande-Grèce*; Batiffol, *L'abbaye di Rossano;* Vaccari, *La Grecia nell'Italia meridionale*; White, *Latin Monasticism*; Charanis, 'On the question'; Scaduto, *Il Monachesimo Basiliano*; Ménager, 'La 'byzantinisation' religieuse'; Cappelli, *Il monaschesimo basiliano*; Pertusi, 'Aspetti Organizzativi'; Borsari, *Il monachesimo bizantino*.

51 Borsari, *Il monachesimo bizantino*, 13–17.

52 Borsari, *Il monachesimo bizantino*, 17.

53 Borsari, *Il monachesimo bizantino*, 22.

54 San Lorenzo in Salerno, the church of San Giovanni in Vietri, the church of San Nicola in Gallocanta, and the church of Santa Sofia in Salerno contained Greek priests, clerics, or monks. III, 55 (CDC II, 309); IV, 6 (CDC II, 382); VIII, 103 (CDC VI, 977); XI, 14 (CDC VIII, 1258); XI, 26 (CDC VIII, 1270); XII, 22 (CDC IX, 1). The monastery of San Benedetto in Salerno had a Greek rector appointed in 1043. Cherubini, *Le Pergamene*, 14–15. Charter evidence survives at the abbey of Cava for numerous Greek foundations in Lucania, and other evidence, written as well as archaeological and toponymic, indicates the existence of an even greater number of Greek-speaking or Greek-inspired foundations in the area. See Pietro Ebner, 'I monasteri bizantini nel Cilento: I Monasteri di S. Barbara, S. Mauro et S. Marina', *Rassegna Storica Salernitana*, 28 (1967), 77–142; Giuseppe Talamo-Atenolfi, 'La Regione di Velia e gli epigoni dell dinastia longobarda salernitana', *Archivi*, 28 (1968), 7–34; Borsari, *Il monachesimo bizantino*, 71–5; Paolo Peduto, 'Insediamenti altomedievali e ricerca archeologica', in *Guida alla storia di Salerno e della sua provincia*, ed. Alfonso Leone and Giovanni Vitolo (Salerno, 1982), 441–73; *La Civiltà rupestre medioevale nel Mezzogiorno d'Italia: Ricerche e Problemi: Atti del primo convegno internazionale di studi, Mottola-Casalrotta, 29 September–3 October 1971*, ed. C. D. Fosenca (Genova, 1975).

placed under the authority of a Greek bishop or archbishop. Little information survives about the liturgy or religious practices in the early Middle Ages for either Greek or Latin foundations so it is hard to know if Greek clerics in the region followed the same practices as clergy in Byzantine territories. Papal letters from the fifth and sixth centuries demonstrate that some popes at this time, such as Leo I, Gelasius I, and Gregory I, attempted to standardize certain practices for all of Christendom, including Sicily and southern Italy. However, it is doubtful they had much success, and after the papacy of Gregory I there was little contact between the pope in Rome and bishops in southern Italy. Neither Greek nor Latin clerics in Salerno were part of a centralized ecclesiastical hierarchy in the early Middle Ages.

Evidence suggests that Greek and Latin practices merged together in southern Italy. In the fifth century popes such as Gelasius I censured bishops in the region for adopting eastern practices, such as baptisms on the Epiphany.[55] In Rome itself popes adopted a number of festivals from the East in the course of the seventh century, including the *Theophania*, the Exaltation of the True Cross, and the Annunciation, Dormition, and Nativity of the Virgin Mary. Greek hymns and chants imported from Constantinople were also introduced at this time.[56] Although we are not as well informed about festivals and religious services in other parts of southern Italy, bi-lingual religious houses were found throughout the region in the early medieval period, as well as calendars that mixed Latin and Greek elements.[57] In Salerno, the monasteries of San Lorenzo and San Benedetto as well as the church of Santa Sofia contained both Greek and Latin clerics. The church of San Giovanni in Vietri, the church of Santa Sofia in Salerno, and the monastery of San Benedetto in Salerno all alternated between Latin- and Greek-speaking rectors in the tenth and eleventh centuries.[58] Even after the Norman conquest hybrid houses could still be found. To take just one example, Bruno of Rheims, the founder of Chartreuse, established an eremitic community in Calabria in the late eleventh century, Santa Maria near Stilo. The monastery was based on local Greek models rather than Benedictine ones and the monastery itself was confirmed and exempted by the local Greek bishop, Theodore of Squillace.[59]

[55] Borsari, *Il monachesimo bizantino*, 18–19. Evidently bishops in Naples likewise performed baptisms on the Epiphany.
[56] Jeffrey Richards, *The Popes and the Papacy in the Early Middle Ages, 476–752* (London, 1979), 278–80.
[57] Vitolo, 'Vescovi e Diocesi', 91; Taviani-Carozzi, *La Principauté*, 815–16.
[58] San Giovanni in Vietri had Latin priests appointed in 974 and 980 and Greek ones in 986. III, 25 (CDC II, 276); III, 69 (CDC II, 323); IV, 6 (CDC II, 382). Likewise the abbot of Santa Sofia in Salerno signed a 1041 document in Greek, while ten years later the new abbot signed in Latin. VIII, 103 (CDC VI, 977); X, 30 (CDC VII, 1147). In 1043 Prince Guaimarius IV appointed a Greek monk from Calabria, Basil, as abbot of San Benedetto, while fourteen years later Alfanus I, the future archbishop of Salerno, was named abbot. Cherubini, *Le Pergamene*, 14–15.
[59] Loud, *The Age of Robert Guiscard*, 269–70.

In addition, Latin foundations could be dependencies of Greek ones, or vice versa. The church of Santa Lucia, for example, was donated to San Nicola of Gallocanta. In the late eleventh and early twelfth centuries a number of Greek foundations were donated to the Latin abbey of Cava. Such donations did not entail any change in religious practices or traditions. Santa Lucia would not have become a Greek foundation upon its donation to San Nicola of Gallocanta. Likewise, the abbey of Cava allowed Greek houses dependent upon it to continue using the Greek language and to follow their own traditional practices, and there is no evidence that Cava or the archbishop of Salerno tried to 'Latinize' Greek foundations in the region in the twelfth century.[60]

The ecclesiastical system that arose in southern Italy in the early medieval period was a local phenomenon, made up of different traditions that combined together to create a unique religious system difficult to categorize as 'Latin' or 'Greek'. In the Principality of Salerno, identifying Greek versus Latin rites is especially difficult since the region lacked any institutions that could standardize practices, be it Greek or Latin. Religious rites appear to have differed not only from one place to another, but even from one church to another. As a result the Latin–Greek dichotomy is probably not very useful for understanding religious practices in the Principality of Salerno since it masks the variety of religious traditions that merged together over centuries as well as the regionalized nature of the early medieval ecclesiastical system.

Hence Santa Lucia was typical of an eleventh-century ecclesiastical foundation in the Principality of Salerno in many ways. First of all it was a small family foundation, built, supported, and administered by two brothers and a group of 'parentes' who lived nearby the church. It was also a community house, serving the religious needs of the small village of Balnearia. In addition, the house was a joint undertaking by members of the clergy and laity and it was free from archiepiscopal control. Thus the administration of Santa Lucia was in the hands of the founding family and surrounding community.

Likewise the career of Raidolfus was typical of that of other clerics in the region of Salerno. He served in a small, family foundation that was administered autonomously by the owners and clergy appointed. He had a wife and children, and he owned property over which he exercised the same rights as other laymen did. He also combined the duties of abbot and priest. Thus Raidolfus's lifestyle did not differ much from that of the laity, nor did it embody the ideals of papal reformers who were active in Italy at the time.

The church of Santa Lucia was also part of the consolidation trend characteristic of the mid-eleventh to mid-twelfth centuries. The *charta libertatis* from 1050 shows the church participating in a newly strengthened diocesan system in which the archbishop asserted power, albeit limited, over the clergy. Then sometime in the late eleventh and early twelfth centuries, Santa Lucia was donated to the church of San Nicola of Gallocanta, which in turn was absorbed by the

---

60 Vera von Falkenhausen, 'I monasteri greci'; Giovanni Vitolo, 'La Latinizzazione'.

abbey of Cava over the course of the first half of the twelfth century. Thus Santa Lucia passed out of the hands of the original founding family after only two generations, and by the twelfth century it was no longer a family-controlled religious house but part of the formidable Cava empire.

4

Lesser Barons and Greater Knights:
The Middling Group within the English Nobility
c. 1086–*c.* 1265

Richard Dace

'More than a knight, yet not a magnate'[1]

This paper argues for the existence of a middling group within the early medieval English nobility. Much of the evidence discussed here concerns six families, the Birminghams, the Du Bois, the Grimbalds, the Montforts, the Cahaignes, and the Verduns. In the twelfth century none were magnates but all were major landowners, predominantly but not exclusively in the English Midlands. They represent a sample of those who might be described as *milites mediae nobiles* rather than *milites gregarii*.[2] The Birminghams, Du Bois, Grimbalds, and Montforts all had their caputs in the Midlands, at Birmingham (Warwicks), Thorpe Arnold (Leics), Little Houghton (Northants) and Beaudesert (Warwicks) respectively. The Cahaignes family – frequently confused with other families bearing similar surnames – had extensive estates in Northamptonshire, but these estates were divided into two main branches with caputs at Tarrant Keynes (Somerset) and Horsted Keynes (Sussex) in the 1130s.[3] The Verduns were exceptional in a number of respects, being very modest landowners in Buckinghamshire in 1086 but verging on magnate status by *c.* 1200 when they held two sizeable English estates centred upon Alton (Staffs) and Brandon (Warwicks) and the Irish lordship of Dundalk (Louth).[4]

Some general genealogical points are worthy of brief comment. No less than seven successive heads of the Du Bois family bore the name Arnold. The Du Bois and Grimbald families were related by marriage in the mid-twelfth century, giving rise to a degree of common history and some legal disputes. The

1   D. Crouch, *The Beaumont Twins: Roots and Branches of Power in the Twelfth Century* (Cambridge, 1982), 102. Professor Crouch supervised my M.Phil thesis 'Towards the Banneret: Studies in Midland Society, 1150–1300' (unpub., Leeds, 1998), of which this article is a distillation. I acknowledge his considerable influence on my thinking here.
2   *Guillaume de Poitiers, Histoire de Guillaume Le Conquérant*, ed. R. Foreville (Paris, 1952), 232.
3   L.F. Salzman, 'William de Cahagnes and the family of Keynes', *Sussex Archaeological Collection*, 63 (1922), 180–202. Cahaignes is the spelling adopted in most recent works.
4   R. Dace, 'Bertran de Verdun: royal service, land and family in the late twelfth century', *Medieval Prosography*, 20 (1999), 75–93.

Birminghams seem to have been related to the Berminghams, an important family in Ireland in the thirteenth and fourteenth centuries.[5] Only two individual members of these families have received the attention of modern historians. Bertran de Verdun II (*c.* 1159–1192) merits an entry in the *Dictionary of National Biography*,[6] whilst Peter de Montfort (*c.* 1217–1265) appears in the *Dictionary of National Biography: Missing Persons.*[7]

The Du Bois, Montfort, Grimbald, and Birmingham families feature to a greater or lesser extent in recent honorial studies by Crouch, Stringer, and Hunt, and thus they may be reasonably described as 'honorial barons' in the twelfth century.[8] Other labels have been applied to the families. Coss describes the Montfort family as 'lesser barons' whilst Maddicott describes the Du Bois family as 'minor barons rather than knights'. Hilton refers to a 'lesser baronial' group which includes the Verdun family. The use of such terms demonstrates these historians' awareness of the existence of a middling group within the nobility, albeit an ill-defined one.[9] This awareness has a long history; the seventeenth-century antiquary Dugdale wrote of the Birminghams 'though none of this ancient Family were reputed Barons till the beginning of Edward III's reign yet were they persons of great note long before'.[10] Eighteenth-century county historians such as Nichols and Bridges certainly recognized that some of the families featured in their works, the Bassets for example, were of exceptional status and significance. The three main branches of the Basset family were all barons inasmuch as they held baronies in the thirteenth century, but as Reedy has shown, the greater part of their holdings were mesne tenancies and 'none . . . ever held really large amounts of land'.[11] Maddicott rightly points out that defining the baronage 'is notoriously difficult in the mid-thirteenth century'. Painter notes that the use of the term 'baron' in a legal sense is apparent by the time of Magna Carta and superseded the twelfth-century usage,

[5] G.H. Orpen, *Ireland under the Normans* (4 vols., Oxford, 1911–20), iii, 113, 211. Sir W. Dugdale, *Antiquities of Warwickshire* (2 vols., London, 1723), 898.

[6] *D.N.B.*, xx, 217. See also Dace, 'Bertran de Verdun', 75–93. M. Hagger's recent and comprehensive study of the Verdun family, *The Fortunes of a Norman Family* (Dublin, 2001), adds an extra generation to the family tree and prefers the form Bertram. Thus my Bertran II is his Bertram III.

[7] *D.N.B.: Missing Persons*, ed. C.S. Nicholls (London, 1993), 520–21.

[8] Crouch, *The Beaumont Twins*, 106–11. D. Crouch, 'The local influence of the early earls of Warwick, 1088–1242: A study in decline and resourcefulness', *Midland History*, 21 (1996), 1–22. K. Stringer, *Earl David of Huntingdon* (Edinburgh, 1985), 128, 143. J. Hunt, *Lordship and the Landscape: a documentary and archaeological study of the honor of Dudley, c. 1086–1322*, B.A.R. British Series, 264 (London, 1997), 52–3.

[9] P.R. Coss, *Lordship, Knighthood, and Locality: A Study in English Society* (Cambridge, 1991), 241. J.R. Maddicott, *Simon de Montfort* (Cambridge, 1994), 70. R.H. Hilton, *A Medieval Society: The West Midlands at the End of the Thirteenth Century* (London, 1966), 49.

[10] Sir William Dugdale, *The Baronage of England* (3 vols., London, 1675–6), ii, 108.

[11] J. Nichols, *The History and Antiquities of the County of Leicester* (4 vols., in 8 parts, London, 1795–1815), passim. J. Bridges, *The History and Antiquities of Northamptonshire* (2 vols., London, 1791), passim. W. Reedy, *Basset Charters, c. 1120–1250*, Pipe Roll Society (London, 1995), xvi.

which had encompassed greater mesne tenants, lesser *curiales* and minor tenants-in-chief.[12]

Stenton's *First Century of English Feudalism* was the first serious attempt to analyse the middling group within the nobility, albiet confined to a narrow time frame and a purely honorial context. His definition of what constituted an honorial baron was cautious but included closeness to a great lord and possession of a significant amount of land and possibly a castle. He recognized that an honorial baron might have a distinguished lineage and a following of his own.[13] He also considered that possession of the rights of legal jurisdiction – specifically, sake and soke, toll, team, and infangenetheof – to be indicative of barony, honorial or otherwise, and he cites the Verdun barony of Alton as an example of a smaller type commonly found in the north of England.[14] Stenton's honorial emphasis has been challenged; Holt for example claims that the 'social and political independence' of some northern knights was evident from the twelfth century and was an attribute of those who challenged King John in 1216.[15] Studies of honorial communities by Crouch and others have demonstrated that families who were important mesne tenants were not necessarily politically or socially subordinated to the lords of the honours from which they held land.[16] In the Midlands the Burdet, Camville, and Foliot families are just a few examples of 'sub-tenants of baronial character'[17] who held lands of different lords. The Burdets were tenants of both the earls of Leicester and Huntingdon, and honorial officials of the latter. The Camvilles were tenants of the honour of Mowbray and prominent royal servants, whilst the Foliots were tenants of the honour of Huntingdon as well as significant tenants-in-chief in their own right.[18] These families may be compared with the greater tenants of other honours outside the Midlands. Mortimer's study of the honour of Clare indicates that tenant families such as the Dammartins and the Baillols were of considerable stature.[19] English's study of the lordship of Holderness gives more examples, including the Ros and Fauconberg families.[20]

It is generally accepted that the term 'honorial baron' has little meaning beyond the twelfth century. English is adamant that honorial barons 'disappeared about 1200 on all but the greatest regalities'.[21] No equivalent collective term has

---

12 Maddicott, *Simon de Montfort*, 70. S. Painter, *Barons and Baronies* (Baltimore 1943), 14–16. D. Crouch, *The Image of Aristocracy in Britain, 1000–1300* (London, 1992), 109–14.

13 F.M. Stenton, *The First Century of English Feudalism, 1066–1166* (1932), chapter 3.

14 Stenton, *First Century*, 109.

15 J.C. Holt, *The Northerners* (1961), 36–7, 55–60.

16 Crouch, *Beaumont Twins*, 101–38. D. Crouch, 'From Stenton to McFarlane: Models of Societies of the Twelfth and Thirteenth Centuries', *T.R.H.S.*, 6th ser., 5 (1995), 179–86.

17 S.J. Harvey, 'The knight and the knight's fee in England', *P.&P.*, 49 (1970), 10.

18 Crouch, *Beaumont Twins*, 130. D. Greenway, *Charters of the Honour of Mowbray, 1107–91* (London, 1972), xxxiv. Stringer, *Earl David*, 136.

19 R. Mortimer, 'Land and Service: The Tenants of the Honour of Clare', *A.N.S.*, 8 (1985), 182 and 194.

20 B. English, *The Lords of Holderness* (Oxford, 1979), 147–9.

21 English, *Lords of Holderness*, 139.

gained general acceptance amongst historians of the thirteenth century. Coss has argued for 'vavasour' and Williams uses it in this sense of the Ashby family, tenants of the honour of Peveril in the East Midlands, but it has not been widely adopted, possibly because it is also freely applied to those below knightly rank.[22] Historians of the fourteenth century, however, use the term 'banneret' to describe the middling group. Saul dramatically describes bannerets as 'an enigmatic group who bestrode the borderland between the higher nobility and the knights',[23] whilst Given-Wilson believes that bannerets were 'somewhere between full baronial rank and knightly rank'.[24] This intermediate condition might be of long standing, one fourteenth-century election to parliament was challenged because the would-be knight of the shire was 'a banneret as were most of his ancestors' and therefore ineligible.[25] Although the term *milites regis bannericiis*, which first appears in 1260, is generally viewed as a military rank,[26] the term 'banneret' was also used by chroniclers of the Baron's War to describe one element of the nobility. William of Rishanger distinguishes *vexilliferos* from *barones*, whilst Robert of Gloucester similarly distinguishes bannerets from knights.[27] The adoption of the banner as a symbol of social elevation can be discerned much earlier. William Marshall is described as *portant banière* in a tournament at Lagny in 1180. This was well before he was elevated to an earldom and high office although the recounting of the event dates to the 1220s.[28] A near contemporary continental parallel can be found in Rigord's biography of Philip Augustus, which refers to 'knights of such nobility that they rejoiced in the insignia of a baron'.[29]

The traditional view that the post-Conquest nobility was predominantly of Norman origin and came over with the Conqueror is difficult to sustain in the light of recent research. That there was a significant Breton and Flemish element has been long recognized, but it is now clear that some French lords had acquired their holdings in England well before the Conquest.[30] It is also evident that members of the pre-Conquest English nobility could find a niche in the new

[22] P.R. Coss, 'Literature and Social Terminology: the Vavasour in England', *Social Relations and Ideas: Essays in Honour of R.H. Hilton*, ed. T. Aston (Cambridge, 1983), 112–17. D. Williams, 'The Peverils and the Essebies', *England in the Twelfth Century*, ed. D. Williams, Harlaxton Symposium, 1988 (Woodbridge, 1990), 247. Crouch, *Image*, 171–3.

[23] N. Saul, *Knights and Esquires: The Gloucester Gentry in the Fourteenth Century* (Oxford, 1981), 7.

[24] C. Given-Wilson, *The English Nobility in the Later Middle Ages* (London, 1987), 61.

[25] Given-Wilson, *English Nobility*, 61. Saul, *Knights and Esquires*, 7.

[26] *Close R.*, 1259–61, 315.

[27] *The Chronicle of William of Rishanger of the Barons' War*, ed. J.O. Helliwell, Camden Society 15 (1840), 44. *The Metrical Chronicle of Robert of Gloucester*, ed. W.A. Wright (R.S., 2 vols., London, 1887), 11501.

[28] D. Crouch, *William Marshal* (London, 1990), 44.

[29] *Recueil des Historiens des Gaules et de la France*, ed. M. Bouquet et al. (24 vols., Paris, 1869–1904), xvii, 99.

[30] C.P. Lewis, 'The French in England before the Norman Conquest', *A.N.S.*, 17 (1994), 121–39.

order, the Arden family being an example in the Midlands.[31] However, four out of the six families studied here can be confidently supposed to have had Norman origins, based on the evidence of their surnames and post-Conquest ownership of land in the Duchy. Members of the Du Bois family were prominent tenants of the honour of Breteuil in southern Normandy before 1071 and remained so until dispossessed in 1202.[32] The Cahaignes family took its name from Cahagnes (Calvados, cant. Aunay-sur-Odon) and certainly held a knight's fee there from the honour of Mortain in 1172. William de Cahaignes I was an important tenant of the count of Mortain in England in 1086 and seems to have been the count's agent in the Midlands. It is reasonable to suppose their close relationship was formed before the Conquest.[33] The Montfort family was fairly certainly a cadet branch of the powerful lords of Montfort-sur-Risle (Eure), and possessed lands at Pithienville, Gauville and Claville (Eure, cant. Evreux Nord et Sud).[34] The Verdun family had strong links with the Breton march. In 1172 Bertran de Verdun II held land at Bouillon (Manche, cant. Granville) and Chavoy (Manche, cant. Avranches), and there is a Verdun place name in Vessey (Manche, cant. Pontorson).[35] The origins of the Grimbald and Birmingham families are unclear. We do know that the Grimbald whose name was adopted as a patronymic by his descendants was not the pre-Conquest lord of the lands he held in 1086 but little more than this. His descendants held land in the Cotentin but this was probably acquired by marriage in the mid-twelfth century.[36] The Birmingham family although clearly important by the 1150s cannot be traced back beyond the 1130s when William of Birmingham I was set up as major tenant of the honour of Dudley.[37]

The earliest recorded members of these families were almost invariably significant individuals. Arnold fitz Popelina, head of the Du Bois family in 1071 was a patron of Lyre Abbey (Eure, cant. Rugles), to which he granted a church and tithes.[38] Orderic Vitalis mentions that he was one of ten knights of the honour of Breteuil captured in fighting at Ivry (Eure) in 1094.[39] The ancestry of

---

[31] A. Williams, 'A Vice-Comital Family in Pre-Conquest Warwickshire', *A.N.S.*, 11 (1988), 279–92. Coss, *Knighthood*, 190–91.

[32] Lyre Cartulary, Collection du Dom Lenoir, Château de Semilly, MS. de la Marquise de Mathan, 2. *Cartulaire Normand de Philippe-Auguste, Louis VIII, St Louis et Philippe-le-Hardi*, ed. L. Deslisle (Geneva, 1978), 71.

[33] L.C. Loyd, *The Origins of Some Anglo-Norman Families*, Harleian Society (Leeds, 1951), 52. *Red Book of the Exchequer*, ed. H. Hall (R.S., 3 vols., London, 1896), ii, 640. *D.B.*, 20b, 223. J.A. Green, 'The Sheriffs of William the Conqueror', *A.N.S.*, 5 (1982), 137. M.J. Crispin and L. Macary, *The Falaise Roll* (London, 1938), 36.

[34] *Complete Peerage*, ix, 130. D. Crouch, 'Normans and Anglo-Normans: a divided aristocracy', *England and Normandy in the Middle Ages*, eds. D. Bates and A. Curry (London, 1994), 62.

[35] Loyd, *Anglo-Norman Families*, 109.

[36] *D.B.*, fol. 228c, 236c. J.H. Round, *Calendar of Documents Preserved in France* (London, 1899), 945.

[37] Hunt, *Lordship and the Landscape*, 52–3.

[38] Ctl. Lyre, 2.

[39] Orderic, *Eccl. Hist.*, iv, 288.

his mother Popelina is not known but, like the Gunnora from whom several prominent Norman families claimed descent, she was evidently a significant figure. Arnold's adoption of a matronymic surname can only mean that he inherited her rights.[40] According to Orderic, Arnold's son, Arnold fitz Arnold, was castellan of Lyre in 1119 when the castle was attacked by the forces of King Henry I.[41] Crouch sees his support for the earl of Leicester in the following year, as crucial to the earl's assimilation of the lordship of Breteuil, and Arnold's reward was a substantial grant of land in Leicestershire and Warwickshire.[42] William de Cahaignes I held over thirty properties of the count of Mortain in Sussex and Northamptonshire in 1086, and was sheriff of the latter county *c.* 1070 to 1106.[43] Grimbald, progenitor of the Grimbald family, held five manors in Northamptonshire and Leicestershire of Countess Judith, widow of Earl Waltheof, in 1086 and subsequently became the steward of her son-in-law, Simon de Senlis I, earl of Huntingdon.[44] Thurstin de Montfort I became a follower of Henry, earl of Warwick in the 1090s and witnessed his charters.[45] Thurstin's descendants held lands of the honour of Warwick in Warwickshire, Rutland, and Berkshire, reckoned at a substantial ten and a quarter knight's fees.[46] Domesday Book indicates that Bertran de Verdun I held only a single manor in Buckinghamshire in 1086, but he subsequently served as sheriff of Yorkshire and *c.* 1100 he was granted a lordship of more than twenty properties in Staffordshire and Leicestershire.[47] In the 1150s Peter of Birmingham, son of William, was both the main tenant and the steward of the Pagnell lords of Dudley. His lands in Warwickshire, Staffordshire, and Buckinghamshire were assessed at nine knight's fees in 1166.[48]

The heads of these families were demonstrably substantial landowners, and as a consequence they had numerous subtenants. Some of these were petty freeholders paying a rent, but others were far from insubstantial figures; the Edgbaston, Enville, and Parles families held land of the Birmingham family by knight's service in the early thirteenth century and have been identified as 'county knights'.[49] The Birminghams seem to have exercised the same rights in respect of fees held by their subtenants, demonstrably wardship but presumably aids and scutage as well, as the lords of Dudley exercised over them.[50] Whilst

[40] D. Bates, *Normandy before 1066* (London, 1982), 108. J.C. Holt, 'What's in a name? Family Nomenclature and the Norman Conquest', *Colonial England, 1066–1215* (London, 1997), 194.
[41] Orderic, *Eccl. Hist.*, vi, 251.
[42] Crouch, *Beaumont Twins*, 108.
[43] *D.B.*, fol. 20b. 223c–d. J.A. Green, *English Sheriffs to 1154*, P.R.O. (London, 1990), 63.
[44] *D.B.*, fol. 228c, 236c, 236d. B.L., Vespasian E. xvii (Ctl. St Andrew's, Northampton), fol. 5d.
[45] *Chronicon Monasterii de Abingdon* (R.S., 2 vols., London, 1858), ii, 21.
[46] *R.B.E.*, 325.
[47] See Dace, 'Bertran de Verdun', 77.
[48] *Magnum Registrum Album*, Staffordshire Historical Collections (London, 1926), 20. *R.B.E.*, 269.
[49] Coss, *Lordship*, 259.
[50] Staffordshire Historical Collections, William Salt Archaeological Society, 4 (1883), 119.

the effectiveness of honorial, and by implication sub-honorial, authority has been questioned,[51] two instances provided by the subjects of this study show that sub-honorial courts did operate as courts of arbitration and record. The earlier of these instances is a grant of the manor of Allexton (Leics) made before *tota curia* of Robert Grimbald *c.* 1160 and documented by his charter. Robert refers to himself as *advocatus* of the fee in question and his seal shows a seated magisterial figure holding a sword in his right hand.[52] Whilst most of the heads of the families studied here were using seals by the mid-twelfth century, they normally bore an equestian image. It was presumably this sort of affectation that prompted Henry II's Justiciar, Richard de Lucy, to comment that every 'little knight' had a seal, although the target of Lucy's splenetic comment, Gilbert de Baillol, was a substantial landowner.[53] The second instance probably dates to the 1180s or 1190s. An entry in the *Curia Regis Rolls* dated 1210–12 records that a claim concerning land in Bushbury (Warwicks) and Upper Penn (Staffs) had previously been disputed in the *curia* of William of Birmingham, lord of the lands in question.[54] The heads of the families appointed officials of their own to manage their estates. Baldwin de Charnelles was acting as Arnold du Bois III's deputy in Normandy *c.* 1150, whilst Arnold of Barton was steward and deputy to Bertran de Verdun II in the 1180s.[55] The next generation preferred clerical stewards; Benjamin rector of Ebrington (Gloucs) was the steward and attorney of Arnold du Bois IV, and Adam the clerk served Nicholas de Verdun in the same capacities.[56]

Perhaps the most enduring reminder of the former influence of the families considered here is in the form of place names. Somerford Keynes (Wilts), Tarrant Keynes and Combe Keynes (Dorset) were all members of the barony of Tarrant, held by Ralph de Cahaignes I and his descendants. Horsted Keynes was the principal manor of Ralph's brother Hugh de Cahaignes I and his successors. Wellesbourne Mountfort (Warwicks) was a Montfort manor. 'Grimbald's Houghton' (now Little Houghton) belonged to the Grimbalds and Newbold Verdon (Leics) to the Verduns. Many of these formulations date to the thirteenth century or later but there are earlier instances. The Du Bois Christian name Arnold forms part of the place names of their head manors in Normandy and England – Bois-Arnault (Eure, cant. Rugles) and Thorpe Arnold respectively – and the former of these is recorded as early as 1125.[57] The Staffordshire section

---

51 Crouch, 'From Stenton to McFarlane', 184–6.
52 *Sir Christopher Hatton's Book of Seals*, ed. L.C. Loyd and D.M. Stenton (Oxford, 1950), 146.
53 Mortimer, 'Land and Service', 194.
54 *Cur.Reg.R.*, vi, 72.
55 Ctl. Lyre, 35. Dace, 'Bertran de Verdun', 86.
56 P.R.O., JUST1/799 m. 6. *Cur.Reg. R.*, i, 239. *Pleas before the King or his Justices, 1198–1212*, Seldon Society (London, 1966), 254.
57 *Dictionnaire Topographique du Département de l'Eure*, ed. M. de Blossville (Paris, 1877), i, 347.

of the 1167 Pipe Roll mentions the place name *Morf Petri*. Morfe was a demesne holding of the Birmingham family so the reference must be to Peter of Birmingham.[58]

Landownership was undoubtedly an important indicator of status but Stenton believed that '(honorial) baronage ... depended far less on the extent of a tenant's fee than on his general social position, his birth, and on the nature of his relations with his lord'.[59] Thurstin de Montfort I who was of good family and was a kinsman of the first earl of Warwick is a good example. However Stenton also stressed that 'household duties, even more than obligation or military service, brought a man into that direct personal relationship with his lord which was the essence of a baron's status'.[60] Robert Grimbald I, son of the steward of Simon de Senlis I, earl of Huntingdon, was steward of the honour of Huntingdon in the 1130s when the King of Scots held it. Robert subsequently transferred his allegiance to Simon de Senlis II, earl of Northampton, who regained possession of his ancestral lands in the 1140s.[61] Arnold du Bois III, son of the Arnold established in England by the earl of Leicester, deputed for the earl when fighting broke out around Breteuil in 1138. Orderic Vitalis calls him the earl's steward in his account of the razing of the nearby rebel fortress of Pont Echanfray and the village of Montreuil, although the earl himself styled Arnold his constable in a charter concerning Breteuil.[62] Arnold was definitely the earl's steward in England during the 1140s, whilst his son Arnold IV held the same office in the 1180s.[63] The Du Bois family were also hereditary prévots of Glos-la-Ferrière (Orne, cant. L'Aigle), a *bourg* within the honour of Breteuil.[64] Willingness to serve as an honorial official persisted throughout twelfth century. William fitz Richard de Cahaignes, a great-grandson of William de Cahaignes I was steward to John of Mortain in the 1190s, although of course in this instance the count was also the King's brother and Lord of Ireland.[65] It is only after *c.* 1200 that the middling sort of nobleman abandoned honorial office, to be replaced by more numerous but less socially prominent professional administrators.[66] However, foregoing ministerial duties did not necessarily mean that the intimate relationship with their lords ceased. The father and son Arnold du Bois VI and VII, were amongst the closest associates of Simon de Montfort, earl of Leicester, and witnessed several of his charters. Arnold VII was made one of the executors of

---

[58] *Pipe R.*, 13 Henry II, 56. *Calendar of Inqusitions Post Mortem*, HMSO (London, 1904–), iii, 813.

[59] Stenton, *First Century*, 95.

[60] Stenton, *First Century*, 110.

[61] W.K. Farrer, *Honors and Knights Fees* (3 vols., London, 1923–5), 302.

[62] Orderic, *Eccl. Hist.*, vi, 513. Ctl. Lyre, 23.

[63] *English Lawsuits from William I to Richard I*, ed. R.C. van Caenegem, Selden Society (2 vols., London, 1990–91), i, 317. *Pipe R.*, 26 Henry II, 6.

[64] Crouch, *Beaumont Twins*, 111.

[65] *Historical and Municipal Documents of Ireland, 1172–1320*, ed. J.T. Gilbert, R.S. (London, 1870), 51–5.

[66] N. Denholm-Young, *Seigenurial Administration in England* (London, 1937), passim.

Earl Simon's will in 1259.[67] Simon de Montfort had succeeded to only part of the lands of the twelfth-century earldom of Leicester; the remainder went to the Quincy family. William du Bois, brother of Arnold VI, served as a knight in the household of Roger de Quincy, earl of Winchester and constable of Scotland.[68] In his study of Quincy's following Simpson identifies William as one the earl's 'inner circle', a term that Maddicot has adopted in his analysis of the following of Simon de Montfort, and applies to Arnold du Bois VI and his son.[69]

Powerful men, like Quincy and Montfort, could attract retainers from outside the traditional honorial connections. Peter de Montfort, a descendant of Thurstin I, had no historic links with the earldom of Leicester, but he became a trusted lieutenant of Simon de Montfort. He was granted land at Ilmington (Warwicks) by the earl, and was also named as an executor of his will.[70] The marriage of William of Birmingham III to Sybil de Coleville in the early thirteenth century can also be seen in terms of forging a new relationship outside the honorial structure. Sybil was daughter and co-heiress of Alice de Coleville, who was the mistress of William Marshal's brother John.[71] It does not seem unreasonable to suggest that this was an attempt by the Birmingham family to become part of the Earl Marshal's affinity; the 'penumbra of men, whom it would be difficult to call followers because they did not follow him on any regular basis'.[72] If some relationships were newly forged in the thirteenth century, long-standing honorial obligations could still be enforced, as is evident from Roger de Somery's impleading of William of Birmingham V regarding fees and suit of court owed to the honour of Dudley in 1262.[73] However at Evesham three years later Roger and William were on opposite sides, and it seems that in this case politics and kinship (William was a grandson of Arnold du Bois VI and a son-in-law of Thomas of Astley, another Montfort 'inner circle' member) prevailed over honorial loyalty.

That William de Cahaignes I and Bertran de Verdun I served as sheriff of Northampton and Yorkshire respectively has already been noted. Successive heads of most of the families considered here undertook royal service of some form, but whether they sought it out or had it forced upon them is not clear from the evidence. Hugh de Cahaignes, a younger son of William de Cahaignes I, was the keeper of Whittlewood forest (Northants) by 1129 and the 1130 Pipe Roll shows that he had been granted the farm of the royal manor of Silverstone

[67] Maddicott, *Simon de Montfort*, 64.

[68] G. Simpson, 'The Familia of Roger de Quincy, Earl of Winchester and Constable of Scotland', *Essays on the Nobility of Medieval Scotland*, ed. K. Stringer (Edinburgh, 1985), 108.

[69] Maddicott, *Simon de Montfort*, 68.

[70] Maddicott, *Simon de Montfort*, 64, 72.

[71] *William Marshal*, 81 n.33. *Bk. of Fees*, 842 and 881.

[72] Crouch, *William Marshal*, 157. Huntingdon Lib. storage box 7, 17. I am grateful to Professor David Crouch for the latter reference.

[73] *Warwickshire Feet of Fines*, ed. E. Stokes et al., Dugdale Society (2 vols., London, 1932–9), i, 842. *Calendar of Inquisitions Miscellaneous*, i (1916), 1176.

within the forest.[74] Robert Grimbald I served as sheriff of Northampton and Huntingdon in the 1140s and 1150s.[75] In 1169 Peter of Birmingham acted as overseer for royal bridge construction in Staffordshire, and he may also have been an agister for the forests in the same county since he accounted for forest pannage in the previous year.[76] Robert Grimbald II undertook some local governmental duties, conducting tax receipts from Northampton to Oxford in 1225 and collecting taxes in 1234.[77] In the latter year he was also nominated as a justice-in-eyre in Rutland.[78] Arnold du Bois VI was appointed a Justice of the Forest in 1253.[79] He had been custodian of the counties of Nottingham and Derby for part of 1239 but surprisingly this seems to have been his only public appointment prior to appointment as Justice. It seems likely therefore that he owed his appointment to his connection with Simon de Montfort.[80] For some service became a career, Bertran de Verdun II and Peter de Montfort are examples from the twelfth and thirteenth centuries respectively. Both served as sheriffs, Bertran of Warwickshire and Leicestershire, and Peter of Shropshire; and both served in ambassadorial capacities, the former to Spain in 1177 and the latter to France on several occasions in the later 1250s. Both served in the retinues of royal princes, the former as steward to John as lord of Ireland in 1185 and the later as a member of Lord Edward's wedding party in Spain in 1254. Bertram de Verdun died on crusade in the Holy Land in 1192.[81] Peter by contrast died in ignominy, a rebel killed at Evesham in 1265.[82]

Notwithstanding the willingness of members of the families to involve themselves in certain types of royal service, none of them undertook the more mundane judicial and administrative duties that most knights performed from the late twelfth century onwards.[83] Both Coss and Crouch have suggested that non-participation was a mark of elevated status, and cite the Montfort family as an example of those who did not serve as jurors.[84] However it does appear that these families sometimes found it desirable to procure a specific royal exemption. William of Birmingham IV and Robert Grimbald II were both granted exemptions from assizes, juries, or recognitions by Henry III.[85] In his analysis of

---

[74] *Regesta,* ii, 1844, 1847. *Pipe R.,* 31 Henry II, 83.

[75] Green, *English Sheriffs,* 49, 64. R.H. Davis, *King Stephen* (London, 1990), 127–8.

[76] *Pipe R.,* 15 Henry II, 68. *Pipe R.,* 14 Henry II, 118. C.R. Young, *The Royal Forests of Medieval England* (Leicester, 1979), 27–9.

[77] *Rot. Litt. Claus.,* ii, 74. *Close R.,* 1232–42, 158.

[78] *Cal. Pat.* (1906–), 1232–47, 77 and 127. D. Crook, *Records of the General Eyre,* HMSO (London, 1982), 89.

[79] Matthew Paris, *Chronica Majora,* (R.S. 7 vols., London, 1872–83), v, 379, 487.

[80] *Cal. Lib. R.,* 1226–40, 387.

[81] *D.N.B.,* xx, 217.

[82] *D.N.B: Missing Persons,* 520–21.

[83] A.L. Poole, *Obligations of Society in the Twelfth and Thirteenth Centuries* (Oxford, 1946), 53–6. K. Faulkner, 'The Transformation of Knighthood in Early Thirteenth-Century England', *E.H.R.,* 111 (1996), 1–5.

[84] Coss, *Lordship,* 241. Crouch, *Image,* 119.

[85] *Patent Rolls,* 1247–58, 82, 310.

the recipients of exemptions Waugh demonstrates that they were often granted to those who engaged in other forms of royal service, which was certainly true of these two. He also concludes that together with respites of knighthood, exemptions were a means for the crown to differentiate those in 'positions of power and profit' from those engaged in 'routine tasks of governance'.[86]

The importance of service in an administrative sense cannot be understated and Hicks rightly points out that most historians agree on this point.[87] However the emphasis on administrative activity should not obscure the fact that the heads of the families were knights and the raison d'etre of the knight was war. Evidence for participation in campaigns, sieges and battles is plentiful. The military activities of the earlier members of the Du Bois family on the southern borders of Normandy have already been mentioned. A William de Cahaignes, described as *miles validissimus*, fought at the battle of Lincoln in 1141 and captured King Stephen, although who he was is not absolutely clear.[88] Norman de Verdun was present at the siege of Stamford in 1153.[89] Bertran de Verdun II, William de Birmingham II, and Ralph de Cahaignes II were all active royalists during the 1173–4 revolt.[90] Bertran and William both accompanied Richard I on the Third Crusade.[91] Arnold du Bois IV, a suspected rebel in 1173–4, was also a Crusader and was amongst those who rescued the earl of Leicester during a skirmish outside Ramlah in November or December 1191.[92] Thurstin de Montfort III, William fitz Ralph de Cahaignes and Nicholas de Verdun fought in several of John's campaigns prior to 1216,[93] although all three turned against him during the Civil War of 1216.[94] Under John's successor Henry III, Arnold du Bois VI mustered at Portsmouth in 1229 for an abortive campaign to Brittany,[95] whilst Peter de Montfort and William de Birmingham IV served in Gascony in 1242 and 1254 respectively.[96] It is perhaps worth noting that none of these individuals were killed in action; but the situation changed drastically at

---

86 S. Waugh, 'Reluctant Knights and Jurors: Respites, Exemptions and Public Obligations in the Reign of Henry III', *Speculum,* 58 (1983), 971–86.

87 M. Hicks, *Bastard Feudalism* (London, 1995) 11.

88 Henry of Huntingdon, *Henrici Archiadiaconi Huntendunensis Historia Anglorum*, ed. T. Arnold (R.S., London, 1879), 274. Salzman, 'William de Cahaignes', 180–202. Dace, 'Towards the Banneret', chapter 3 and appendix 2.

89 *Regesta,* iii, 492.

90 *Jordan Fantosme's Chronicle*, 111, 114. *Pipe R.*, 20 Henry II, 14, 139.

91 Benedict of Peterborough, *Gesta Regis Henrici Secundi* (R.S. 2 vols., London, 1867), ii, 150. *Pipe R.*, 2 & 3 Richard I, 152.

92 Ambroise, *L'Estoire de la Guerre Sainte*, ed. G Paris, Collection de Documents Inedits (Paris, 1897), 201.

93 *Cur. Reg. R.*, iv, 164. *Rot. Litt. Claus*, i, 43. B. Smith, 'Tenure and locality in North Leinster', *Colony and Frontier in Medieval Ireland*, ed. T.B. Barry, R. Frame, and K. Simms (London, 1995), 32.

94 *Rot. Litt. Claus.*, i, 242–3, 272, 277, 287, 294, 300.

95 I. Sanders, *Feudal Military Service in England* (Oxford, 1956) 125.

96 *Patent Rolls*, 1232–47, 366; 1247–58, 242.

Evesham in 1265 where both Peter de Montfort and William de Birmingham V were amongst those who died supporting Simon de Montfort.[97]

Although members of the families can be shown to have been fighting men, it is not always certain on what basis they served. In the twelfth century there is no explicit evidence that any of the families performed military service in person under a defined feudal obligation, or that they operated as a military contractor in the manner that Harvey suggests important vassals might be expected to.[98] Historians are in broad agreement that there was radical change in the nature of military obligation in the thirteenth century whereby service was linked to status not tenure, and it can be demonstrated that this was the case for the families studied here.[99] The Montfort, Du Bois, and Birmingham families held the bulk if not all of their lands as mesne tenants. Yet in royal campaigns under John and Henry III the heads of these families were found serving alongside the heads of the Verdun and Cahaignes families, who were tenants-in-chief to a more significant degree. Thurstin de Montfort III served in royal expeditions to France in 1206 and 1214.[100] Although none of his ancestors had been tenants-in-chief, inexplicably he was stated to be holding one fee in-chief in 1212.[101] Conceivably this was an attempt by King John to break the Montfort's tenurial link with the enfeebled earldom of Warwick; if so it did not succeed and they remained Warwick tenants. Arnold du Bois VI held only a tiny fraction of his land in chief yet he mustered for a royal expedition to Brittany in 1229.[102] William of Birmingham IV served on the royal campaign to Gascony in 1254 although none of his lands were held in chief.[103] In the thirteenth century the Tarrant branch of the Cahaignes family disputed the extent of their liability in respect of the barony they held, claiming it was two fees not three, but were nonetheless regular attendees at royal musters.[104] Participation in warfare was not invariably at royal behest. The heads of the families were just as likely to be in arms in support of private conflicts or rebellions. Arnold du Bois I and his son were active supporters of Eustace de Breteuil, the popular but illegitimate claimant to the honour of Breteuil, and fought against his various enemies including Henry I.[105] When Thomas de Verdun and Hugh de Lacy formed an alliance in the late 1190s, one of the provisions of the alliance was that they would share any conquests in 'the land of war'.[106]

[97] *Cal. Inq. Misc.*, i, 928.
[98] Harvey, 'The knight and the knight's fee', 12.
[99] M. Powicke, *Military Obligation in Medieval England* (Oxford, 1962), chapter 4. Sanders, *Feudal Military Service*, chapter 4.
[100] *Cur. Reg. R.*, iv, 164. *Rot. Litt. Claus.*, i, 201.
[101] *R.B.E.*, 550.
[102] Sanders, *Feudal Military Service*, 125.
[103] *Patent Rolls*, 1247–58, 338 & 348.
[104] Sanders, *Feudal Military Service*, 83. *R.B.E.*, 218.
[105] See Crouch, *Beaumont Twins*, 108–9.
[106] *Calendar of the Gormanston Register*, ed. J. Miller and M. McEnery (Dublin, 1916), 144.

The exercise of military command was always expected of the nobility.[107] Arnold du Bois III's prominent role during the fighting around Breteuil in 1138 has already been mentioned. In the 1140s his *homines* disturbed the holdings of Reading Abbey at Wigston (Leics).[108] During the civil war of 1173–4 Bertran de Verdun II commanded a force of *milites* and *pedites* which included mercenaries and armed townsmen. Bertran was subsequently made constable of the important castle of Pontorson on the frontier of Normandy and Brittany, and possibly also of the similarly strategic fortress of Drogheda in Ireland.[109] As a leading *curialis* he obviously could not spend much time at either in person, but he could be relied on to appoint suitable surrogates such as his relative Ralph de Verdun, who may have acted as Bertran's deputy at both places.[110] Bertran's appointment as governor of Acre in 1190 is another example of the trust placed in his qualities as a military commander.[111] Bertran's son Nicholas also exercised military command effectively. In 1217 a number of his kinsmen and tenants are found amongst the former rebels presumably mustered by him the previous year.[112] In 1228 he was entrusted with guarding the marches of Ireland whilst a major expedition was launched into Connaught.[113] Peter de Montfort seems to have been another notable leader. He was custodian of Abergavenny in 1259 with responsibility for defence of the border against Prince Llewelyn.[114] He commanded the Montfortian force in Northampton in 1264[115] and at Evesham a year later his following included his two sons, both of whom were knights.[116] On a more modest scale, the participation of William de Birmingham IV and his brother Brian, both knights, in the 1254 Gascony campaign may be an instance of a greater knight manning his following from amongst his kin and acting as a banneret in the sense of leading a force.[117]

The families rapidly adopted the imagery of aristocratic knighthood in the thirteenth century, in conscious imitation of their magnate overlords. The surviving seals of the various members of the Du Bois family serve as examples of the trend. Those of Arnolds III, and IV show the mounted knight typical of the twelfth century although the latter boasted a counterseal, an antique oval intaglio gem surrounded by the text *secretum Hernaldi de Bosco*.[118] However a seal of

---

[107] L. Génicot, 'Recent research on the medieval nobility', *The Medieval Nobility*, ed. and trans. T. Reuter (Amsterdam, 1978), 24.

[108] *Regesta*, iii, 682.

[109] *Recueil Des Actes de Henri II*, ii, 179. *Calendar of Documents in Ireland, 1171–1251*, ed. H. S. Sweetman, HMSO (London, 1875), 2302.

[110] Dace, 'Bertran de Verdun', 87.

[111] Benedict, *Gesta*, ii, 149–50.

[112] Dace, 'Bertran de Verdun', 91.

[113] A.J. Otway Ruthven, 'Knight service in Ireland', *Royal Society of Antiquaries of Ireland*, 89 (Dublin, 1959), 4.

[114] *Patent Rolls*, 1247–58, 14, 39

[115] *Annales Monastici*, ed. H.R. Luard (R.S., 5 vols., London, 1864–9), iii, 229.

[116] *Annales Monastici*, ii, 265; iv, 171.

[117] *Patent Rolls*, 1247–58, 242 & 338.

[118] B.L., Harl. Charters 84. H.46, H.52.

Arnold VI (*fl.* 1223–1255) dating to no later than 1236 is heraldic, comprising a shield with two horizontal bars and a canton containing a lion passant.[119] Two decades later, Matthew Paris records Arnold's arms as *argent two bars a canton gules*.[120] A seal of Robert II Grimbald dating to *c.* 1260 has a combination image, an armoured equestrian figure with a visible shield of arms.[121] There are also surviving examples of horse furniture that bear the arms of the Montfort and Cahaignes families although these may date to the early fourteenth century.[122]

The families also supply instances of use of the language of aristocratic knighthood, specifically the terms *dominus* and *miles*. Fleming points out that in the context of attestations these were explicit indications of high status. He also suggests that employment of the term *miles* represented a deliberate proclamation of the military ethos.[123] There are numerous instances of the use of the terms by heads of the six families studied here. Nicholas de Verdun is styled *dominus Nicholaus de Verdona* and *Nicholaus de Verdun miles* in the early thirteenth-century.[124] William de Cahaignes III is styled *miles c.* 1203–6, and his son William IV appears as *dominus* in 1246–7.[125] Both Arnold du Bois VI and his brother William are styled *domini* in the witness list of a charter *c.* 1235–7.[126] The Anglo-Norman honorific *Sire* is used of two of the more prominent individual figures. Jordan Fantasome refers to *Sire Bertram de Verdun* when recording the events of the 1173 rebellion.[127] He is also *Sire* in the History of William Marshal written in the second quarter of the thirteenth century.[128] *Sire Peres de Montfort* appears in the Song of the Barons of 1264.[129]

Stenton took the ownership of a castle to be one of the signifiers of the status of baron in the twelfth century.[130] At this date a castle might still be a comparatively modest edifice, essentially of earth and timber construction, although often embellished with a stone tower or gatehouse.[131] Hugh de Cahaignes' castle

---

[119] B.L., Harl. 84 H.55.

[120] Matthew Paris, *Chronica Majora*, vi, 470.

[121] B.L., Harl. 86, C.43.

[122] The first object, a suspension-mount bearing the arms of the Cahaignes family, was found in the vicinity of Tarrant Keyneston by Mr Julian Adams. The second, a small pendant bearing the arms of the Montfort family, was found in the vicinity of Compton Wynyates (Warwicks), information provided by Mr Jerry Warren. I am grateful to these gentlemen for allowing me to record these finds and to Mr Nick Griffiths who brought them to my attention. See N. Griffiths, *Horse Harness Pendants,* Finds Research Group 700–1700 Datasheet 5 (1986).

[123] D. Fleming, '*Milites* as Attestors to Charters in England, 1101–1300', *Albion*, 32 (1990), 187, 191.

[124] *Roll of Hugh de Welles*, ed. W. Phillimore and F. Davis, Canterbury and York Society (3 vols., 1907–9), ii, 283, 301.

[125] *Lincoln Episcopal Acta*, ed. D. Smith (2 vols., London, 1986), ii, 298. *Cartulary of Daventry Priory*, ed. M.J. Franklin, Northampton Records Society, 35 (1988), 583.

[126] *Book of Seals*, 67.

[127] *Jordan Fantosme*, 112.

[128] *Histoire de Guillaume le Maréscal*, 8226.

[129] *Anglo-Norman Political Songs*, ed. I. Aspin (1953), 16.

[130] Stenton, *First Century*, 200.

[131] D.J. Cathcart King, *The Castle in England and Wales* (1988), 42–76.

of *Bosco* at or near Silverstone (Northants) is mentioned in a thirteenth-century document but with reference to the reign of Stephen. It does not appear to have survived the accession of Henry II and the site is now lost. Substantial surviving earthworks at Thorpe Arnold may perhaps be the remains of a twelfth-century castle of the Du Bois family, although there is no contemporary documentary mention of it. The castle of Birmingham is referred to only once in an 1166 charter but its moated site remained in use as a residence a century later.[132] The English castles of the Verdun family, Alton and Brandon first recorded in 1176 and 1136 respectively, were rather more durable since both were regarded as castles a century later although neither were major fortifications. At the former there are traces of an early masonry wall and the latter boasted a simple keep, probably of early thirteenth century date.[133] Despite being a garrison in hostile territory the Verdun's Irish castle at Castletown near Dundalk, which was in existence by *c.* 1195, seems to have been of purely earth and timber construction.[134] However in 1236, Bertran's granddaughter, Rohesia de Verdun constructed an impressive new masonry castle at Roche (Louth) on a strong natural site three miles north-west of Dundalk.[135] The Montfort castle at Beaudesert (Warwicks) probably dates to the late eleventh century and was certainly in existence by 1141. Refurbishment of the defences was underway in 1262 although only earthworks now remain.[136] The Grimbald family acquired the manor of Little Houghton in the mid-twelfth century and there are two earth-work fortifications there, but neither have a documented history.[137] Strangely the Cahaignes of Tarrant, barons in the thirteenth century do not appear to have possessed a castle.

All of these six families were patrons of religious houses to a greater or lesser degree. Mirroring Mortimer's findings with the tenants of the honour of Clare, patronage was at first confined to the foundations of others, principally those houses founded by their own lords, but after the mid-twelfth century several of the families founded their own religious houses.[138] Arnold fitz Popelina and his son granted the church of Corneuil (Eure, cant. Damville) and tithes of the demesne and woodland to Lyre, founded by William fitz Osbern, lord of Breteuil.[139] Arnold du Bois III made grants to St Mary du Pré, Leicester, and Garendon Abbey (Leics) both founded by the earl of Leicester.[140] Bertran de Verdun II granted the church of Great Limber (Lincs) to the abbey of

---

132 *Cartae Antiquae*, 11–20, Pipe Roll Society (1957), 613. L. Watts, 'Birmingham Moat, its history, topography and destruction', *Transactions of the Birmingham Archaelogical Society*, 89 (1980).

133 D. Renn, *Norman Castles* (London, 1973), 352, 115–16.

134 Renn, *Norman Castles*, 177.

135 T. McNeill, *Castles in Ireland* (London, 1997), 85–8.

136 Renn, *Norman Castles*, 104. *Close R.*, 1261–4, 130.

137 D.J. Cathcart King, *Castellarium Anglicanum* (2 vols., London, 1983), 316.

138 Mortimer, 'Land and Service', 195–6.

139 Ctl. Lyre, 2, 45.

140 Nichols, *Leicester*, i(1), appx 56. *Book of Seals*, 4. Nichols, *Leicester*, iii(2), 815.

Aunay-sur-Odon (Calvados), founded by his patron Richard de Hommet.[141] Grimbald and his son Robert Grimbald I made grants to the priory of St Andrew's, Northampton, founded by Simon de Senlis I.[142] William de Cahaignes I and his son Hugh were benefactors of Lewes Priory (Sussex) that had also received grants from the count of Mortain, and Hugh ended his life a monk there.[143] The Cahaignes family also supported Luffield Priory (Bucks), to which they granted the church of Dodford (Northants). Dodford was held of the earl of Leicester, founder of Luffield.[144] Lescelina, widow of Norman de Verdun, made grants from her dower to Kenilworth Priory founded by her father Geoffrey de Clinton the elder.[145] Robert de Montfort I atypically was a patron, and eventually a monk, of the ancient English abbey of Thorney (Cambs), to which he gave land and a mill at Wing (Rutland).[146]

The Du Bois, Verdun, Grimbald, and Cahaignes families were monastic founders in their own right. Biddlesden (Bucks) and Croxden (Staffs) Abbeys, founded by Arnold du Bois III and Bertran de Verdun II respectively in 1147 and 1178, were Cistercian houses. Although Cistercian houses did not have patrons in the strict sense, it is evident that Biddlesden and Croxden maintained strong links with their founder's descendants. Arnold du Bois VI was buried at Biddlesden in 1255,[147] whilst Croxden recorded Verdun family births and deaths in its own chronicle, and included the family coat of arms on its seal.[148] Owston Abbey (Leics) founded by Robert Grimbald I before 1161 was Augustinian, and Robert Grimbald II was described as patron in the 1230s.[149] The Augustinian nunnery of Grace Dieu (Leics) was founded by Rohesia de Verdun in *c.* 1239,[150] whilst the nunnery of Tarrant (Dorset) was probably founded by Ralph de Cahaignes II in the late twelfth century. The early history of the latter is obscure, shortly after its foundation it was described as a house of White nuns but a few years later it was said to be home to three ladies and their servants living as anchoresses under no particular rule.[151] The Verdun family were also the founders of hospitals at Lutterworth (Leics) *a.* 1219 and Dundalk (Louth)

---

[141] *Cal. Docs. France, ed. Round*, 531.

[142] Ctl. St Andrew's, Northampton, fol. 5d.

[143] *The Chartulary of the Priory of St Pancras of Lewes*, ed. L.F. Salzman, Sussex Record Society (2 vols., London, 1933–5), 75. *Monasticon Anglicanum*, ed. Sir W. Dugdale and R. Dodsworth (6 vols. in 8, London, 1817–30), v, 14. *Cal. Docs. France*, ed. Round, 510–11.

[144] *Luffield Priory Charters*, ed. G.R. Elvey, Northamptonshire Record Society (2 vols., London, 1957–75), i, 24–6; ii, 292–4.

[145] C. Watson, 'An Edition of the Kenilworth Cartulary', Unpub. Ph.D. thesis, University of London, 1966., 763. *Pipe R.*, 26 Henry II, 29.

[146] Cambridge University Library, Add. Ms 3021 (Ctl. Thorney), fol. 233r. I am grateful to Professor David Crouch for this reference.

[147] Matthew Paris, *Chronica Majora*, v, 487.

[148] *Monasticon*, v, 662.

[149] *Hugh de Welles*, i, 266.

[150] *Monasticon*, vi, 567.

[151] D. Knowles and R.N. Hadcock, *Medieval Religious Houses in England and Wales* (Harlow, 1971), 276.

a. 1190.[152] At Biddlesden at least the foundation of the house was as much to do with expediency as piety. The foundation narrative in the Biddlesden cartulary recounts that the land on which the house was founded had been granted to Arnold du Bois III after the original tenant was dispossessed but Arnold feared his title was weak and sought to protect it by establishing a monastery there.[153] His precedent was the earl of Leicester's foundation of Garendon Abbey in 1133, which was built on land claimed by the earl of Chester.[154] Superior lords could play an important role in the foundation of monastic houses by their men. The earl of Leicester confirmed both his grant to Arnold and Arnold's grant to the monks; and he used his influence to settle the dispute over title that Arnold had anticipated.[155] Biddlesden's first monks came from the earl's own foundation at Garendon, and there was a similar arrangement at Croxden whose original monks were from Aunay-sur-Odon, founded by Richard de Hommet.[156]

The founder was obliged to provide land for his new community although the original endowments of these foundations seem to have been adequate rather than generous. Cistercian houses required land to cultivate directly and were theoretically prohibited from accepting church livings and land held in fee.[157] Arnold du Bois III's foundation charter for Biddlesden refers only to unspecified land in Biddlesden, whilst a subsequent grant contains a similarly vague reference to land in nearby Syresham. The charter of confirmation issued by Stephen describes the Biddlesden lands as a manor, and indicates that the Syresham holding, known as Maryland, comprised three carrucates. The foundation chronicle of Biddlesden adds that the manor of Biddlesden included a member called Whiteland, which comprised five virgates.[158] Presumably the manor of Biddlesden soon went the way of Smite in Warwickshire, cleared to make way for a grange of Combe Abbey.[159] However, the prohibitions against acceptance of church livings and land held in fee were soon being ignored. At the behest of his wife Emma, Arnold du Bois IV granted Biddlesden his share of the church of Little Houghton that was held jointly with the Grimbald family, as well a mill and a small amount land there.[160] Biddlesden also acquired land in North Witham (Lincs) which, in the thirteenth century at least, was held as one-twelfth part of a knight's fee.[161] The 1178 foundation charter of Croxden

---

[152] Knowles and Hadcock, *Religious Houses*, 376. A. Gwynn and R.N. Hadcock, *Medieval Religious Houses of Ireland* (Dublin, 1970), 212.

[153] *English Lawsuits*, i, 317.

[154] E. King, 'Mountsorrel and its region in King Stephen's reign', *Huntingdon Library Quarterly*, 44 (1980), 2–6.

[155] *Monasticon*, v, 367. *English Lawsuits*, i, 317.

[156] J. Burton, *Monastic and Religious Orders in Britain, 1000–1300* (Cambridge, 1994), 72. Knowles and Hadcock, *Religious Houses*, 112.

[157] Burton, *Monastic and Religious Orders*, 223.

[158] *Monasticon*, v, 367. *Regesta*, iii, 103. *English Lawsuits*, i, 317.

[159] *Monasticon*, v, 584. Dugdale, *Warwickshire*, 222.

[160] B.L., Harl. 84 H.47, H.48, H.50.

[161] *C.R.R.*, xii, 2039. *Book of Fees*, 1050.

Abbey gives a very full picture of the endowment granted by its founder Bertran de Verdun II. The bulk of the lands granted to the house were in the immediate vicinity of Croxden itself and were described as *in territorio patrimonii mei* by Bertran. Much was marginal upland suitable for sheep rearing, like that at Musden where a grange was established.[162] His other gifts were extremely varied, more land in Tugby (Leics) and Hartshorn (Derby), a salt pit in Middlewich (Cheshire), a messuage in Stamford (Lincs) and the churches of Alton and Tugby.[163] Robert de Grimbald I's foundation charter for Owston Abbey, indicates the original endowment included the church and vill of Owston, together with their respective appurtenances.[164] The subsequent confirmation charter granted to Owston by the bishop of Lincoln also records the grant of the church of North Witham by Robert and eight virgates of land in Knossington (Leics) by Walter de Chevrecurt, a Grimbald tenant. The latter was soon turned into a grange.[165] The endowment of Grace Dieu comprised the manor and advowson of Belton (Leics) and three parts of a knight's fee in Kirkby-la-Thorpe (Lincs).[166] Grants to other foundations were more modest. The original endowment of Tarrant seems to have been a moiety of the manor, comprising the church of All Saints, an adjacent site for the nuns' house, a mill, small parcels of arable, meadow, pasture, and wood, and an unspecified amount of downland.[167] The founders's endowments of the hospitals at Lutterworth and Dundalk appear to have consisted of only of very small amounts of land and gifts of tithes.[168]

Compared to the other families the Montforts and Birminghams were not generous to the church. Robert de Montfort's fairly modest gift to Thorney has already been mentioned, and his brother Thurstin II made a similarly small grant of a rent from a mill in Great Aydon (Yorks), which he had acquired by marriage, to Guisborough Priory (Yorks) for the soul of his younger sibling Henry, *c.* 1160.[169] Thurstin's son Henry granted the mill of Henley-in-Arden to Wootton Wawen Priory (Warwicks), a cell of Conches Abbey, *c.* 1185–1199.[170] Surprisingly the Birmingham family appears to have made only a single grant to a religious house. William of Birmingham II's gift of land at Tilstone Fearnall (Ches) to Chester Abbey is very unusual in so far as it was made expressly for the maintenance of a chaplain who would conduct divine service behalf of him and his wife in perpetuity.[171] The establishment of a chantry, for this is what it

[162] C. Platt, *The Monastic Grange in England* (London, 1969) 119.

[163] *Monasticon*, v, 662.

[164] *Monasticon*, v, 424.

[165] *Lincoln Acta*, i, 215. Platt, *Monastic Grange*, 214–15.

[166] *Monasticon*, vi, 567. *Book of Fees*, 1110.

[167] *Charter Rolls, 1226–57*, 272.

[168] Knowles and Hadcock, *Religious Houses*, 376. Gwynn and Hadcock, *Religious Houses of Ireland*, 212.

[169] W.K. Farrer, *Early Yorkshire Charters* (3 vols., Edinburgh, 1914–16), ii, 1045.

[170] *Cal. Docs. France, td. Round*, 415.

[171] *The Chartulary or Register of the Abbey of St Werburgh, Chester*, ed. J. Tait, Chetham Society (2 vols., London, 1920–23), ii, 552.

appears to be, was at this date very much an aristocratic undertaking. The immediate inspiration may have been the earl of Chester's establishment of six chantry priest-monks at Bordesley Abbey (Worcs) in the late twelfth century.[172] Crusading and pilgrimage were also favoured by the families and seem likely to have had an element of social aspiration as well as pious intent. Bertran de Verdun II, William of Birmingham II, and Arnold du Bois IV all went on the Third Crusade, whilst Peter de Montfort was a pilgrim to Compostela, shrine of St James in the early thirteenth century.[173]

This article opened with a quotation from Crouch regarding the intermediate position of the honorial baronage in the twelfth century with which the heads of families studied here can undoubtedly be equated *c.* 1150. By *c.* 1265, when their descendants may be tentatively described as bannerets, they still occupied a position above the knight but below the magnate. Whilst the fact of their individual intermediate positions within the nobility can hardly be challenged, the evidence also seems to support the view that these families are representative of a middling group within the nobility. The families were certainly endogamous, evidently taking pride in their kinship connections, which tended to be regional rather than national in scope. In this respect at least these families were more like knights than magnates. The recurrence of Christian names such as Arnold, Thurstin, or Bertran generation after generation also suggests a strong sense of lineage. They were important honorial figures, demonstrating loyalty and even affection for the lords of the honours from whom they held land, whom they frequently served as honorial stewards. However the connection to a particular honour was not perpetual, as the migration of several of the families into the orbit of Simon de Montfort in the 1240s shows. They were important lords in their own rights, with followings and even monastic foundations of their own to which ordinary knights could not aspire. There is good evidence to suggest that their *curiae* were effective courts of record, and that their dependants could form a cohesive sub-honorial body in some circumstances. Their status derived from land, which they held in quantities significantly greater than those of the majority of the nobility. Expressing this in meaningful terms is difficult, but the table on page 76 indicates the number of fees held by the families *c.* 1200.[174] Quantification of the families' worth in monetary terms is not possible from the available evidence, but the annual revenue of around £100 suggested by Hilton for a 'lesser baronial' group at the close of the thirteenth century seems reasonable.[175] It can be compared with the £20 annual revenue deemed sufficient to oblige a man to become a knight a few years earlier and the £1000 per annum

172 D. Crouch, 'The Culture of Death in the Anglo-Norman World', *Anglo-Norman Political Culture and the Twelfth-Century Rennaissance*, ed. C.W. Hollister (Woodbridge, 1997), 175–77.

173 Benedict of Peterborough, *Gesta*, ii, 150. *Pipe R.*, 2–3 Richard I, 152. Ambroise, *L'Estoire*, 201. *Patent Rolls*, 1232–47, 140.

174 Dace, 'Towards the banneret', 65–66.

175 Hilton, *A Medieval Society*, 49.

Family	England	Other
Du Bois	23¾	11
Birmingham	10	–
Montford	14⅓	1
Grimbald	10¾	¾
Verdun	18 (at least)	23½
Cahaignes (Tarrant)	14¾	1
Cahaignes (Horsted)	6¾	–

that an earl aspired to in the eleventh and twelfth centuries.[176] Where the family can be said to be Norman in origin, the preservation of Norman toponymic surnames and the retention of patrimonial lands in Normandy suggests they may have considered themselves as much Norman as English at least until the later twelfth century. However, with the exception of the Du Bois family's estates at Breteuil, these Norman holdings were of very modest extent and value in comparison with the English ones, and their loss after 1203 caused no discernable harm to the family fortunes. There is even some evidence to suggest that the Normans holdings of the Montfort and Grimbald families were alienated in the fourth quarter of the twelfth century, presumably because their value did not justify the effort of holding onto them.[177]

The events of 1173 show that loyalty to, or perhaps more realistically, fear of the crown could override honorial connections. When circumstances were different, as in 1216 or 1265, lesser nobles could stand against royal authority with remarkable solidarity, in some cases taking an opposing stance to their own lords.[178] There is probably no significant conclusion to be drawn from their shifting loyalties; the heads of these families were players in a volatile political game. In normal conditions they were willing to serve the crown, not in the mundane but onerous role that was the lot of the county knight from the 1160s onwards, but as sheriffs, justices, or in a few individual cases as *curiales*. They were most definitely knights in the functional sense, participating in numerous campaigns, sieges, and battles and frequently serving as military leaders. They enthusiastically embraced chivalry and the trappings of aristocratic knighthood in the thirteenth century.

It seems likely that the middling group existed almost from the point at which the Anglo-Norman nobility was established: the Oath of Salisbury of 1086 was sworn by 'people occupying land who were of any account over all England,

---

[176] Powicke, *Military Obligation*, 73. Crouch, *Beaumont Twins*, 178.

[177] Henry de Montfort granted his Norman lands to his brother Hugh for a rent of two gilt spurs a. 1199. *Report on the MSS. of Lord Middleton*, HMC (London, 1911), 35–6. Maud of Houghton, a Grimbald widow, gave her Norman property to the Abbey of St Mary de Voto, Cherbourg *c.* 1175. for a small rent payable at Little Houghton. *Cal. Docs. France, ed. Round*, 945.

[178] *Rot. Litt. Claus*, i, 242–3, 272, 277, 279, 287, 294, 300, 358. *Rotuli Litterarum Patentium in Turri Londinensi asservati*, ed. T.D. Hardy, Record Commission (London, 1835), 169.

whosoever's vassal they might be'.[179] Having suggested that there was a middling group, it is necessary to ask whether membership was dynamic. Based on the evidence of the families studied here, it was. The Verdun family were clearly inconsequential in 1086, but steadily rose in status through the period under consideration. By the late thirteenth century they were magnates. The Cahaignes family were major landowners in 1086 but seem to have declined in status over the following two centuries. The heads of the two main branches in the late thirteenth century were by no means ruined, but they were not the powerful figures their ancestors had been. However, the place in the society of the Birminghams, the Du Bois, the Grimalds and the Montforts seems to have remained remarkably steady.

---

[179] *E.H.D.*, ii, 161–2.

Appendix – Family Trees

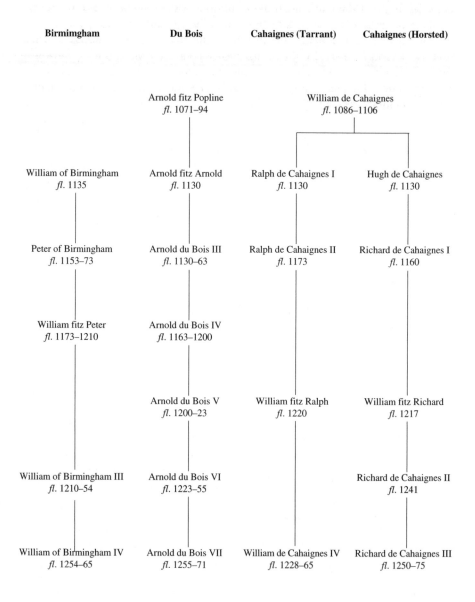

Birmimgham	Du Bois	Cahaignes (Tarrant)	Cahaignes (Horsted)
	Arnold fitz Popline *fl.* 1071–94	William de Cahaignes *fl.* 1086–1106	
William of Birmingham *fl.* 1135	Arnold fitz Arnold *fl.* 1130	Ralph de Cahaignes I *fl.* 1130	Hugh de Cahaignes *fl.* 1130
Peter of Birmingham *fl.* 1153–73	Arnold du Bois III *fl.* 1130–63	Ralph de Cahaignes II *fl.* 1173	Richard de Cahaignes I *fl.* 1160
William fitz Peter *fl.* 1173–1210	Arnold du Bois IV *fl.* 1163–1200		
	Arnold du Bois V *fl.* 1200–23	William fitz Ralph *fl.* 1220	William fitz Richard *fl.* 1217
William of Birmingham III *fl.* 1210–54	Arnold du Bois VI *fl.* 1223–55		Richard de Cahaignes II *fl.* 1241
William of Birmingham IV *fl.* 1254–65	Arnold du Bois VII *fl.* 1255–71	William de Cahaignes IV *fl.* 1228–65	Richard de Cahaignes III *fl.* 1250–75

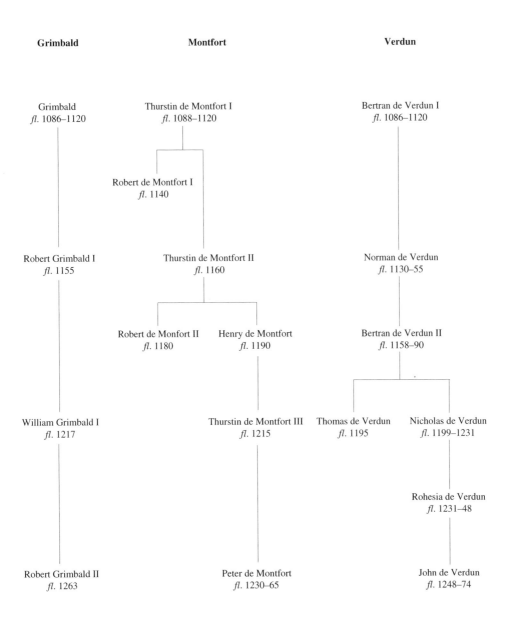

Grimbald

Grimbald
fl. 1086–1120

Robert Grimbald I
fl. 1155

William Grimbald I
fl. 1217

Robert Grimbald II
fl. 1263

Montfort

Thurstin de Montfort I
fl. 1088–1120

Robert de Montfort I
fl. 1140

Thurstin de Montfort II
fl. 1160

Robert de Monfort II
fl. 1180

Henry de Montfort
fl. 1190

Thurstin de Montfort III
fl. 1215

Peter de Montfort
fl. 1230–65

Verdun

Bertran de Verdun I
fl. 1086–1120

Norman de Verdun
fl. 1130–55

Bertran de Verdun II
fl. 1158–90

Thomas de Verdun
fl. 1195

Nicholas de Verdun
fl. 1199–1231

Rohesia de Verdun
fl. 1231–48

John de Verdun
fl. 1248–74

5

Norman Institutions or Norman Legal Practices? Geoffrey le Bel and the Development of the Jury of Recognition

Robert Helmerichs

Almost a century ago, Charles Homer Haskins published his study of 'The Early Norman Jury,' which was reprinted fifteen years later in his *Norman Institutions*.[1] That book remains a landmark in the study of Norman institutional history, and especially so for the reign of Duke Geoffrey le Bel (1114–1151; duke 1144–1150). For Haskins was the first to attribute correctly a number of crucial documents to Duke Geoffrey, and he was thus the first to realize the significance of Geoffrey's reign to the development of the jury of recognition. But Haskins was searching specifically for 'institutions,' and his findings were colored by the questions he asked. He began with the later conception of the recognition as an established legal device, and worked backward to find its origins. This led him to generalize from scattered and partial evidence and to disregard or explain away examples that did not fit his scheme. Thus, he was able to see a relatively clean and direct evolution of the recognition as an institution or, in his view, a devolution of the regalian right of the recognition into a component of the regular system of justice.[2]

---

[1]   Charles Homer Haskins, *Norman Institutions*, Harvard Historical Studies, 24 (Cambridge, MA, 1918); the relevant chapter is a slightly revised reprint of Charles Homer Haskins, 'The Early Norman Jury,' *A.H.R.*, 8 (1903), 613–40. Any examination of the development of the jury of recognition must begin with Haskins, since he was the first to attribute correctly some important charters dealing with the recognition found in the cartulary of Bayeux Cathedral, published as *Antiquus cartularius ecclesiae Bajocensis (Livre noir)*, edited by Victor Bourrienne, Société de l'Histoire de Normandie 34 (2 vols., Rouen, 1902–3). The first letter for each charter in that cartulary was left blank for rubrics, which were never added. Several of the documents used only the initial of the duke in question; thus, they begin '__, dux normannorum.' Earlier historians had attributed various of these documents to Henry II, Geoffrey le Bel, or even Henry I. In the edition of the cartulary edited by Bourrienne, most of them were attributed to Henry II. But Haskins examined the manuscript more carefully and found the initial letters lightly but clearly sketched in the margin, for the benefit of the rubricator. Twelve of the *Antiquus cartularius* documents begin with the letter 'G,' and thus are Geoffrey's. *Antiquus cartularius*, nos. 16–19, 23, 24, 39, 43, 44, 89, 90, 100; Haskins, *Norman Institutions,* 200–1 and n. 15. This discovery eliminated old misconceptions and red herrings concerning the development of the recognition and allowed Haskins to make a fresh start.

[2]   Haskins, *Norman Institutions*, 198.

But recent scholarship has taken a less legalistic view of medieval institutions, showing them as less rigid and more plastic than historians of Haskins's
time saw them.[3] In this spirit, I will approach the problem from another angle,
depicting a long-standing tradition of using sworn inquests, not only in royal and
ducal courts, but also in episcopal courts. I will show the recognition as being
not a regalian right, but a legal tool, available for use by anyone with the power
to enforce his will. It was only after the time of Duke Geoffrey, perhaps during
the reign of his son, Henry II, that we can see the recognition begin to develop
into something rightly called an institution.[4] But I will suggest that Haskins was
correct in principle if not in detail when he gave Geoffrey credit for furthering
the development of the recognition. For it was during Geoffrey's rule that the
use of the recognition became a tool of choice, thus building the foundation for
an institution underneath the existing legal tradition. I will examine Haskins's
discussion of the recognition under Geoffrey, suggesting places at which he can
be corrected. I will also look at the work of later historians who have dealt with
Geoffrey's recognitions, especially Josèphe Chartrou and Sarell Everett
Gleason.[5] I will demonstrate how, in their attempts to move beyond Haskins,

---

[3] For non-monolithic views of medieval legal structures, see, among others, Geoffrey Koziol,
Begging Pardon and Favor: Ritual and Political Order in Early Medieval France (Ithaca, 1992);
Stephen D. White, *Custom, Kinship, and Gifts to Saints: The Laudatio Parentum in Western
France, 1050–1150* (Chapel Hill, 1988); and the articles collected in *The Settlement of Disputes in
Early Medieval Europe*, ed. Wendy Davies and Paul Fouracre (Cambridge, 1986). Modern legal
practice, as opposed to theory, is also less structured than one might think; see Robert C.
Ellickson's stimulating *Order without Law: How Neighbors Settle Disputes* (Cambridge, MA,
1991).

[4] Robert Besnier, ' "Inquisitiones" et "Recognitiones": Le nouveau système des preuves à
l'époque des Coutumiers normands,' *Revue historique de droit français et étranger*, 4e série, 28
(1950): 181–212, suggested an even later date for the 'institutionalization' of the recognition:
'Quoi qu'il en soit, c'est bien vers cette époque, c'est-à-dire depuis le milieu du XIIIe siècle, que
les requenoissants semblent s'établir comme une institution régulière, encore n'apparaissent-ils
sans doute pas tout à la fois.' It is not my purpose to assign a specific date for the birth of the
recognition as an institution; indeed, such a date might be impossible to fix. I intend only to
suggest that in Geoffrey's time, the recognition was not yet what could be termed an institution.

[5] Josèphe Chartrou, *L'Anjou de 1109 à 1151: Foulque de Jerusalem et Geoffroi Plantegenêt*
(Paris, 1928); Sarell Everett Gleason, *An Ecclesiastical Barony of the Middle Ages: The Bishopric
of Bayeux, 1066–1204*, Harvard Historical Monographs, 10 (Cambridge, MA, 1936). Victeur
Bourrienne, *Un grand bâtisseur: Philippe de Harcourt, évêque de Bayeux (1142–1163)* (Paris,
1930), discusses Geoffrey's recognitions at length, but his discussion is virtually an uncited translation of Haskins. Besnier, 'Inquisitiones', although primarily interested in the later development
of the recognition, briefly discussed Geoffrey's role. His views will be cited as appropriate in the
notes below. R.C. van Caenegem, *Royal Writs in England from the Conquest to Glanvill: Studies
in the Early History of the Common Law*, Publications of the Seldon Society, 77 (London, 1959),
discussed the recognition, but had nothing to say about its use under Geoffrey; on the other hand,
his handling of technical aspects of the recognition are important and will be cited as necessary.
Lucien Valin, *Le duc de Normandie et sa cour (912–1204): Étude d'histoire juridique* (Paris,
1910), discussed Norman ducal authority in a broad-ranging if summary manner, but his section
on the recognition (194–219) is crippled by his acceptance of Bourrienne's misdating of key documents, despite the existence several years earlier of Haskins' *A.H.R.* article correcting these dating
errors. Jean Yver, 'Les premières institutions du duché de Normandie,' *I Normanni e la loro*

they distorted or misrepresented the evidence to make insupportable claims, and thus muddied the waters rather than clearing them.[6]

Definitions of terms

First, it will be useful to establish the background for this study by defining some important terms, especially 'recognition,' and by describing the *Antiquus cartularius,* the most important source for the recognition under Duke Geoffrey. The jury of recognition was a process by which rights over certain lands, as they existed at a specific time in the past, were determined. In different cases, the recognition might have been intended to clarify and/or restore these rights, or to determine which party held them. Thus, the recognition could be a tool by which someone in power might recover lost rights, on his own behalf or on behalf of one of his men, or it could be a tool by which he might settle a dispute between his men. In its mature form, a recognition consisted of old and legal men of the neighborhood (*antiqui et legitimi homines de vicinio*), who would be expected to have personal knowledge of the facts of the case (*se hoc vidisse et audisse et novisse testabantur*), being gathered before an official or officials. These men would then testify under oath as to the issue in question, perhaps concerning who held a fief, or how the customs of a tenement were divided, or its boundaries. Their decision was binding. In later customaries, it is stressed that the parties involved in the case must either request the recognition or consent to it.[7]

---

espansione in Europa nell'alto medioevo, Settimane di studio del Centro italiano di studi sull'alto medioevo, 16 (Spoleto, 1969), 299–366, 589–98, went far towards supplanting Valin, but unfortunately was concerned almost exclusively with pre-Conquest Normandy. Jean Yver, 'Contribution à l'étude du développement de la compétence ducale en Normandie,' *Annales de Normandie*, 8 (1958), 139–83, went from the Carolingian period to Henry II, but never mentioned Geoffrey and did not discuss recognitions. Michel de Boüard, 'Le duché de Normandie,' *Institutions seigneuriales (Les droits du Roi exercés par les grands vassaux)*, ed. Ferdinand Lot and Robert Fawtier, Histoire des institutions françaises au Moyen Age, 1 (Paris, 1957), 1–33, finished his survey of Norman ducal institutional history with two short paragraphs on the recognition under Geoffrey derived from Haskins.

6 I would like to stress that in this article, I am not directly addressing the issue of the crystallization of Norman customary law. A great deal of work has been done in this area, culminating in Emily Zack Tabuteau's forceful argument that this crystallization had taken place by the death of the Conqueror. Emily Zack Tabuteau, *Transfers of Property in Eleventh-Century Normandy* (Chapel Hill, 1988), chapter 12. The notes to this chapter give a thorough summary of previous work in this area. I do not dispute this argument, but a distinction must be drawn between the existence of a coherent body of customary law, and the existence of institutions by which such a body of law is regulated and enforced. My argument is that the recognition does not constitute such an institution until after the reign of Duke Geoffrey. I am also not addressing the issue of the origin of the jury. Whether it originated in Normandy or in England and whether it was a hybrid of Norman and English practices is irrelevant here. The jury was clearly in use in Normandy during Geoffrey's reign and earlier, regardless of its origin, and it is the nature of the jury of recognition under Geoffrey that I am investigating.

7 Caenegem, *Royal Writs*, 51–3, made a sharp distinction between the *inquisitio* (the actual

A further note on terminology: in Geoffrey's time, there does not seem to have been a noun to describe the procedure carried out by a sworn jury. The earliest known uses of the word *recognitio* to refer to a jury of inquest occur in the 1160s; that is, in the reign of Henry II.[8] Instead, during Geoffrey's reign and before, verbal forms were invariably used. Thus, we find *fecit recognosci* or *inquiri* for 'he ordered a recognition' or 'inquest.' In Geoffrey's documents, a form of the verb *recognoscere* is always used. For the sake of convenience, I will use the modern convention of 'recognition'. Also, in examining possible cases of recognition, one must be careful to distinguish the recognition from proof by co-swearer, in which the oath-takers are partisans of one party to the case and not third-party witnesses with actual knowledge of the details of the case.

Duke Geoffrey's recognitions

The reign of Geoffrey le Bel is especially fertile for early evidence of the recognition because of the relentless efforts of Bishop Philip of Bayeux to recover the vast, lost fortunes of his diocese. Duke Geoffrey co-operated in these efforts, and his tool of choice was the jury of recognition. Fortunately for institutional historians, ten documents concerning these recognitions, issuing from Geoffrey or his agents, were collected into the *Antiquus cartularius*. Although the chance survival of this collection may skew our perception of the recognition in Normandy as a whole due to possible local eccentricities, the laser-beam focus of the Bayeux documents makes them an excellent case-study; a casual examination of them reveals that they represent only a part, possibly a small part, of the paperwork generated by Geoffrey's recognitions.[9]

Four of the documents involve the recognition held to determine the boundaries and customs of Cambremer, a privileged enclave of Bayeux located within the diocese of Lisieux.[10] The first is Duke Geoffrey's order for the recognition to take place; the second and third are his justices' reports to Geoffrey of the results; and the fourth is Geoffrey's report of the recognition and his confirmation to Archbishop Hugh of Rouen.[11] Two more of the Bayeux documents are Geoffrey's justices' reports concerning the results of a recognition held to

---

inquest) and the *recognitio* (the finding and giving of the jury's verdict). Within the context of Glanvill's sharply regulated recognition this distinction is probably valid and useful. As noted above, however, no such distinction is made in the documents of Duke Geoffrey's recognitions, and thus I will not make the distinction here. For a more detailed description of the recognition in its mature form, see *Glanvill*, 148–70; Caenegem, *Royal Writs*, 51–103.

[8] J.F. Niermeyer, *Mediae latinitatis lexicon minus* (Leiden, 1984), s.v. *recognitio*, where several uses occur between *c.* 1160 and *c.* 1174.

[9] To cite only one example, *Antiquus cartularius*, nos. 89 and 90 are reports to Geoffrey of a recognition held by his order. The order itself does not survive, nor does Geoffrey's confirmation.

[10] See appendix below.

[11] *Regesta*, 3, nos. 53 and 56; *Antiquus cartularius*, nos. 43–4.

determine the holdings, rights, and privileges of the bishops of Lisieux and Bayeux at Cheffreville.[12] The other documents consist of a general order by Duke Geoffrey that all disputes between Bishop Philip and Philip's men concerning tenements will be resolved by recognition;[13] two writs directed to specific justices of Geoffrey's and each ordering two recognitions to be held;[14] and the confirmation of a general recognition of the lands of Bayeux.[15]

The problem of novelty

Haskins was the first correctly to attribute all these documents, and his analysis of them remains the state of the question. There are, however, several problems with that analysis, which I will now discuss. The first of these is the problem of novelty. Haskins wrote,

That Geoffrey's reign begins a new stage in the development of the jury in Normandy may also be argued from such rare instances of the sworn inquest as we find under his predecessors. . . . When we leave these fiscal inquiries, we no longer find clear examples of inquests of the later type.[16]

Chartrou concurred, stating that 'the procedure is little-applied from the end of the 11th century to 1144.'[17] The fact that few documents survive from before Geoffrey's reign is less impressive than the fact that ten documents survive from his reign. All these documents come from one single source, the *Antiquus cartularius,* and even that collection is demonstrably incomplete. Given the exigencies of documentary transmission in the twelfth century, an argument purely from silence can carry little weight.

Internal evidence in one of the Bayeux documents suggests that the recognition was an established practice in Geoffrey's time, and probably before: in the returns of the Cambremer recognition, Geoffrey's justices inform him that 'we had more oath-takers than we are accustomed to in other matters gather and swear in our presence.'[18] The authors of this report were Robert de Courcy and Robert du Neubourg. Robert de Courcy is known to have been involved in three other recognitions under Geoffrey and Robert du Neubourg in one;[19] would

---

[12] *Antiquus cartularius*, nos. 89 and 90.

[13] *Regesta*, 3, no. 52.

[14] *Regesta*, 3, nos. 54–5.

[15] *Regesta*, 3, no. 57.

[16] Haskins, *Norman Institutions*, 222.

[17] Chartrou, *L'Anjou*, 141: 'En Normandie, la procédure est peu appliquée de la fin du XIe siècle à 1144.'

[18] *Antiquus cartularius*, no. 43: 'Plures quam in caeteris rebus soleamus juratores . . . in praesentia nostra convire et jurare fecimus.'

[19] Both men participated in the general recognition of Bayeux's demesne lands at Bayeux. *Regesta*, 3, no. 56. In addition, Robert de Courcy oversaw the recognition concerning the fief of William Bersic and that involving the dispute between Vauquelin de Courseulles and Robert son of Erneis. *Regesta*, 3, no. 55.

these three cases be enough to establish a precedent strong enough for a departure to be noteworthy? It seems likely that they were involved in other cases, and thus that the extent of the recognition under Geoffrey was greater than the documentary evidence suggests. Robert de Courcy served as *dapifer* under Henry I, as did Robert du Neubourg's father; it is conceivable that the experience to which they allude in this document extends back as far as Henry I's reign, although I will not press this theory too far.[20] Although there seems to have been a definite expansion of the recognition's beneficiaries, its form may not have developed as much under Geoffrey as Haskins suggested.

But we need not rely on such circumstantial evidence for early examples of non-fiscal inquests. Other cases exist, although they are not as clear-cut and vivid as the recognitions under Geoffrey. The most famous inquest of the pre-Geoffrey era was the one held by Henry I in 1133 to determine the fees, services, rights, possessions, customs, and liberties of the church of Bayeux.[21] This fits neatly with Haskins' theory that the jury of recognition before Geoffrey was used solely by the duke for his own fiscal benefit, because the 1133 inquest took place during a vacancy in the see of Bayeux, when the diocese's revenues were in Henry's hands. After the glory days of Bishop Odo, the fortunes of Bayeux had suffered a dramatic decline at the hands of later bishops, and Henry took advantage of the vacancy to attempt to restore the church to its ancient wealth.[22] The only part of the returns from the 1133 inquest that survive deal with the knights' fees. A jury of twelve men gathered and testified as who held what lands from the church of Bayeux, and what services they owed. This is clearly consistent with the procedure of the recognition, although the verb *inquirere* is used instead of *recognoscere*. Haskins accepted the 1133 inquest as a part of the recognition's development.[23]

Chartrou did not; she seems to have believed that Henry I's inquest did not

---

[20] For Robert de Courcy and Roger du Neubourg as Henry I's *dapiferes*, see *Regesta*, 2, xii. Working both for and against this theory is the probability that Robert de Courcy was the author of this document: two versions exist, with the names reversed in the *salutatio*, and it is the version with Robert de Courcy named first that comments on the unusual number of oath-takers. On the one hand, Robert de Courcy is the one who served personally as *dapifer* under Henry I; on the other, he is the one who is recorded as presiding over three other recognitions, which could conceivably account for his noting the difference in procedure.

[21] Edition of returns concerning knights' fees and services with discussion, Henri Navel, 'L'enquête de 1133 sur les fiefs de l'évêché de Bayeux,' *Bulletin de la Société des Antiquaires de Normandie*, 42 (1934), 5–80. Duke Geoffrey's account of Henry's inquest, *Regesta*, 3, no. 56. Henry II's account, *Regesta*, 3, no. 61. Some confusion exists among historians as to exactly what was covered in Henry I's inquest and in Geoffrey's later recognitions; this confusion will be dealt with below.

[22] For a general description of Bayeux's shifting fortunes, see Gleason, *Ecclesiastical Barony*, 8–31.

[23] Haskins, *Norman Institutions*, 207–8. Besnier, 'Inquisitiones,' 193–4, mentioned Henry II's general recognition without noting that Henry was repeating the action of his father in the 1140s and his grandfather in 1133.

include a general recognition of fiefs.[24] But her argument is based in part on a misreading of Haskins: where Haskins questioned 'whether Geoffrey also imitated the example of Henry I in ordering a general inquest with regard to the fiefs of the bishop,'[25] Chartrou reversed the question, asking, 'Did Henry I order a general inquest, as much concerning the fiefs as the goods of the bishop?'[26] Yet the acknowledgment of fiefs is implicit in the surviving returns, which list fiefs held of the bishop and their fees. We must attribute Chartrou's argument purely to confusion.

Two other examples of recognitions before Duke Geoffrey's time have survived. At some point between 1107 and 1133, a recognition was held (*recognitum est*) before Bishop Richard fitz Samson to determine what pertained to the chancellor of the chapter in the time of Bishop Odo, attested by ancient men and the bishop himself.[27] Another recognition was held (*recognoverunt*) between 1135 and 1142, in which four men of Hérils determine that a land at Hérils, with its church, had been given to Joscelin, *succentor* of Bayeux, *in elemosina,* and that he should always hold it thus.[28] Neither case has anything whatsoever to do with ducal prerogative.

A still earlier case, mentioned by both Haskins and Chartrou, involved an inquest ordered by William the Conqueror. In this instance, William ordered the 'barons of the honour' of Fontenay Abbey to gather and record under oath all

---

[24] Chartrou, *L'Anjou*, 146–7.

[25] Haskins, *Norman Institutions*, 208.

[26] Chartrou, *L'Anjou*, 146: 'Henri I avait-il, lui aussi, ordonné une enquête générale, tant des fiefs que des biens de l'évêque?' Chartrou was further confused by a footnote in Haskins, which claims to cite an example of a charter of Henry I, but actually refers to a charter of Henry II that does not relate to the issue at hand. Haskins, *Norman Institutions*, 208 and n. 52. Clearly Haskins erred, either in the text or in the citation; I cannot deduce his true intention.

[27] Excerpts, Haskins, *Norman Institutions*, 226, n. 114:

> Ceterum, dilecte nobis fratre Anulphe, cancellarie ecclesie nostre, cum de hiis que ad ius personatus tui pertinent in capitulo coram Ricardo episcopo et fratribus ageretur, antiquorum virorum et eiusdem episcopi attestatione recognitum est ea que hic subnotata sunt ex institucione Odonis episcopi et tuorum antecessorum continua possessione ad ius personatus tui iure perpetuo pertinere. . . . Hec autem omnia in capitulo nostro coram Ricardo episcopo, Sansonis filio, et nobis recognita sunt et postmodem coram successore eius altero Ricardo publica attestione firmata.

Haskins went on to suggest that 'the mention of the attestation of the bishop along with that of the ancient men might appear to contradict the view that a sworn inquest was held, but the last sentence makes it plain that the attestation spoken of is that of the subsequent bishop, Richard of Kent, while the facts had been recognized under Richard fitz Samson.' This is clearly wrong; the document explicitly refers to 'eiusdem episcopo attestatione,' or Richard fitz Samson. But his attestation only need disqualify the event as a recognition if we take a needlessly institutional definition of what constitutes a recognition. Central to Haskins's own argument is that during this period, the 'institution' was still developing. While at a later date the direct participation of the bishop would have been highly irregular, here it should only be taken as evidence for the plastic nature of the recognition as a legal tradition, not a rigid institution.

[28] *Antiquus cartularius*, no. 102, discussed in Haskins, *Norman Institutions*, 225.

the things that Ralph Taisson I and Ralph Taisson II gave to the abbey.[29] Thus it is clear that although the evidence is spotty and vague, and the precise nature of the procedure is often unclear, some form of sworn inquest was taking place before the reign of Duke Geoffrey, and not always a purely fiscal inquest.[30]

The problem of continuity

Another problem surrounding the recognitions is the problem of continuity: given that something involving the use of sworn jurors existed before Geoffrey's reign, to what extent were Geoffrey's recognitions similar or dissimilar to what had gone on before? Henry I's inquest covered both the bishop's demesne and his fiefs, and Haskins doubted that Geoffrey's recognitions contained a general inquest of the bishop's fiefs.[31] He acknowledged that Henry II explicitly stated this to be the case ('[Geoffrey] had recognized by sworn oath . . . demesne lands, and fiefs, and all the tenements of the church of Bayeux'[32]) but noted that no record of such an inquest for Geoffrey survives, and that the *Red Book of the Exchequer* went back to Henry I's inquest. This argument from silence, however, ignores positive evidence. Not only did Henry II state that Geoffrey held a recognition of Bayeux's fiefs, but Pope Lucius II ordered Geoffrey to hold a recognition in the same manner (*eodem modo*) as Henry I,[33] and Geoffrey himself says that he is following in Henry I's footsteps:

We have had recognized whatever rights, possessions, customs and liberties that the said

---

[29] Printed with discussion as *Regesta Regum Anglo-Normannorum: The Acta of William I, 1066–1087*, ed. David Bates (Oxford, 1998), no. 149:

[King William] praecepit Ricardo vicecomiti Abrincarum quatinus de parte eiusdem regis, ante se et Willelmum abbatem Cadomensem, predictaque Mathilde jubente, barones honoris in Cadomo convenire jussisset, et omnia quae praedicti duo Radulfi Taxones huic Fontanetensi ecclesie dederant sacramento super Santum Evangelium facto veraciter recordari fecisset. Quod et factum est. Itum fuit Cadomum juxta preceptum regis et electi sunt quattuor legitimi viri communi assensu qui omnia hec que predicta recordati sunt, et se illa verissime recordatos fuisse super Sanctum Evangelium iuraverunt.

Discussed in Haskins, *Norman Institutions*, 222–3; Chartrou, *L'Anjou*, 142; Valin, *Le duc de Normandie*, 200–1; *Les actes de Guillaume le Conquérant et de la Reine Mathilde pour les abbayes caennaises*, ed. Lucien Musset, Mémoires de la Société des Antiquaires de Normandie, 37 (Caen, 1967), 11–15.

[30] Both Haskins and Chartrou examined the possibility of Angevin origins for the recognition; Haskins decided that very little resembling a Norman recognition can be found in Anjou, and Chartrou saw examples of Angevin inquests before Geoffrey's reign, but agreed that the Norman inquest owed nothing to its Angevin counterpart. Haskins, *Norman Institutions*, 230–32; Chartrou, *L'Anjou*, 151–7.

[31] Haskins, *Norman Institutions*, 208.

[32] 'dominica, et feoda, et omnes Baiocensis ecclesia teneduras . . . juramento fecit recognosci.' *Regesta*, 3, no. 61.

[33] *Antiquus cartularius*, no. 106.

church had in the time of Bishop Odo, following in the footsteps of King Henry, who had this same thing recognized by the oaths of ancient men.[34]

Geoffrey went on to say of his own recognition, which dealt with 'the rights, possessions, customs and liberties' of the church, that 'the occupations of the rest of the manors [that is, other than Cambremer] . . . were recognized, entirely as is contained in the document that was made following the oath that King Henry had ordered to be made.'[35] Therefore, not only did Geoffrey's inquest have a deliberately similar scope to Henry's, but Geoffrey had in his possession a document containing returns from 1133 beyond what has survived to us. The only difference seems to be that Geoffrey did not gather information on the military service owed, but this indicates only that Geoffrey's recognition was more specialized than Henry's, and this can easily be attributed to different objectives: while Henry I was trying to determine all the possessions and obligations of the diocese so that he personally could enjoy them, Geoffrey was merely attempting to restore the diocese's possessions. Within this context, the military services are irrelevant.

Assisia mea

One problem that arises directly from examining Geoffrey's recognitions is the mention in two documents of his assize (*secundam assisiam meam*).[36] Haskins noted the difficulties involved with this word:

'[M]y assize' may refer to an ordinance of Geoffrey regulating procedure, it may denote the procedure so established, or it may conceivably mean only the prerogative procedure of the duke – his not in the sense of origination but of exclusive possession.[37]

But Haskins went on to identify, if somewhat tentatively, 'my assize' with *Regesta*, 3, no. 52, a document of Geoffrey's in which Duke Geoffrey confirms to Bishop Philip the lands held by Bishop Odo, and orders that if a dispute should arise between the bishop and one of his men, it should be resolved by a recognition, the results of which should be upheld unless the tenant can show, either in the bishop's court or in the duke's, that the tenement came into his hands legitimately after the time of Odo.[38]

This identification does not hold water. The two documents containing this phrase order four recognitions to be held.[39] Three of them do, indeed, involve

---

[34] *Regesta*, 3, no. 56: 'vestigiis regis Henrici inherentes, qui hoc idem juramento antiquorum hominum fecerat recognosci post mortem Ricardi episcopi filii Sansonis.'

[35] *Regesta*, 3, no. 56: 'Ceterorum maneriorum occupationes jurate sunt . . . ita omnino recognitum est, sicut continebatur in scripto quod factum fuerat secundum juramentum quod rex Henricus antea fieri preceperat.'

[36] *Regesta*, 3, nos. 54–5.

[37] Haskins, *Norman Institutions*, 211–12.

[38] Of course, to Haskins this document was *Antiquus cartularius*, no. 16.

[39] *Regesta*, 3, nos. 54–5. It is interesting to note that these, the only two surviving documents

disputes between the bishop and his men, but the fourth does not. Duke Geoffrey orders Guy de Sablé and Robert de Courcy to hold a recognition (*recognosci faciatis*) to determine who was seized of Cramesnil and Rocquancourt in the time of King Henry, according to Geoffrey's assize. And if they should determine that Vauquelin de Courseulles was seized, they should allow him to hold it in peace and prevent Robert son of Erneis from interfering. If *Regesta*, 3, no. 52 is Geoffrey's assize, then the Vauquelin case clearly does not follow it, since it does not involve a dispute between the bishop and one of his men. Thus, *Regesta*, 3, no. 52 cannot be Geoffrey's assize, and we must accept that 'my assize,' whatever it is, is not a particular document that has survived; indeed, Haskins's (rejected) alternate suggestion that it may refer in general to a procedure seems more likely.[40]

Whose benefit?

The Vauquelin de Courseulles case also calls into question Haskins's statement that the recognition under Geoffrey was held for the bishop's benefit alone.[41] Haskins said that since at least one of the fiefs in question is known to have been a fief of the bishop, this document is within 'the sphere of the bishop's interests,' but this interpretation seems overly technical. This is a clear case of somebody other than the bishop benefiting from the recognition, namely Vauquelin, who from the wording is assumed to be in the right. Certainly all the cases somehow involved the bishop, since they were recorded in his cartulary, but here the connection is quite tangential. Thus, in this respect Haskins understated his case: the use of the recognition was expanded not only to the bishop's benefit, but also, in one documented case, to the benefit of one of his tenants against a rival. We cannot simply assume that no cases existed that did not involve the bishop at all, simply because they did not survive through recording in the *Antiquus cartularius*.

Both Chartrou and Gleason tried to take the issue of episcopal benefit a step further: they suggested that Geoffrey had granted to Bishop Philip the right to hold a recognition in the episcopal court whenever a dispute arose between the bishop and one of his tenants.[42] This is simply wrong. The portion of *Regesta*, 3, no. 52 in question reads as follows (the translation is Haskins's):

If a dispute should arise between the bishop and any of his men, it shall be recognized by the oath of lawful men of the vicinage who was seized of the land in Bishop Odo's time, whether it was the bishop or the other claimant; and the verdict thus declared shall be

---

issued by Geoffrey to mention 'my assize,' were both issued at Le Mans with Paganus de Clairvaux as sole witness, and thus they were likely issued at the same time.

[40] Besnier's discussion of the assize adds nothing of importance. Besnier, 'Inquisitiones,' 200.

[41] Haskins, *Norman Institutions*, 209.

[42] Chartrou, *L'Anjou*, 147–8; Gleason, *Ecclesiastical Barony*, 92–3 and 101.

firmly observed unless the tenant can show, in the duke's court or in the bishop's, that the tenement came to him subsequently by inheritance or lawful gift.[43]

Clearly, the only matter to be taken up in the episcopal court is the proof by the defendant that, despite the findings of the recognition concerning tenure *in tempore Odonis,* he later came by the land in question legitimately. The recognition is to be held by Geoffrey's authority, not the bishop's, and even a casual reading of the documents involved reveals that the recognitions never took place in anybody's court, but rather at a predetermined location near the land in question; neither Geoffrey nor the bishop was present.[44]

Gleason thought he saw two examples of Philip exercising this power. But one of these is a case in which Philip was resolving differences between his own subordinates, and thus should not be seen as infringing on the ducal prerogative. The other involves a dispute within the diocese of Lisieux; the document describing this procedure has not been published, and the excerpt supplied by Gleason is insufficient for analysis.[45] Ironically, Gleason ignored an example given by Haskins that better supports his argument. In this case of 1153, Philip created a prebend from various lands, concerning one of which he had earlier held a recognition to establish that it belonged to the bishop's demesne.[46] But this notice does not describe the initiation and process of the recognition; it may well have fallen under the ducal license given in *Regesta*, 3, no. 52.

---

[43] Haskins, *Norman Institutions*, 208; *Regesta*, 3, no. 52:
> Si de aliqua tenedura orta fuerit contentio inter episcopum et aliquem de suis hominibus per juramentum legitimorum hominum vicinie in qua hoc fuerit, sit recognitum quis saisitus inerat tempore Odonis episcopi, vel ipse episcopus vel ille cum quo erit contentio. Et quod inde recognitum fuerit firmiter teneatur nisi ille qui tenet poterit ostendere quod tenedura illa in manus suas postea venerit jure hereditario aut tali donatione que juste debeat stare, et hoc in curia episcopi vel in mea.

[44] The recognition of Cambremer was held at Falaise before Robert de Courcy and Robert du Neubourg. *Regesta*, 3, no. 56; *Antiquus cartularius*, nos. 43–4. The general recognition was held at Bayeux before Richard de La Haie, Robert du Neubourg, Robert de Courcy, and Engelgerius de Bohon. *Regesta*, 3, nos. 56–7. None of Geoffrey's other recognitions indicate where they were held, but he clearly was not present. *Regesta*, 3, nos. 54–5; *Antiquus cartularius*, nos. 89–90.

[45] Gleason, *Ecclesiastical Barony*, 101 n. 62. The cases are found in *Antiquus cartularius*, no. 63, and in the Collection Mancel, Caen, MS. 75, fol. 244. In the *Antiquus cartularius* case, the procedure was markedly different from that of the ducal recognitions: the oath-takers are chosen from the parishioners of the disputed church by the disputants. Haskins had also mentioned the *Antiquus cartularius* case, in greater detail, as an example of the use of the recognition by the bishop, but without implying that this use infringed on ducal prerogative. Haskins, *Norman Institutions*, 223–4.

[46] Haskins, *Norman Institutions*, 224; *Antiquus cartularius*, nos. 148–9.

The place of the recognition in institutional history

This raises the larger issue of ducal prerogative. Haskins was cautious: 'One of the most interesting problems in the history of the jury is to determine how and when the procedure by recognition ceased to be an exclusive privilege of the king and became part of the regular system of justice.'[47] Haskins was looking at a long-term perspective, from the Carolingian period to the reign of Henry II; he did not directly state that in Geoffrey's day, the recognition remained a regalian right, although elsewhere he acknowledged the possibility that it may have been.[48] Chartrou took it a step further: 'The reign of [Geoffrey] Plantagenet marks a stage in the evolution of the inquest, reserved until now for the recognition of the fiscal rights of the sovereign, and which, under the reign of Henry II, was generalized through the procedure of the assize.'[49] She used the same basic words as Haskins, but lost was the Carolingian context; thus she came closer to suggesting, deliberately or otherwise, that in Geoffrey's day ducal prerogative over the recognition was accepted. Gleason made the final leap: 'Geoffrey's grant marks the earliest known case of the extension of the prerogative procedure of the sworn inquest from the duke's courts to those of any of his vassals.'[50] For this, Gleason cited Haskins's reference to the possibility that a 'prerogative procedure of the duke' may have existed. Elsewhere, Haskins stated that this document extends the recognition to benefit the bishop, not the duke,[51] but nowhere did he imply that a ducal vassal receives the 'prerogative procedure of the sworn inquest.' But as we have already seen, the recognition was used by people other than the duke even before Geoffrey's time. It had already devolved from a regalian right to a procedure available to anyone who had the power to adjudicate disputes between his men.

Furthermore, although as we have seen in Geoffrey's reign and earlier the recognition was not exclusively a ducal prerogative, nevertheless by the time of the compilation of the *Très Ancien Coutumier* in about 1200, it clearly was, for there we read: 'No recognition shall be made unless by the brief of the duke or his justice.' Thus, by suggesting that the development of the recognition was from ducal prerogative to general procedure, Haskins, Chartrou, and Gleason had it nearly backwards. Instead, the recognition changed from being a legal tradition available to anyone with the power to enforce his will, to a general procedure held only under ducal authority. The devolution Haskins postulated must have already occurred by the Anglo-Norman period.

---

[47] Haskins, *Norman Institutions*, 198.
[48] Haskins, *Norman Institutions*, 212.
[49] Chartrou, *L'Anjou*, 143: 'Le règne du Plantegenêt marque une étape dans l'évolution de l'enquête réservée jusqu'ici à la reconnaissance des droits fiscaux du souverain et qui, sous le règne d'Henri II, se généralisera par la procédure de l'assise.'
[50] Gleason, *Ecclesiastical Barony*, 92–3.
[51] Haskins, *Norman Institutions*, 209.

Conclusion

Contrary to Haskins, Chartrou, and Gleason, the recognition existed as a legal tradition outside the ducal prerogative before the reign of Geoffrey le Bel. Geoffrey himself attempted no innovation, but rather ordered recognitions to be held in the same manner as had his predecessor Henry I. We can no longer see the recognition in the time of Geoffrey or earlier as a regalian right devolving into an institution; rather, it was a legal tradition that would later evolve into an institution. Duke Geoffrey contributed to this evolution by strengthening the tradition. Where earlier dukes had used the recognition sporadically and inconsistently, Geoffrey made a conscious effort to have it used on a more regular basis; it was his tool of choice when dealing with tenurial issues. Geoffrey was an outsider, and could not be expected to know who was right and who wrong in such cases. Thus, the recognition was an extremely logical tool for him. By using the knowledge of 'ancient and legitimate men,' he could be assured of being seen as just and fair in cases about which he personally could know nothing. For Geoffrey, the recognition would thus be not an institution, but rather an existing tradition that could be of particular use to him. Furthermore, Geoffrey's repeatedly stated motivation to restore things to the way they were in the time of Henry I would favour the use of recognitions.[52] Since Henry I's reign was easily within living memory of Geoffrey's new subjects, the most logical way to pursue this goal would be to collect sworn testimony from those who remembered the way things used to be.

Haskins's contributions to Norman legal history were enormous. But he was locked into a pattern of thought in which the institutional conception of government dominated. By breaking away from this pattern, and by looking at the tools of government in Geoffrey's reign not as legal institutions, but as legal traditions, we can achieve a deeper and more accurate view of this period of Norman history.

Appendix: The *leugata* of Cambremer

The history of Cambremer is complicated, well-documented, and untold. The *leugata* of Cambremer was an *exemption* of Bayeux within the diocese of Lisieux. The boundaries of the *leugata* as given in Geoffrey's recognition cannot be traced exactly; several of the place-names given cannot be found on a modern 1:50,000 topographical map. A discussion of the composition and history of Cambremer can be found in H. de Formeville, *Histoire de l'ancien évêché-comté de Lisieux* (Lisieux, 1873), 1, vii–x. The *exemption* consisted of

---

[52] I count forty-two extant Norman ducal charters of Geoffrey's, all contained in the *Regesta*. Of these, thirty-six involve Geoffrey attempting to restore conditions to those of Henry I's reign or earlier, confirming gifts made by Normans, or adjudicating disputes. Only six charters show Geoffrey making an original gift or concession.

nine parishes: Cambremer, Crèvecoeur, Grandouet, Manerbe, Saint-Laurent-du-Mont, Saint-Pair-du-Mont, Montreuil-en-Auge, Saint-Ouen-le-Pin, and le Pré-d'Auge. Formeville's discussion of the history of the *leugata's* development needs some adjustment. He gives evidence that Saint-Ouen-le-Pin did not become part of the *exemption* until 1186, and Pré-d'Auge until 1207; this probably fits with Duke Geoffrey's recognition, in which the boundary seems to jog around those parishes. Formeville cites a charter of King Henry II which states that the church of Cambremer was given to Bayeux during the time of Bishop Philip; he gives no citation for this charter, which is not found in the *Recueil des actes de Henri II*, and it does not make sense, since Cambremer is noted in the recognition as being held by Bayeux in the time of Bishop Odo. Formeville suggests that Manerbe was acquired by Odo, but both Manerbe and Cambremer are listed as possessions of Bayeux in a charter of Bishop Hugh II, dating from 1035–7 (*Antiquus cartularius*, no. 21). Finally, the boundaries given in Duke Geoffrey's recognition seem to indicate that additional parishes may have been included in the western portion of the *leugata*.

The *leugata* of Cambremer was also the site of le Val-Richer, a Cistercian abbey translated from Souleuvre in 1150 at the request of Bernard of Clairvaux. For a discussion of the translation and early history of le Val-Richer, see Bourrienne, *Bâtisseur*, 84–7 (cited in footnote 5), apparently derived from Gustave Dupont, *L'abbaye du Val-Richer, étude historique* (Caen, 1866), which I have not seen. A bull of confirmation to le Val-Richer from Pope Alexander III (*P.L.*, cc, no. 253) contains a list of early gifts to the abbey; this bull and the data revealed in Duke Geoffrey's recognition contain a wealth of information about the landholders of the Cambremer area that could profitably be mined.

6

The Denis Bethell Prize Essay
Forging Communities:
Memory and Identity in Post-Conquest England[1]

Jennifer Paxton

The century following the Norman Conquest of England has justly been described as the great age of English forgery. Michael Clanchy suggests that on the basis of recent research, we might soon conclude that forgery in this period was 'the rule rather than the exception.' Not surprisingly, a large percentage of these forgeries stemmed from the great monastic communities that were seeking to secure their rights to land and privileges in the wake of the change of regime.[2] Previous work on these forgeries by scholars such as Wilhelm Levison,[3] Christopher Brooke,[4] and Richard Southern[5] and, more recently, David Bates,[6] and Susan Kelly,[7] has tended to focus narrowly on the charters themselves. However, forgeries were often produced alongside other kinds of writing, and although Clanchy hints at the relationship between literary invention and the forging of documents when he discusses forgery in general terms,[8] there has

---

[1] The author wishes to thank Robert Berkhofer, Alan Cooper, Bruce O'Brien, and Emily Tabuteau for helpful comments and suggestions.

[2] Michael Clanchy, *From Memory to Written Record: England 1066–1307* (2nd edn., Oxford, 1993), 318. For a good general treatment of medieval forgery, with accompanying bibliography, see Olivier Guyotjeannin, Jacques Pycke, and Benoît-Michel Tock, *Diplomatique médiévale* (Turnhout, 1993), 367–95.

[3] Wilhelm Levison, *England and the Continent in the Eighth Century* (Oxford, 1946; repr. 1956), appendix 1, 174–233.

[4] C.N.L. Brooke, 'The Canterbury Forgeries and Their Author,' *Downside Review,* 68 (1950), 462–76; 69 (1951), 210–31.

[5] R.W. Southern, 'The Canterbury Forgeries,' *E.H.R.,* 73 (1958), 193–226.

[6] David Bates, 'The Land Pleas of William I's Reign: Penenden Heath Revisited,' *Bulletin of the Institute of Historical Research,* 51 (1978), 1–19.

[7] Susan Elisabeth Kelly, 'Some Forgeries in the Archives of St Augustine's Abbey, Canterbury,' in *Fälschungen im Mittelalter, Teil IV, Diplomatische Fälschungen (II)* (Hanover, 1988), 347–69.

[8] Of course, not all houses that forged charters also produced other kinds of historical texts. Coventry, for example, engaged in a sustained campaign of forgery in the early years of Henry I's reign without assembling any historical works. James Tait, 'An Alleged Charter of William the Conqueror,' in *Essays in History Presented to Reginald Lane Poole,* ed. H.W.C. Davis, 151–67 (Oxford, 1927; repr. 1969, Freeport, NY); Joan C. Lancaster, 'The Coventry Forged Charters: A Reconsideration (1100–1140),' *Bulletin of the Institute of Historical Research,* 27 (1954), 113–40. See Clanchy, 318–21, for general comments on forged narrative and forged charters.

been only very scattered work on the relationships among these texts.[9] In addition, forgery in England has usually been studied in an exclusively legal context. Valuable work has been done to assess the role of forgery in the birth of the common law,[10] but forgery can also be used to gain a wider understanding of early Anglo-Norman culture. While specific legal disputes were quite often the precipitating factor in cases of forgery, there were other, less tangible causes for monastic communities to resort to the fabrication of documents.[11]

This article argues that forged documents were often created as an integral part of a broad textual effort to use the (often distorted) memory of the Anglo-Saxon past as a means not just of protecting monastic rights and privileges but of solidifying the identity of the monastic community in the present. When considered together, the forgeries and their associated historical narratives cast a new light on the famous shift from memory to written record. Whereas Clanchy and other scholars emphasize the administrative and legal uses of literacy, these sources reveal that texts constituted an increasingly powerful tool for constructing links between the present and the past that bound monastic communities together. Furthermore, a comparison between narrative and charter (both genuine and spurious) reinforces the now widely accepted notion that distinctions between written genres in this period were fluid, although certainly not entirely absent. Indeed, the line of demarcation between charter and narrative is not at all clear, as Marjorie Chibnall has made plain in her discussion of foundation charters and pancartes in Normandy and England in the eleventh and early twelfth centuries;[12] still, both charter and narrative were seen as complementary elements in constructing a tissue of rights, privileges, and claims to sanctity that made a monastic community unique.

The English were not the first to construct a close link between narrative and forged charter. As for so much else in the post-Conquest English church, there are Norman precedents from the mid-eleventh century onwards. Leah Shopkow

---

[9] 'Le problème se complique quand c'est le faussaire (ou le groupe de faussaires) lui-même qui, parallèlement à la confection de faux actes, a eu une production historiographique et hagiographique. Les faussaires ont souvent cherché à se garantir en croisant les pistes, en accumulant les références; mais cette cascade de citations entrecroisées permet parfois de mieux les confondre.' Guyotjeannin, Pycke, and Tock, 377.

[10] Bruce O'Brien, 'Forgery and the Literacy of the Early Common Law,' *Albion*, 27 (1995), 1–18.

[11] For example, the Battle forgeries, which were precipitated by an effort to assert exemption from diocesan control. Eleanor Searle, 'Battle Abbey and Exemption: The Forged Charters,' *E.H.R.*, 83 (1968), 449–80. In her edition of the Battle chronicle, Searle recognizes the intimate connection between forgery and narrative, but she attributes the creation of narrative largely to a need to 'protect' forgeries by providing them with a narrative context. Searle, ed. and trans., *The Chronicle of Battle Abbey* (Oxford, 1980), 5. This is certainly true as far as it goes, but it neglects other factors I attempt to explore in this article.

[12] Marjorie Chibnall, 'Charter and Chronicle: The Use of Archive Sources by Norman Historians,' in *Church and Government in the Middle Ages: Essays Presented to C.R. Cheney on His Seventieth Birthday*, ed. C.N.L. Brooke, D.E. Luscombe, G.H. Martin, and Dorothy Owen (Cambridge, 1976), 1–17; 'Forgery in Narrative Charters,' in *Fälschungen im Mittelalter, Teil IV, Diplomatische Fälschungen (II)* (Hanover, 1988), 331–46.

notes that historical texts produced in connection with legal disputes or other controversies were more likely to include charters.[13] For example, in 1053, in an effort to prove that the relics of St Vulfran resided at St-Wandrille rather than at St-Peter in Ghent, the author of the *Inventio sancti Vulfranni* incorporated a forged charter that seemed to prove that the monks of St-Wandrille had celebrated the feast of the translation of St Vulfran since 1027.[14] At Fécamp, an early eleventh-century history of the house was enhanced, in the midst of a dispute with the archbishop of Rouen, with information from privileges forged at the same time to stake a spurious claim to exemption from archiepiscopal control.[15] In this case, the privileges were merely plundered for details, not included *verbatim* in the text. However, there could also be discrepancies between the charters and the chronicle tradition at a single house, as, for example, at Bec, where it is hard to tell which account of the foundation of the dependent church of Notre-Dame-du-Pré, the chronicle or the pancarte, represents the earlier witness.[16]

Nonetheless, there is abundant evidence of co-ordination between forged charters and the narrative texts with which they became associated, in England as well as Normandy, though the best-known English examples are somewhat later. A famous case is the *Vita beati Edwardi regis* by Osbert de Clare, prior of Westminster. In connection with a trip to Rome in 1139–42 to ask the pope's aid in reforming the abbey, Osbert inserted his own forged charters in favour of his house into the *Life*.[17] During the second half of the twelfth century, this pattern was further elaborated at some of the important black monk houses in England, particularly in the Fens, into a new genre: the 'charter-chronicle' that incorporated large numbers of documents, both forged and genuine, into a narrative that covered the whole history of the monastic community.[18]

There would thus appear to be a substantial gap in time between the Norman

---

[13] Leah Shopkow, *History and Community: Norman Historical Writing in the Eleventh and Twelfth Centuries* (Washington, DC, 1997), 200.

[14] Elisabeth M.C. van Houts, 'Historiography and Hagiography at Saint-Wandrille: The *Inventio et Miracula Sancti Vulfranni*,' *A.N.S.*, 12 (1989), 233–51, at 240–41.

[15] Marjorie Chibnall, *The World of Orderic Vitalis* (Oxford, 1984), 111–12.

[16] Chibnall, 'Forgery in Narrative Charters,' 333–4.

[17] Osbert de Clare, *Vita Beati Edwardi Regis Anglorum*, in Marc Bloch, 'La Vie de S. Edouard le Confesseur par Osbert de Clare,' *Analecta Bollandiana*, 41 (1923), 5–131. Reprinted in Bloch, *Mélanges historiques* (2 vols., Paris, 1963), ii, 948–1030. Bloch discusses the interpolated texts at 974–8. Pierre Chaplais argues convincingly that the documents were forged at the same time as the *Life* was composed. Chaplais, 'The Original Charters of Herbert and Gervase, Abbots of Westminster (1121–1157),' *Essays in Medieval Diplomacy and Administration* (London, 1981), xviii, 89–112, at 91–5.

[18] The best-known examples are the *Liber Eliensis*, ed. E.O. Blake, Camden 3rd ser. 79 (London, 1963); the *Chronicon abbatiae Rameseiensis*, ed. W. Dunn Macray (R.S., London, 1886); the *Chronicle of Hugh Candidus*, ed. W.T. Mellows (Oxford, 1949) (hereafter *HC*); and the *Chronicon monasterii de Abingdon (A.D. 201–1189)*, ed. Joseph Stevenson (2 vols., R.S., London, 1858). See my thesis, 'Charter and Chronicle in Twelfth-Century England: The House-Histories of the Fenland Abbeys' (Harvard University, 1999), for extended analysis of the first three of these.

examples I have cited and the English ones, but there is, in fact, an earlier English example[19] of the juxtaposition of forgery with narrative that may suggest a path of transmission for this method of textual manipulation. It is a sort of proto-charter-chronicle called the 'Relatio Heddae,'[20] which is contained in the earliest Peterborough cartulary, the Liber Niger (LN), dating from the 1130s. The 'Relatio' purports to be an account of the foundation of Peterborough in the seventh century written by Abbot Hedda, supposed successor of the first abbot. It includes several important privileges granted by the founders, followed by confirmations of these privileges by all the important English kings from Edgar 'the Peaceable' to William the Conqueror. As I attempt to demonstrate, Peterborough did not create the 'Relatio' in isolation; the production of this text was associated with the abbacy of a great Norman cleric, Abbot Ernulf (1107–14), who brought his preoccupation with monastic history and privileges with him from his previous post at Christ Church, Canterbury. A close study of the texts Ernulf fostered at Peterborough sheds light on a network of textual production (including forgery) that had its centre at Christ Church, the most important church in the land.

The case of this otherwise obscure work at a remote (if powerful) house can help to illuminate how such a network could help monastic communities use their past to protect their privileges and to create a sense of a shared communal identity. The 'Relatio' can illuminate some of the major currents in early Anglo-Norman culture: the increased emphasis on historical narrative,[21] the perceived need to counter with written texts the great insecurity of title that followed the Norman Conquest,[22] and the effort by many monastic communities to construct an identity for themselves that stressed specific connections with the past that served their present needs. Peterborough perfectly embodies all these trends. After suffering greatly in the aftermath of the Norman Conquest because

---

[19] Chibnall, 'Forgery in Narrative Charters,' 336, proposes that a lost Shrewsbury chronicle that incorporated individual grants to the abbey served as the basis for the surviving pancartes, so the Peterborough text may not in fact be the earliest example of this genre.

[20] London, Society of Antiquaries, MS. 60, fols. 48v–71. For a description of the manuscript, see Janet D. Martin, *The Cartularies and Registers of Peterborough Abbey,* Northamptonshire Record Society, 28 (Peterborough, 1978), 1–7.

[21] For this now much-studied subject, see, among others: Sir Richard Southern, 'The Place of England in the Twelfth-Century Renaissance,' *Medieval Humanism and Other Studies* (Oxford, 1970; paperback edn., 1984), 158–80; James Campbell, 'Some Twelfth-Century Views of the Anglo-Saxon Past,' *Essays in Anglo-Saxon History* (London, 1986), 209–28; Nancy Partner, *Serious Entertainments: The Writing of History in Twelfth-Century England* (Chicago and London, 1977); Monika Otter, *Inventiones: Fiction and Referentiality in Twelfth-Century English Historical Writing* (Chapel Hill, NC, 1996). The starting-place should always be Antonia Gransden, *Historical Writing in England, Vol. I: c. 550–c. 1307* (Ithaca, 1974). For Normandy, see Shopkow, *History and Community.*

[22] See Robin Fleming, 'What Can Now Be Said About Land, Law and Lordship in the Kingdom of England,' paper delivered to the Medieval Academy of America, Washington, DC, April 1999.

of its close ties to the previous regime,[23] It fashioned a complicated, multi-faceted textual response, drawing on the elements – both chronicle and charter – that made up a newly emerging written culture, each of which was embellished or, if you will, forged, to help authenticate the other.

The 'Relatio' has never been studied in detail, partly because it has never been published in a way that makes clear its character as a work that was conceived from the outset as a combination of charter and narrative.[24] By the 1130s at the latest, it had assumed the form of a free-standing work: The hand in the LN changes just before and after the 'Relatio,' suggesting that it was written in one bout and conceived of as a whole. Moreover, the rubric, in the same hand as the text, refers explicitly to the privileges as if they are an integral part of the 'Relatio.'[25]

The 1130s is very much a *terminus ad quem*, however, since the privileges contained in the 'Relatio' certainly existed in some form before 1122, when they were translated into Old English and inserted into the E version of the Anglo-Saxon Chronicle, which was written at Peterborough.[26] The question, then, is whether the privileges were forged separately before the E Chronicle was written or whether the whole 'Relatio' already existed by 1122. The answer I propose is somewhat speculative, but I hope it will suggest that the connection between forged charters and narrative was an intimate one in England as early as the first decades of the twelfth century.

A brief summary of the 'Relatio' will help to demonstrate how it accomplishes several related polemical goals for the abbey. First, its narrative introduction constitutes the first step in altering Peterborough's historical profile in order to give it a royal Anglo-Saxon pedigree, which it otherwise lacked.[27] The text begins by stating that during the reign of the infamous pagan King Penda of Mercia, his son Peada, prompted by his wife Alchfled, the daughter of King Oswy of Northumbria, accepted baptism and endowed the monastery of Medeshamstede (as Peterborough was then called), with a man named Seaxwulf at its head. There are no pre-Conquest sources that mention any connection

23 See Edmund King, *Peterborough Abbey, 1086–1310: A Study in the Land Market* (Cambridge, 1973), 15–20.
24 Mellows, *HC*, 159–61, prints the introductory narrative only, from the fourteenth-century Book of Walter of Whittlesey, where the charters have been abstracted from the text and included elsewhere in the cartulary; he makes a note of the original text in the Liber Niger (see below) but does not reproduce it.
25 'Relatio Hedde abbatis, quomodo incipiente Christianitate Mediterraneorum Anglorum initiatum sit Medeshamstedense monasterium et subsequentibus priuilegiis confirmatum.' LN, fol. 48v.
26 For an edition of the Peterborough interpolations and associated bibliography, see *The Peterborough Chronicle 1070–1154*, ed. Cecily Clark (2nd edn., Oxford, 1970), 115–27 (hereafter A.S.C. E).
27 Robin Fleming's paper, 'What Can Now Be Said About Land, Law and Lordship,' suggests that post-Conquest landholders, including the great abbeys, were attempting to stress that they derived their tenure from royal grants because they believed the king was the best guarantor of their rights in the land.

between Medeshamstede and the royal house of Mercia, and though such an association is certainly not impossible, there is no sign that Peterborough preserved any evidence of this in the twelfth century. The author of the 'Relatio' forges this link by extracting information from Bede about the Mercian and Northumbrian kings and grafting onto it Bede's otherwise unrelated account of the foundation of Medeshamstede by Seaxwulf. The author first paraphrases Bede's account in Book Three of the *Historia ecclesiastica*[28] of how Peada, the son of the pagan King Penda, brought back four priests to preach the Gospel in Mercia after his conversion in Northumbria. He then adds: 'Their companion and fellow-worker was the distinguished Seaxwulf, a man who was very prominent in both the world and in religious life, and who was very well-regarded by both the church and the king.'[29] Bede does not mention Seaxwulf in this context at all, but instead refers to him only in passing, during his discussion of the deposition of Bishop Wilfrid in Book Four.[30] The Peterborough writer merely inserts him into the story as the fifth member of Peada's troop of preachers. By linking two passages in Bede, the 'Relatio' allowed the monks of Peterborough in the early twelfth century to claim an association with one of the most powerful of the early Anglo-Saxon kings.

The 'Relatio' ties the fortunes of Medeshamstede not just to the Mercian royal house, but to that of Northumbria as well.[31] The 'Relatio' states that after King Oswy had slain Penda in battle, he ruled Mercia for three years, during which time he also fostered the development of Medeshamstede ('regaliter prouexit').[32] According to Bede,[33] Peada was for that period king of the South Mercians, presumably under his father-in-law's overlordship, but the 'Relatio' glosses over this fact and proceeds straight to a terse mention of Peada's treacherous murder and the accession of his brother Wulfhere, who becomes for the author of the 'Relatio' the true founder of Medeshamstede. Of course, Wulfhere was known to have been an exceptionally strong king, during whose reign Mercian dominance extended over much of southern England. The 'Relatio' states that Wulfhere granted great privileges to Medeshamstede, which Seaxwulf, due to his great sagacity, ensured were committed to writing. The narrative introduction thus provides the context for Peterborough's acquisition of charters of enormous authority, backed by a great Anglo-Saxon ruler.[34]

---

[28] Bede, *Ecclesiastical History of the English People*, ed. Bertram Colgrave and R.A.B. Mynors (Oxford, 1969), bk. iii, c.21, 278–81 (hereafter *HE*).

[29] 'Hic accessit comes et cooperator illustris Saxulfus, uir prepotens et seculo et religione regisque et ecclesie acceptissimus.' LN, fol. 58v.

[30] *HE*, bk. iv, c.6, 354–5.

[31] One possible reason for this emphasis on a Northumbrian link is Peterborough's claim to possess the arm of St Oswald. I deal with this relic in my thesis, pp. 100–2.

[32] LN, fol. 59r.

[33] *HE*, bk. iii, c.24, 294–5.

[34] The story of Wulfhere's involvement with the foundation of Medeshamstede received further elaboration at some unknown date, possibly in the late twelfth or early thirteenth centuries. This tale is told in a text preserved now only in The Book of Walter of Whittlesey (B.L., Additional

The privileges that follow are clearly intended to provide secure title to Peterborough's estates. They constitute a 'dossier' comparable to the collections of documents relating to a particular controversy that were common among monastic houses in eleventh-century France.[35] The documents include: (1) a charter of King Wulfhere[36] confirming Peterborough's estates and privileges with a confirmation by his brother and successor Ethelred;[37] (2) a bull of Pope Agatho that confers sweeping exemptions from diocesan control;[38] and (3) a confirmation by King Edgar 'the Peaceable', as well as confirmations of this latter document by succeeding English kings down to William the Conqueror.[39]

MS. 39758, fol. 8), though it was also to be found in B.L., Cotton MS. Otho A.XVII, from which it was printed by Dugdale. This manuscript was destroyed in the Cotton fire of 1731, but a description of it can be found in Thomas Smith, *Catalogue of the Manuscripts in the Cottonian Library (Catalogus librorum manuscriptorum bibliothecae Cottonianae)* (1696), edited by C.G.C. Tite and reprinted (Cambridge and Totowa, NJ, 1984), 68–9. The Otho manuscript also contained a text of *HC* that was the source for a seventeenth-century transcript by George Davenport, on which Mellows based his edition. The text in question tells the story of the king's murder of his sons, Sts Wulflad and Rufinus, whom he slew in rage at their stubborn adherence to Christianity (remorse for this deed led to his own conversion and repentance). Whittlesey seems to be condensing the account in the Otho text. While Hugh Candidus quotes the Wulfhere privilege, and gives information about Wulfhere's family drawn from Bede, he nowhere mentions Wulflad and Rufinus. The absence of any reference to this story could be explained in two ways: either Hugh knew the text and was suspicious of its many anachronistic features, which Gunton pointed out long ago, or it had not yet been composed at the time he wrote his chronicle. In the absence of any better manuscript evidence, perhaps only a detailed stylistic analysis could attempt to fix a date to this text. One feature may possibly localize the text in the late twelfth or early thirteenth century, namely the pope's reluctance to use the relics of St Wulflad, brought to Rome by the procurator of Stanes, to test the truth of his claims. The pope says one should not tempt God. This is an attitude that could belong to the period of growing scepticism about the ordeal that culminated in the withdrawal of church participation at the Fourth Lateran Council in 1215. At any rate, since it appears neither in the LN nor in the body of Hugh's chronicle, and since no relics of the two martyrs are recorded in Hugh's relic list, I think it is safe to regard it as a rather late elaboration on the story of the origins of Medeshamstede.

[35] Robert Berkhofer, 'Forging Community in Medieval France,' paper delivered to the American Historical Association, Chicago, Illinois, January 2000.

[36] P.H. Sawyer, *Anglo-Saxon Charters: An Annotated List and Bibliography*, Royal Historical Society Guides and Handbooks, 8 (London, 1968), no. 68 (hereafter S68, etc.).

[37] S72, though Simon Keynes, *A Handlist of Anglo-Saxon Charters: Archives and Single Sheets* (Oxford, forthcoming), notes that Sawyer does not make clear that the 'original' Latin version of this charter occurs here, in the LN. I am grateful to Dr Keynes for allowing me to consult his manuscript before publication. As the manuscript has no continuous pagination, all references to this work will lack precise page numbers.

[38] *Cartularium Saxonicum: A Collection of Charters Relating to Anglo-Saxon History, A.D. 430–975*, ed. Walter de Gray Birch (3 vols., London, 1885–93), no. 48 (hereafter *CS*); P. Jaffé, et al., *Regesta pontificum Romanorum* (2nd edn., Leipzig, 1885–8), no. †2111. Walther Holtzmann, *Papsturkunden in England* (3 vols., Berlin, 1930), cites this bull in vol. i, 207–8 and vol. ii, 95, but does not print or discuss it, since, as he reports in vol. ii, 93–4, his visit to Peterborough in 1929 proved unproductive due to the absence of W.T. Mellows, who had promised to review the archives with him.

[39] The (very brief) confirmations of Edgar's charter by Edward the Martyr, Ethelred, Cnut, and Edward the Confessor are not noted by Sawyer; William the Conqueror's charter is printed in

Not a single scholar will defend the authenticity of Wulfhere's charter or even claim that it is based on genuine materials.[40] The charter claims that it wishes to confirm and add to what Peada and Oswy had granted to the monastery. The estates it lists comprise almost all of the two hundreds of Nassaburgh in Northamptonshire, which became the Soke of Peterborough.[41] The charter also provides a Biblical pretext for exempting Medeshamstede and any churches dependent upon it from all royal dues. It quotes Christ's question to St Peter, 'Does one accept tribute from sons or from foreigners?' Peter's response is, of course, 'from foreigners.'[42] The author of the charter thus invokes the authority of the titular patron of the church[43] in creating a spurious privilege. Needless to say, such a grant cannot be genuine, but it might have been of the greatest value if it could have been deployed in the twelfth century against those who had seized Peterborough estates. The charter of Wulfhere is followed by a lengthy confirmation by his brother, Ethelred, who was also a powerful king; this confirmation, spurious in its turn, of course, serves to demonstrate that the grant was accepted at the time it was issued.

The 'Relatio' provides Peterborough with not only secular but also ecclesiastical authority for its rights and privileges. The next document in the text is a spurious bull of Pope Agatho.[44] It is a similarly breathtaking forgery that confers liberties on Peterborough never dreamed of by a seventh-century pope, including a provision exempting Peterborough from the jurisdiction of its diocesan bishop, who was presumably then Seaxwulf, the very founder of the abbey, who had by then become bishop of the Mercians. Indeed, Seaxwulf witnesses the document and explicitly concedes jurisdiction.[45] Seaxwulf's consent to the exemption in the privilege provides an important precedent that could potentially be used against the bishops of Lincoln in the early twelfth century, and the value of Seaxwulf's approval is reinforced by the flattering portrait already painted of him in the narrative of the 'Relatio.' Thus, the combination of charter and narrative is stronger than either text alone.

The dossier of privileges seems to have been designed to highlight turning points in the abbey's history, because the text jumps from the initial foundation to a confirmation of the abbey's estates by Edgar 'the Peaceable' (959–975),

David Bates, ed., *Regesta Regum Anglo-Normannorum: The Acta of William I (1066–1087)* (Oxford, 1998), no. 216.

[40] See Sawyer's summary of critical opinion on this charter, note 39 above.

[41] *The Early Charters of Eastern England*, ed. C.R. Hart (Leicester, 1966), no. (1), 110.

[42] 'A quibus accipiunt [reges gentium] tributa, a filiis an ab alienis? Ab alienis, inquit Petrus.' LN, fol. 51v.

[43] Peterborough sources throughout the twelfth century emphasize the community's special relationship with St Peter. See chapter 3 of my thesis.

[44] *CS*, no. 48.

[45] 'Ego humilis Saxulfus regali beneficio ejusdem monasterii fundator, ita ipsius in omnibus libertatem et prerogativam corroborare gaudeo, sicut ei specialius optima omnia cupio, ut nichil usurpem uel de rebus uel officiis ipsius monasterii preter uoluntatem abbatis et postulationem, nec ego nec successores mei; ego quoque omnem violentie abusionem anathemate hinc excludo.' LN, fols. 66v–67; *CS*, no. 48.

during whose reign the abbey was restored and refounded after the disruption in monastic life due to the Viking invasions of the ninth century. This charter, which is certainly spurious,[46] is followed by confirmations of subsequent kings – Edward the Martyr, Ethelred, Cnut, and Edward the Confessor – which have clearly been constructed simply to demonstrate continuity between the reigns of Edgar and the Conqueror.

These forgeries are followed by a writ of William I[47] that has been slightly altered in order to make it conform better to the previous charters. It confirms specific estates to the abbey at the request of Abbot Brand (1066–9).[48] Hugh Candidus, writing a century later, states explicitly that these estates were given to the abbey by Brand and his relatives in the period between the death of Harold and William's coronation.[49] Davis felt that the confirmation of William I, 'while irregular in form (perhaps translated),' could be accepted in substance, and suggested that it may be identical to the charter that, according to the A.S.C. E, Abbot Brand purchased from the king for 40 marks of gold to buy back his good will after Brand's initial overtures to the atheling.[50] Similarly, David Bates, in his recent edition of the Conqueror's charters, also cites the story in the A.S.C. E and states: 'The charter is idiosyncratic. But it resembles other Peterborough documents, and may well be a charter written by its beneficiary and presented to William for confirmation.'[51] However, it has been very slightly altered to lend authenticity to the forged charters that precede it in the 'Relatio': 'Ego Will(el)m(us) Dei beneficio rex Anglorum, petente abbate Brand, istud privilegium in omnibus laudo et confirmo *sicut suprascripti reges ante me.*' The wording of the opening clause thus implies that William had been shown the charters of his predecessors, which, of course, did not exist at the time this writ was issued. The compiler of the 'Relatio' has taken a genuine writ of the Conqueror and altered it to stand at the end of a series of forgeries. The confirmations in the 'Relatio' thus provide an interesting example of how monastic authors could blend the genuine and the fictitious in an attempt to construct a continuous chain of authority.

In sum, then, this narrative with supporting documentation provides the abbey with the legal basis for holding both its rights and its property and manufactures a chain of authority, both royal and papal, that stretches from the earliest history of the abbey to its recent past. The 'Relatio' thus serves both to safeguard the abbey's rights and privileges and to raise its profile as a distinguished, royal foundation.

This much about the 'Relatio' in its current form is straightforward, but the

---

[46] See Sawyer S787 for a summary of critical opinions.

[47] Bates, *The Acta of William I*, no. 216. The charter survives only in Peterborough cartularies.

[48] Scotter, Scotton, Manton, Ragenaldetorp, Messingham, Cleatham, Hibaldstow, Walcot (all Lincs); and North Muskham (Notts).

[49] King, *Peterborough Abbey*, 9.

[50] *Regesta*, i, no. 8.

[51] Bates, *The Acta of William I*, no. 216.

picture becomes significantly more complicated when we take into account the other texts produced at Peterborough at around the same time, for, as I have already mentioned, some of the privileges included in the 'Relatio' were incorporated about a decade earlier into the E version of the Anglo-Saxon Chronicle as vernacular epitomes. The charter of Wulfhere (s.a. 656),[52] the bull of Pope Agatho (s.a. 675), and the confirmation of Edgar (s.a. 963) (though not, as I have noted, the privilege of William the Conqueror) can all be found among the Peterborough interpolations that characterize the E Chronicle. It is usually presumed that in about 1122, perhaps as a result of having lost their own copy of the Anglo-Saxon Chronicle during the great abbey fire of 1116, the monks of Peterborough set about copying and interpolating a new version, based on an exemplar that may have been borrowed from Christ Church, Canterbury.[53] The present manuscript, now Oxford, Bodleian Library, Laud Misc. MS. 636, has been written in a single hand through the annal for 1121 and continued thereafter in several hands down to 1154.[54] The interpolations relating to Peterborough in the first section of the manuscript can thus be safely assumed to predate 1121.

Many of these are based on documents preserved in the LN, including some of those contained in the 'Relatio,' so these would presumably have been gathered and/or forged before 1121. The English chronicler clearly combed through the records of the house in order to gather the material necessary for putting a distinctly Peterborough stamp on the new manuscript. Among these records are several eighth-century leases that appear to be completely authentic.[55] Their inclusion in the A.S.C. E, despite their only rather peripheral relevance to Peterborough, indicates that the chronicler was eager to make use of whatever he could that would forge a link to Peterborough's Anglo-Saxon past.

By grafting the Peterborough documents, some of which were audacious forgeries, onto the narrative framework of the Anglo-Saxon Chronicle, the Peterborough chronicler was locating their production in time and helping to legitimize them. The most interesting example of this phenomenon concerns the 'Relatio Heddae' itself. The A.S.C. E records s.a. 963[56] that when Æthelwold came to Medeshamstede, he found in the old walls remaining from the original monastery documents written by Abbot Hedda telling how the abbey had been

[52] A.S.C. E, 115–19.
[53] David Dumville, 'Some Aspects of Annalistic Writing at Canterbury in the Eleventh and Early Twelfth Centuries,' *Peritia*, 2 (1983), 23–57, states at p. 35 that it is currently impossible to prove whether the A.S.C. E is derived directly from a Canterbury exemplar, but that is one of the hypotheses he offers.
[54] Neil Ker, *Catalogue of Manuscripts Containing Anglo-Saxon* (Oxford, 1957), no. 346; *The Peterborough Chronicle*, ed. Dorothy Whitelock, Early English Manuscripts in Facsimile, no. 4 (Copenhagen and London, 1955).
[55] F.M. Stenton, 'Medeshamstede and its Colonies,' in *Preparatory to Anglo-Saxon England* (Oxford, 1970), 179–92 at 189–92.
[56] Keynes, *Handlist*, points out the actual date of foundation is more likely to have been 970. The Peterborough chronicler is perhaps here attempting to claim that Peterborough was the earliest Fenland foundation.

founded by Wulfhere and his brother and freed from all royal and episcopal obligations. Æthelwold then had the monastery built, installed an abbot and monks, and showed the documents he had found to King Edgar, who thereupon granted a charter of immunity, which the text cites in a vernacular epitome.

The literal truth of this story is rendered somewhat suspect, however, by the existence of a Biblical analogy: the story of the discovery of the scrolls of the Torah during the restoration of the temple in 2 Chronicles 34:14–28. In this story, the priest Hilkiah finds the scroll and brings it to King Josiah. When the king hears the newly recovered text read aloud, he is distressed to discover that the people have not been living in accordance with the law. He summons the people to the temple and swears to abide by the commandments and makes all those present do the same. There are some striking parallels between this story and the account of the restoration of Peterborough in the A.S.C. E. In 2 Chronicles, the temple in Jerusalem is being repaired after its desecration during the reigns of the apostate kings Manasseh and Amon, while Peterborough is being restored after its destruction by the pagan Vikings. Bishop Æthelwold stands in for the priest Hilkiah, and King Edgar plays the role of Josiah. The documents found in the walls become the equivalent of the Scriptures discovered in the temple, and in each case, the king 'authenticates' the newly uncovered documents: Josiah pledges to abide by the Torah, and Edgar issues a charter of confirmation. To readers familiar with the story in 2 Chronicles, the parallel being drawn between the Peterborough charters and the law of Moses itself would have been clear.

Simon Keynes maintains that the story of old documents being found in the walls is not wildly improbable, since, as has just been noted, some of the early Peterborough charters are indeed genuine, and thus he suggests that the 'Relatio' 'is obviously the actual embodiment of the same story.'[57] It is quite possible that the 'Relatio' was composed to conform to a story current in the abbey about the discovery of old charters in Æthelwold's day, and that the entry interpolated into the A.S.C. E was written with reference to the 'Relatio,' but whether this refers to the charters with or without their narrative introduction is impossible to say. If this story formed part of the oral tradition current in the abbey in the early twelfth century, then the documents were perhaps forged in order to authenticate it, and were in turn authenticated by a written narrative. Indeed, the Peterborough interpolations make of the early section of the A.S.C. E itself a virtual charter-chronicle of the house. The narrative and the documents in the A.S.C. E reinforce each other, lending legitimacy to the story they tell, just as they do in the 'Relatio' itself.

Thus, Peterborough produced both an Old English version of its history in which documents and narrative interpenetrate each other and a Latin version in which a narrative precedes a series of documents. This complicated production of forged charters and narrative indicates that legal documents and historical accounts were both seen as vital to the creation of an authentic past for the

---

[57] Keynes, *Handlist.*

Peterborough community. It was not enough to enumerate the rights and privileges of the abbey; the monks had to know and understand the context in which they were granted so that they could fully appreciate the greatness of their 'gildene burch,' as Peterborough came to be known.[58]

It is thus indisputable that the charters in the 'Relatio' existed before the compilation of the Liber Niger. But can we go further? Can we suppose that the 'Relatio' in its current form, with its narrative introduction already in place, was available to the Peterborough interpolator of the A.S.C. E in the early 1120s? There is not enough textual evidence for a firm conclusion, but there is at least one phrase in the E Chronicle that suggests that the compiler is writing with the 'Relatio' itself in front of him. In the 'Relatio,' as I have said, Seaxwulf is referred to as 'uir prepotens et seculo et religione regisque et ecclesie acceptissimus.' In the E Chronicle, he is described thus: 'He wæs swyðe Godes freond. 7 him luuede al þeode. 7 he wæs swyðe æþelboren on weorulde 7 rice.'[59] Both texts thus stress the fact that Seaxwulf is powerful and respected in both the religious and the secular spheres, an important component of abbatial leadership in twelfth-century England.[60] Admittedly, there is a slightly different emphasis in the two formulations, but the similarity is enough to suggest either that the interpolator of the E Chronicle had access to the 'Relatio' or that the material the 'Relatio' was later based on already existed at Peterborough a decade before the text itself was composed.

Such a verbal echo is not, of course, strong evidence by itself, but there is another link between the forged charters in the 'Relatio' and the manuscript of the A.S.C. into which they were interpolated that, if it does not prove that the 'Relatio' existed before 1122, at least suggests that there was a close connection between charter and narrative at Peterborough in this period. The common element is an association with Canterbury. The manuscript on which the E Chronicle was based came from Christ Church, though it had spent a considerable time in the eleventh century at St Augustine's.[61] Levison argued that one of the principal documents in the 'Relatio,' the bull of Pope Agatho, may have been forged by Guerno, who fabricated charters for St Augustine's, Canterbury, in the immediate post-Conquest period, or by someone very familiar with his work.[62] This charter is based on a genuine bull of Pope John XII from St Augustine's.[63] Susan Kelly has questioned the attribution of all the St Augustine's forgeries to Guerno, whose death between 1119 and 1131 makes him an improbable candidate for such a lengthy career in document-tampering. Instead, she argues that the forgeries were produced over many years by different hands, but

---

[58] A.S.C. E, s.a. 1052.

[59] A.S.C. E, s.a. 654.

[60] See my discussion of the *Narratio de abbate Gualtero, tempore regis Stephani* of Ramsey Abbey in chapter 4 of my thesis, 144–55.

[61] For a discussion of the relationship between the A.S.C. E and various Canterbury manuscripts, see Dumville, 'Annalistic Writing at Canterbury.'

[62] Levison, *England and the Continent*, 200–1.

[63] Ibid.

she suggests that the charter in question for Peterborough, the second of two privileges in the name of John, was produced late in the series,[64] making it more likely that the forger was Guerno. The important point, though, is not the attribution to a specific forger but the fact that there was a connection between St Augustine's and Peterborough. At first glance, it may seem incongruous to propose a connection between a forgery from St Augustine's and a chronicle text from Christ Church, since the two Canterbury houses were fierce rivals,[65] but by the end of the eleventh century, Christ Church was assembling chronicle texts from all over England and seems, in David Dumville's words, to have served as 'something of an academic clearing-house,'[66] so the charter may have come to Peterborough via Christ Church just as the exemplar of the E Chronicle did.

Now, the person presiding over this 'clearing-house' was a Frenchman from Beauvais named Ernulf, who had been a pupil of Lanfranc at Bec along with Anselm and then a monk of St Symphorien at Beauvais, before going to Christ Church in 1073 to serve under Lanfranc and rising to the office of prior under Anselm in 1096.[67] He may also have been a disciple of Ivo of Chartres.[68] Ernulf served as the schoolmaster at Christ Church while prior and may have been responsible for the library there.[69] In 1107, he was made abbot of Peterborough, where he served with distinction for seven years. After leaving Peterborough, Ernulf became bishop of Rochester (Canterbury's only true suffragan see), where he was almost certainly involved in the compilation of the *Textus Roffensis*.[70] Thus, he was connected to the compilation of various kinds of texts at both Christ Church and Rochester. Ernulf may well have been the conduit for the transfer of the Anglo-Saxon Chronicle and the forged bull of Pope Agatho,

---

[64] S.E. Kelly, ed., *Charters of St Augustine's Abbey Canterbury and Minster-in-Thanet*, Anglo-Saxon Charters, vol. iv (Oxford, 1995), 22.

[65] For a discussion of how the rivalry between Christ Church and St Augustine's is reflected in Christ Church sources, see Robin Fleming, 'Christ Church Canterbury's Anglo-Norman Cartulary,' *Anglo-Norman Political Culture and the Twelfth-Century Renaissance*, ed. C. Warren Hollister (Woodbridge, Suffolk, 1997), 83–155, at 99–102.

[66] Dumville, 38.

[67] For a useful summary of Ernulf's career, see Peter J. Cramer, 'Ernulf of Rochester and Early Anglo-Norman Canon Law,' *Jnl. Eccl. Hist.*, 40 (1989), 483–510, at 483–93.

[68] R.W. Southern, *Saint Anselm and His Biographer* (Cambridge, 1963), 269–70. For a more extended discussion of Ernulf's membership in a circle of friends that included Anselm and Ivo of Chartres, see Lynn K. Barker, 'Ivo of Chartres and the Anglo-Norman Cultural Tradition,' *A.N.S.*, 13 (1990), 15–33, at 18, 21, 23, 26; and Peter J. Cramer, 'Ernulf of Rochester and the Problem of Remembrance,' *Anselm Studies: An Occasional Journal*, 2 (1988), 143–63.

[69] Cramer, 'Ernulf of Rochester and Early Anglo-Norman Canon Law,' 489.

[70] The connection is not absolutely certain, but the editor, Peter Sawyer, points out that a fourteenth-century attribution calls the manuscript 'Textus de ecclesia Roffensi per Ernulfum episcopum.' *Textus Roffensis: Rochester Cathedral Library Manuscripts A.3.5* (2 vols., Copenhagen, 1957, 1962), ii, 18. Patrick Wormald makes a persuasive case for Ernulf's likely involvement in the compilation of the text in 'Laga Eadwardi: The *Textus Roffensis* and Its Context,' *A.N.S.*, 17 (1994), 243–66, at 263–5.

and possibly the driving force behind the compilation of the 'Relatio' itself. We need not actually date these movements of texts to the years of Ernulf's abbacy, since it is easy to imagine that he kept up his contacts with his old monastic community, where he was remembered with great affection.[71]

A further link between Ernulf and the 'Relatio' comes from another text in the Liber Niger that bears on the central controversy of his period at Christ Church, namely the great controversy between Canterbury and York, when Canterbury tried, ultimately unsuccessfully, to assert its primacy over York. The bull of Pope Agatho allows for only one exception from Peterborough's direct subordination to the pope, namely the jurisdiction of the archbishop of Canterbury, and Peterborough in turn seems to have been especially concerned with the primacy of Canterbury. A copy of William the Conqueror's writ confirming Canterbury's primacy, which must have come from Canterbury originally, was copied into the LN,[72] and indeed is placed just before the 'Relatio.'

Now, Ernulf may simply have brought the Canterbury documents with him to Peterborough, where they were then only incorporated into the LN during the reign of Martin de Bec (1133–55). But since the forgeries had to have existed by 1122, they are likely to have been composed either under Ernulf or under Ernulf's immediate successor, John de Seez (1114–25), an abbot who, unlike Ernulf, had no particular literary proclivities.[73]

One question remains. It is easy to understand why Abbot Ernulf would be concerned to provide his house with crucial privileges; the task of an abbot was, after all, to protect the resources of his house. It is also reasonable to imagine him as the instigator of the composition of the 'Relatio,' which, as I have tried to demonstrate, anchored those privileges more securely in the past. It is less immediately obvious why a Norman cleric would be so deeply involved in the effort to produce an updated, customized version of an English vernacular chronicle. There is no definitive proof, but I think it is fair to speculate that the A.S.C. E was designed for the Anglo-Saxon component among the Peterborough community, which probably still predominated in the early twelfth

---

[71] 'Erat bonus monachus et sapiens, et pater monachorum.' *HC*, 90; A.S.C. E, s.a. 1114: 'When the monks heard tell of [the king's decision to make Ernulf bishop of Rochester], they were more grieved than they had ever been, because he was a very good and gentle man, and did much conducive to good within and without while he was there. God Almighty be with him always!' *The Anglo-Saxon Chronicle: A Revised Translation*, trans. Dorothy Whitelock with David C. Douglas and Susie I. Tucker (New Brunswick, NJ, 1961), 184. Ernulf may have accomplished even more than the chroniclers give him credit for at Peterborough; in addition to building a new dormitory, finishing the chapter house and beginning the refectory, as Hugh Candidus states, he may actually have begun work on the new monastic church that is usually assumed to date from after the disastrous fire of 1116. Lisa Reilly, *An Architectural History of Peterborough Cathedral* (Oxford, 1997), 50–6. William of Malmesbury describes his extensive building activities as both prior of Christ Church and abbot of Peterborough. *Gesta pontificum Anglorum*, ed. N.E.S.A. Hamilton (R.S., 52, London, 1870), 137–8.

[72] Bates, *The Acta of William I*, no. 68.

[73] See Hugh Candidus's unflattering portrait of Abbot John, whom Hugh blames for the 1116 fire, *HC*, 97–9.

century, although there is no solid evidence of the ethnic background of the monks at the time the text was written. Ernulf may have wanted to aid in maintaining the Anglo-Saxon tradition that contributed to the community's sense of belonging to a proud past.

In conclusion, when taken together, this evidence of Ernulf's involvement in the Peterborough texts suggests that Canterbury served as the centre of a network not just of forgery but of textual production in general that extended to Rochester and north to the Fens. A salient feature of this network was clearly the conviction that narrative and charter belonged together, whether they were forged or not, and that both were required in order not just to guarantee a community's rights but to create a completely authentic picture of its past.

7

The Experience of Reform: Three Perspectives

William L. North, Jay Rubenstein, and John D. Cotts

Few scholars now deny that the powerful impulse towards the reform of the institutional church and its members in the eleventh and twelfth centuries played a significant role in reshaping the political and intellectual climate of western Europe. So far-reaching are these implications, however, that the very notion of 'reform' has lost some of its precision, as the term can be used in discussions of married priests, lax monasteries, and relations between the secular and ecclesiastical spheres. Still, unlike other abstractions applied to the Middle Ages, most notoriously 'feudalism', few would suggest that the term 'reform' be jettisoned from our scholarly vocabulary. Our imprecision, rather, reflects a medieval imprecision. 'Reform' was a goal which churchmen constantly sought, but whose achievement, and whose precise meaning, always eluded them. The three articles that follow illustrate that shifting meaning by showing how the ideas of reform operated in localized settings. While the reform movement is often discussed in terms of nearly irreconcilable dichotomies (church and state, purity and filth), when churchmen imbued with the prevailing ideology set out to confront moral and professional dilemmas, such distinctions could blur rapidly. We also suggest how intellectual biography can be directed towards complicating – in a productive fashion – our understanding of reform. With this in mind, the following three articles choose specific instances in which an individual monk or cleric confronted or manipulated reforming ideals in the course of his career, and in their chronological and geographical scope they provide a broad survey of the reach of these ideals during the High Middle Ages.

Focusing on the Roman curia under Gregory VII and Urban II, William North challenges the tendency to assume a homogeneity of attitudes and approaches towards reform within the papal curia (and hence to understand difference of opinion as full scale opposition) using hitherto unappreciated evidence in the *Libellus de simoniacis* by Bruno, Bishop of Segni (1079–1123). Prefacing his traditional treatment of this traditional reform issue with a brief life of Pope Leo IX, Bruno at the same time portrays a curia of individuals with shared loyalties but distinctive approaches to the task of reform, a place where the popes were, and knew themselves to be, in dialogue with the ideas and talents of their collaborators rather than in command over them. Far from the simple expressions of a monolithic institutional ideology that brooked no dissent, many of the policies and polemics of the Gregorian curia, North's analysis suggests, resulted from the intellectual and social negotiations of individuals about what was important and how to achieve it within a complex and increasingly self-conscious institution.

Jay Rubenstein's contribution to the survey explores how the precepts of the reform movement were greeted with a sense of irony and ambivalence by an abbot in the midst of professional and political difficulties. While previous scholarly treatments have taken Guibert of Nogent's criticism of simony and nicolaism as evidence of his reformist sympathies, Rubenstein places such reforming sentiments into their local context, and shows that Guibert's commitment to reform is tempered by immediate practical concerns. The experience of the abbot of Nogent should warn scholars not to confuse the language of reform with the language of everyday ecclesiastical politics.

Finally, John D. Cotts explores how a member of prominent ecclesiastical circles, Peter of Blois, articulated a programme of clerical conduct and episcopal duty in the shadow of the late twelfth century's most powerful symbol of radical reform – the martyred archbishop of Canterbury, Thomas Becket. Struggling to make ideal bishops out of Becket's less radical successors, Peter drew on ideals of wide-ranging provenance, including some taken from radical reformers, to construct a model of episcopal duty that worked within the interrelated contexts of a rising feudal monarchy in England and a new self-perception among the literate clergy.

Taken together, these approaches present three figures who were, at once, profoundly aware of the larger intellectual and institutional issues of ecclesiastical reform literature and movements of reform yet also acutely sensitive to the local impact of reform on their careers and communities. All three of these case-studies also blur the neat dichotomies to which the history of medieval ecclesiastical reform can so easily be reduced, insisting that the ideals of reform gained their shape and meaning not through their passive acceptance but by being brought into dialogue with and being challenged by individual minds and local milieus.

It is only proper to note, by way of introduction, that the authors of these three articles share, in addition to their concern with medieval ecclesiastical reform, a common *Doktorvater*, Gerard E. Caspary of the University of California at Berkeley. The work presented here stems ultimately from dissertation research conducted under his care and guidance. Through his own work on medieval exegesis and political theology he has provided all scholars of the medieval church with challenging new avenues for study, and through his erudition and vigilant criticisms he has endowed the present articles with much of whatever value or insight they might offer. The authors dedicate the fruits of these reflections to him with admiration and affection.

7a

Polemic, Apathy, and Authorial Initiative in Gregorian Rome: The Curious Case of Bruno of Segni

William L. North

One of the most distinctive and important features of the period commonly called the Investiture Controversy was the emergence of a sizeable and sophisticated public literature of controversy in which contemporaries of various ideological stripes skilfully deployed authorities and arguments while undermining those of opponents with evidence, analysis or, if all else failed, invective, satire, and scandalous rumor.[1] Starting with a trickle and growing in the 1070s, 1080s, and 1090s to flood-like proportions, the letters, pamphlets, collections of authorities, and historical and biographical works designed to attack or to defend, to explain or to criticize, seem to have filled all corners of society with heated discussion of weighty issues of politics and religion. Whether it be Sigebert of Gembloux's weaving women and *engagés* craftsmen discussing a papal call for clerical celibacy[2] or Manegold of Lautenbach's pamhleteers stuffing samizdat copies of Wenrich of Trier's letter to (against?) Pope Gregory VII into the hands of people passing by in town squares and back alleys,[3] polemical literature circulated to inform and woo the ignorant and the uncertain, to exhort and educate the faithful, and to blacken the opponent in the minds of members of communities, secular and religious, across Europe.

---

[1] C. Mirbt, *Die Publizistik im Zeitalter Gregors VII* (Leipzig, 1894) remains the most comprehensive survey of the polemical literature of this period; see esp. 4–6 and 611–29 for Mirbt's conception of 'publizistische Literatur' and its dominant characteristics. See also the more recent synthetic discussions of K. Leyser, 'The Polemics of the Papal Revolution', *Trends in Medieval Political Thought*, ed. B. Smalley (Oxford, 1952), 42–64 (repr. in idem, *Medieval Germany and Its Neighbors, 900–1250* (London, 1982), 138–61); and I.S. Robinson, *Authority and Resistance in the Investiture Contest: The Polemical Literature of the Late Eleventh Century* (Manchester, 1978).

[2] *Epistola cuiusdam adversus laicorum in presbyteros coniugatos contumeliam*, ed. E. Sackur, M.G.H., *Libelli de Lite*, ii (Hannover, 1892), 437–48, at 438 ll. 4–13; new edn., E. Frauenknecht, in idem, *Die Verteidigung der Priesterehe in der Reformzeit*, M.G.H., Texte und Studien, 16 (Hannover, 1997), 219–39, at 219 ll. 13–220 l. 4.

[3] *Liber ad Gebhardum*, ed. K. Francke, M.G.H., *Libelli de Lite*, i (Hannover, 1891), 308–430, at 311 ll. 13–20. The letter of Wenrich of Trier, written *c.* 1080 ostensibly by Dietrich, bishop of Verdun, outlined the accusations being made against Gregory VII and asked the pope to exculpate himself so that he, Dietrich, might be entirely loyal to and confident in him. On these texts, see the sensitive comments of Robinson, *Authority and Resistance*, 154–6.

The characteristics, and indeed the very existence, of this body of polemical literature have led scholars frequently to understand these conflicts in terms of 'parties' or 'factions', each populated by passionate and talented adherents prepared to suffer, to die, and certainly to write for the cause. Nowhere has the tendency to see a coherent ideological 'party line' and centrally directed action been stronger than in scholarly discussions of the circle of reformers who assembled around Pope Gregory VII in Rome and their abundant production of texts, polemical and canonical, in the service of the papacy and ecclesiastical reform. Yet such a tendency, although certainly legitimate to an extent, risks transforming what was, it will be argued, a flexible and intellectually diverse and dynamic human community – the Roman curia – into a rigid ideological and institutional monolith. Through the sustained analysis of two pieces of contemporary evidence by Bishop Bruno of Segni that have hitherto been overlooked in the scholarship on the 'Gregorian party' in Rome, the following discussion hopes to reveal at once the desire for coherent and directed ideological action within Gregory VII's curia and the possibilities within that institutional setting for apathy, diversity of opinion and approach, and even resistance.

Charismatic, outspoken, visionary, indefatigable – Hildebrand or Pope Gregory VII (1073–85) has long been viewed as a kind of polemical muse, urging and inspiring, if not actually writing, many of the treatises and canon law collections that most clearly articulated principles of ecclesiastical reform or papal authority before, during, and even after his pontificate.[4] There is good reason for this reputation. Early in his Roman career, Gregory VII, then archdeacon Hildebrand, had already made clear to contemporaries that he possessed a unique capacity to envision the intellectual resources necessary to implement central elements of ecclesiastical reform. Thus, when reporting to Hildebrand in December of 1059 on the progress of his legatine visit to Milan, Peter Damian recalled the archdeacon's precocious and repeated exhortation to compile from his reading of canonical texts and Church Fathers a collection of authorities that would fortify the ecclesiastical supremacy of the Apostolic See. It had been an exhortation to which he had initially turned a disdainful and uncomprehending ear.

Minutely considering this matter, as was your custom, you frequently asked me on many occasions . . . that as I read through the decrees and statutes of the Roman pontiffs, I should thoughtfully excerpt from here and there whatever was seen to pertain especially to the authority of the Apostolic See, and assemble them all in a small volume as a new collection. I neglected your pressing request, thinking it to be of little importance and judging it to be superfluous rather than necessary.[5]

---

[4] On Gregory VII, see H.E.J. Cowdrey, *Pope Gregory VII, 1073–1085* (Oxford, 1998), and Uta-Renate Blumenthal, *Gregor VII: Papst zwischen Canossa und Kirchenreform* (Darmstadt, 2001), each with a comprehensive bibliography.

[5] *Die Briefe des Petrus Damiani*, 65 (December, 1059), ed. K. Reindel, M.G.H., *Die Briefe der deutschen Kaiserzeit*, 4:2 (Munich, 1988), 228–47, at 229 ll. 10–230 l. 3 (= *The Letters of Peter Damian*, trans. O. Blum, The Fathers of the Church, Mediaeval Continuation, 3 (Washington, DC, 1992), 25 c. 2).

Coming early in the history of the reform papacy, Peter Damian's words have long been regarded as valuable testimony for Hildebrand/Gregory VII's long-standing commitment to defining and asserting the rights of the Roman church using canon law.[6] What has perhaps been less well noted is that this incident also reveals that, from early on, Hildebrand recognized more clearly than many contemporaries that the reformers' agenda, and particularly the increasingly vigorous assertion of Roman primacy within Christendom, would require the production of new texts in order to be successful in the long run. Advancing reform and ecclesiastical order, in other words, was not simply a matter of spurring the right kinds of action but was seen to demand the composition and dissemination of the right kinds of texts. In this regard Gregory embodied the pragmatic idealism of the Carolingian reformers who had long before recognized that the foundation of Christian unity rested upon a solid foundation of shared texts. Indeed, it was to their canonical compilations and pastoral works that eleventh-century writers were often indebted.[7]

Sketched vividly by Peter Damian in the 1050s, the image of Hildebrand as a textual impresario reappears in an older Hildebrand, now Pope Gregory VII, in the descriptive *incipit* prefacing the twelfth-century copy of the first seven books of Bishop Anselm of Lucca's *Collectio canonum* contained in MS. Vat. Barberini 535. The text reads: 'Here begins an authentic and succinct collection of rules and opinions of the holy fathers and authoritative councils made at the time of the most holy Pope Gregory VII by the blessed Anselm, bishop of Lucca, the diligent disciple and imitator of the one at whose order and command he completed this work'.[8] Although the meaning and ultimate reliability of this text remain contested,[9] scholars agree that its assertion of Gregory's involvement in the final production of the collection offers reliable evidence at the very least for contemporaries' larger perception of the pope's active role in the production of reform texts. In essence, even if Gregory VII did not, in fact, commission the collection, in the eyes of contemporaries, it was something that they could have imagined him doing.

Interestingly, though not surprisingly, Gregory's role as patron and *spiritus*

---

6   In particular, the Collection in 74 Titles has long been viewed – though not by all scholars – as the fulfillment of Hildebrand's desire for a canonical collection that emphasized Roman authority; see the literature cited in Reindel, 230–31 n. 8.

7   For an overview of the production of texts as a dimension of Carolingian ecclesiastical reform, see the excellent study of Rosamond McKitterick, *The Frankish Church and the Carolingian Reforms, 789–895*, Royal Historical Society Studies in History, 2 (London, 1977).

8   Città del Vaticano, Bibliotheca Apostolica Vaticana, MS. Barberini lat. 535, fol. 14v: 'Incipit authentica et compendiosa collectio regularum et sententiarum sanctorum patrum et auctorabilium conciliorum facta tempore VII. Gregorii sanctissimi papae a beato Anselmo Lucensi episcopo eius diligenti imitatore et discipulo, cuius iussione et precepto desiderante consummavit hoc opus'; ed. F. Thaner, *Anselmi episcopi Lucensis Collectio canonum una cum collectione minore* (Innsbruck, 1906, 1915), 2.

9   For the most recent discussion of this text and its problems, see K. Cushing, *Papacy and Law in the Gregorian Revolution: The Canonistic Work of Anselm of Lucca* (Oxford, 1998), 7 n. 27; see also Robinson, *Authority and Resistance*, 43–4 and n. 179.

rector of canonical and polemical projects finds its strongest confirmation in the polemics written by former members of Gregory's own curia who had broken with the pope in 1084.[10] In Wido of Ferrara's *De scismate Hildebrandi* (composed probably sometime between 1085 and 1100), for example, this former member of Gregory's inner circle deployed a range of canonical authorities that paralleled those that were being collected at the same time by Cardinal Deusdedit in Rome, a fact that clearly suggests, as I.S. Robinson noted long ago, that investigation into canonical authorities related to reform was not just the occupation of an isolated few but the collective concern of the curia more generally.[11] In another *libellus* that has been ascribed to Beno, cardinal priest of the church of Sts Martin and Sylvester and was clearly written during Urban II's pontificate, Gregory and 'his disciples' Anselm of Lucca, Deusdedit, and 'Turbanus' (Odo, bishop of Ostia and later Pope Urban II) were portrayed ransacking the Lateran archives and the *turris cartularia* near the Arch of Titus for textual booty and then cutting up authentic canons to suit their own tastes and pasting them together in *compilationes fraudulentes*.[12] Recurring repeatedly in these tracts, the phrase *Hildebrandus et eius discipuli* was clearly intended to make the reader see in the Rome of Gregory VII a closed, and ultimately distorted, intellectual world in which pope and loyal entourage were marching to their damnation in ideological and literary lockstep. Within such a smoothly functioning, highly energized propaganda machine, Beno implied, dissent and the honest interpretation of texts was impossible. Loyalty to the truth of the Gospel and the Fathers could mean only one thing: flight.

While the tracts of the schismatic cardinals offer the reader, at best, a hostile caricature of the kinds of social and intellectual relationships available within the Roman curia, the underlying image of curial consensus and collaboration to achieve the pope's own ideals has been an often reflexive assumption. Over the last decades, however, scholars have come increasingly to question the existence of this consensus as they have uncovered distinct differences in ideology and emphasis among the cardinalate. Deusdedit, in particular, has proven to be a far more complex and controversial figure than previously imagined. For example, in a series of recent studies on Deusdedit's *Collectio canonum*, which was dedicated to Pope Victor III in 1087,[13] Uta-Renate Blumenthal has made clear that this cardinal, one of the *discipuli Hildebrandi*, actually used his

---

[10] For the structure and composition of the curia and the careers of its members at this time, see R. Hüls, *Kardinäle, Klerus und Kirchen Roms, 1049–1130*, Bibliothek des Deutschen Historischen Instituts in Rom, 48 (Tübingen, 1977), passim.

[11] Ed. R. Wilmans, revised E. Dümmler, M.G.H., *Libelli de Lite*, i (Hannover, 1891), 529–67. See the discussion in Robinson, *Authority and Resistance*, 46–7 with further literature.

[12] *Benonis aliorumque cardinalium scripta*, 3, ed. K. Francke, M.G.H., *Libelli de Lite*, ii (Hannover, 1892), 380–403, at 399 c. 13 ll. 14–15. The author goes on to accuse Hildebrand and his disciples of being 'perversores scripturarum' (400, c. 15 l. 1). On these texts, see the insightful analysis of I.S. Robinson, *Authority and Resistance*, 46–9.

[13] *Die Kanonessammlung des Kardinals Deusdedit*, ed. V. Wolf von Glanvell (Paderborn, 1905; Aalen, 1967).

Collectio to articulate and defend an ecclesiology of the Roman church dramatically different from that held by Pope Gregory VII himself, one that stressed the power and authority of the Roman church as a whole rather than that of the person of the pope.[14] Likewise, the brief record of a *'conventus'* of Roman clergy in 1082 that met to discuss the legality of mortgaging church property to pay for mercenaries to fight Wibert of Ravenna, has revealed the presence of opinions within the curia that seem to have been strongly at odds with those of the pope himself.[15] Thus, the members of Gregory's curia have come to be understood less as *discipuli Hildebrandi* (or *Gregorii*) than as clerics zealous to defend and advance their own ecclesiologies and agendas for reform. No longer master of a coherent Roman 'school' of reform easily encouraging his 'students' to undertake literary projects in the service of reform, Gregory VII has come to seem but one voice, albeit a powerful and loud one, trying, at times desperately, to bring into harmony the discordant choir of cardinals each singing his own song.[16]

In developing these distinct understandings of the intellectual and personal dynamics of the Gregorian curia, scholars have consistently, oddly, excluded from consideration the works of one long-standing member of the Roman curial circle: Bruno, bishop of the small Latian diocese of Segni south of Rome and member of the Roman curia from 1078/79 to his death in 1123. This is unfortunate because, although his extensive literary corpus reveals much about the interests and sensibilities operative among Roman reforms, two of his works – the *Life of Leo IX* that prefaces his *libellus de simoniacis* in one manuscript[17]

---

14 'Fälschungen bei Kanonisten der Kirchenreform des 11. Jahrhunderts', *Fälschungen im Mittelalter*, M.G.H., *Schriften*, 33:2 (Hannover, 1988), 241–62; 'Rom in der Kanonistik', *Rom in hohen Mittelalter: Studien zu den Romvorstellungen und zur Rompolitik vom 10. bis zum 12. Jahrhundert*, ed. B. Schimmelpfennig and L. Schmugge (Sigmaringen, 1992), 29–39; and 'History and Tradition in Eleventh-Century Rome', *The Catholic Historical Review*, 79 (1993), 185–96; all repr. in *Papal Reform and Canon Law in the 11th and 12th Centuries*, Collected Studies Series, 618 (Aldershot, 1998), Studies IV, V, & VI respectively. It should be noted that I.S. Robinson, *Authority and Resistance*, 49, had already sketched Deusdedit's distinctive ecclesiological stance and its implications for ideological fissures within Gregory's curia.

15 For the edition of the brief report of this meeting and commentary, see Z. Zafarana, 'Sul conventus del Clero Romano nel maggio 1082', *Studi Medievali*, 3rd ser., 7 (1966), 399–403. For recent interpretations, see Robinson, *Authority and Resistance*, 45, and more optimistically, Blumenthal, *Gregor VII*, 322, and Cowdrey, *Gregory VII*, 321–6.

16 In his new study of Gregory VII, Cowdrey, *Gregory VII*, 314–30, esp. 320–26, likewise emphasizes the Roman clergy as a community of diverse interests and opinions, though one fundamentally united in their loyalty to Gregory, at least prior to 1084.

17 Ed. E. Sackur, M.G.H., *Libelli de Lite*, ii (Hannover, 1892), 543–52; text of the life of Leo at 544–54, cc. 2–9. On this text see the full study of B. Gigalski, *Bruno, Bischof von Segni, Abt von Monte-cassino (1049–1123): Sein Leben und seine Schriften. Ein Beitrag zur Kirchengeschichte im Zeitalter des Investiturstreits*, Kirchengeschichtliche Studien, 3:4 (Münster, 1898), 155–84; and the summary discussion with more recent bibliography in R. Grégoire, *Bruno de Segni: Exégète médiévale et théologien monastique*, Studi del Centro Italiano di studi sull'alto medioevo, 3 (Spoleto, 1965), 108–10.

and his preface to his *Expositio in Isaiam*[18] – shed an unusually penetrating light on the intellectual and literary dynamics of Gregory VII's curia.

Born *c.* 1045 in Asti,[19] Bruno probably gained his clerical training in one of the cathedral schools of northern Italy in the 1060s. A member of the cathedral canonry of Siena prior to his arrival in Rome in 1078/9, Bruno owed his ascent to the episcopacy of Segni a short time later to both Gregory VII's active patronage and his own abilities as a preacher and Biblical exegete. From the outset of his episcopate, Bruno played an active role in the Roman curia. He participated in the above-mentioned '*conventus*' of Roman clergy in 1082 and suffered with it during the periods of duress and exile brought on by King Henry IV's presence in Italy from 1081 to 1084. Yet in his literary endeavors, it was to the explication of the Bible rather than to the excavation and organization of canon law or the elaboration of pro-reform polemics that Bruno devoted the majority of his time and attention. Whence his general neglect in the scholarship on the 'Gregorian reform' circle.[20] For although attempts have been made to fit his exegesis into a polemical mold, he remains in the eyes of most scholars a Gregorian who was, in the words one of his most recent students, 'more concerned to nourish the soul than to ignite a quarrel',[21] and consequently a personality of little interest in assessing the dynamics of what now seems to have been a singularly assertive and quarrelsome lot – Gregory VII and his curia.

Scholarly neglect of Bruno's 'life' of Leo IX, though equally unfortunate, is more explicable. Drawing as it did on contemporary accounts of Leo IX, like that of Libuin, subdeacon of the Roman church[22] and offering little new information on the first reform pope, Bruno's brief panegyric on Leo IX has held little interest for scholars of that pope. Indeed, composed probably around 1094/5, Bruno's 'life' of Pope Leo IX was, in fact, more a brief commemoration of the pope intended for use in liturgy than a fully fledged hagiography, such as had been produced by a close companion and Lotharingian contemporary of Leo IX in the 1050s.[23] The real importance of Bruno's work, however, lies not so

---

[18] The text of the preface, long believed to be lost, was discovered and edited by A. Amelli, *S. Bruno di Segni, Gregorio VII ed Enrico IV dal 1081 al 1083 in Roma illustrati da un documento inedito della biblioteca capitolare di Verona* (Montecassino, 1903), text at 8–9.

[19] For the biographical sketch that follows, see Grégoire, 16–41, and Gigalski, 25–49. See also W. North, 'In the Shadows of Reform: Exegesis and the Formation of a Clerical Elite in the Works of Bruno, Bishop of Segni (1078/79–1123)', Ph.D. dissertation (University of California, Berkeley, 1998), 29–82.

[20] I.S. Robinson's article 'Political Allegory in the Biblical Exegesis of Bruno of Segni', *Recherches de théologie ancienne et médiévale*, 50 (1983), 69–98, is the exception that proves the rule.

[21] Grégoire, 332.

[22] Ed. J. Watterich in *Pontificum Romanorum . . . Vitae*, i (2 vols., Leipzig, 1862; repr. Aalen, 1966), 170–77.

[23] *La Vie du Pape Léon IX (Brunon, évêque de Toul)*, ed. M. Parisse and trans. M. Goullet, Les Classiques de l'Histoire de France au Moyen Age, 38 (Paris, 1997). Although the author of this life has been traditionally named 'Wibert', M. Parisse leaves the matter open in expectation of the new M.G.H. edition of the life by H.G. Krause.

much in what he relates about Leo IX himself as in what the bishop of Segni reveals to his audience about the origins of the text: that he had had no choice but to compose his panegyric of the pope because it had been divinely commanded by that pope himself. Woven together from Bruno's reminiscences, his *apologia* for his papal portrait vividly reveals a vibrant literary milieu within the curia, one even graced, perhaps, with a bit of humor. It is worth recounting at length.

[O]ne day this past Lenten season, when we were in Rome and had gathered together at the church, that truly venerable man, Bishop John of Tusculum, came up to me where I was standing and, in the presence of Hubald, that most religious fellow and bishop of Sabina, and certain others, said to me: *I have been sent to you as a messenger.* So I stood there, interested in what he wished to say to me. Then he said: *Pope Leo orders you to give him one hundred thousand solidi.* And I said: *What are you saying?* And he said: *I am telling you the truth; thus does he command you,* and then he began to recount to me what he had seen in order. *Last night when I was sleeping, the blessed Leo appeared to me in my dreams in his pontifical garb saying: 'Go and tell the bishop of Segni that he should give me one hundred thousand solidi.' And when I thought to myself that you are not so wealthy that you would be able to give him so much money, sensing my thoughts he said: 'Go and tell him to give me one hundred thousand or fifty thousand.' He commands this of you. Therefore attend to what you are going to answer him.*[24]

Initially stunned by the solidi-seeking phantasm, Bruno quickly applied interpretative skills honed by long years of analysing the Biblical text to discover the meaning of the vision and thereby confirm the precise nature of the oneiric Leo's words. He asked his episcopal interlocutor, John of Tusculum, whether the blessed Leo had ordered him specifically to give, to lend, or to pay back that money. When John responded: *No, it was 'to give'*, Bruno was relieved, remarking that it made a big difference whether one has to give something or to pay it back.[25] Had Leo said 'owed', Bruno would have known that he had somehow offended the venerable pope and would now have of necessity to render due satisfaction for the slight. And, indeed, Bruno knew several very good reasons why Leo might suddenly have appeared, demanding such satisfaction from him. As he related to his audience:

I recalled that his feast was formerly celebrated in our church, but because I behaved negligently, the entire feast had ceased [to be celebrated] there. May he have mercy on me because I recognize that I have sinned not a little in this.[26]

In addition to his failure to maintain Leo IX's liturgical feast in his own suburbican diocese since the late 1070s, Leo's demands also conjured in Bruno's memory another deed undone, another request unfulfilled: the explicit request of Pope Gregory VII himself for someone to commemorate Leo IX.

---

[24] *Libellus de simoniacis*, c. 9, 553, ll. 6–18.

[25] Ibid., ll. 19–22.

[26] Ibid., ll. 24–6.

Thus, amidst recounting Leo's miracles, many of which he claimed to have heard from Gregory personally, he recalled:

Sometimes when [Gregory] spoke about him to those of us listening, he would start to rebuke us, and especially me (or so I believed because he kept his eyes intent upon me) because we were allowing the deeds of the blessed Leo perish in silence and because we were not writing things which would be to the glory of the Roman church and [serve] as an example of humility to the many who listened. But because he poured out his words to no one in particular (*in commune*), no one wrote what he ordered to be written by all. Nor even now would I have written these things, if I had not been forced in a certain way to write them, as I shall make clear in what follows. May both popes have mercy on me, because I recognize that I have offended both in this.[27]

Bruno's eyewitness testimony has hitherto been completely neglected in the scholarship, perhaps because it was 'just a dream'.[28] Yet his evidence is of the greatest importance for our understanding of the the intellectual and literary dynamics of the Gregorian curia for several reasons. First, Bruno's first-hand recollection of Gregory VII's exhortation to members of the curia to write something – anything – commemorating Pope Leo IX resonates strikingly with Peter Damian's memory of the young Hildebrand's exhortation to compile a new collection of canons in support of Roman primacy. Bruno's text, in other words, offers historians explicit, first-hand, and friendly testimony which confirms that Gregory VII, like archdeacon Hildebrand of twenty or more years before, did, in fact, view the curia as a kind of scriptorium of reform, the task of which was to produce new texts – canonical, polemical, hagiographical – that could be put to use to further the project of reform and support or extend the authority of the Roman church.

Furthermore, Bruno's recollections offer valuable new evidence for a contemporary attempt to enact that most problematic of claims made by the *Dictatus papae*, item 23: 'That the Roman pontiff, if he has been canonically ordained, is indubitably made holy by the merits of St Peter.'[29] Moreover, these

---

[27] *Libellus de simoniacis*, c. 3, 548 ll. 33–43.

[28] This particular dream-vision has, to my knowledge, not been discussed in the scholarship on medieval dreaming, but for the importance of visions as a form of argument with Roman reform milieu see R. Pauler, 'Visionen als Propagandamittel der Anhänger Gregors VII', *Mediaevistik*, 7 (1994), 155–79. Whether this dream actually occurred to John of Tusculum is a tantalizing but ultimately unanswerable question. There is no reason to doubt, however, that John narrated such a dream to Bruno in the public context of the curia; indeed, through the circumstantiality of the narrative and his inclusion of eyewitnesses, Bruno offered his contemporary audience the opportunity to corroborate his story. I am grateful to Valerie Ramseyer of Wellesley College for pressing me on this point.

[29] *Das Register Gregors VII*, ii. 55a, ed. E. Caspar, M.G.H., *Epistolae Selectae*, 2:1 (Berlin, 1920; repr. Munich, 1990), 207: 'Quod Romanus pontifex, si canonice fuerit ordinatus, meritis beati Petri indubitanter efficitur sanctus testante sancto Ennodio Papiensi episcopo ei multis sanctis patribus fauentibus, sicut in decretis beati Symachi pape continetur'. On this *capitulum*, see W. Ullmann, 'Romanus Pontifex Indubitanter Efficitur Sanctus: Dictatus Papae 23 in Retrospect and Prospect', *Studi Gregoriani*, 6 (1959–61), 229–64. Ullmann, too, makes no use of the evidence offered by Bruno's testimony.

comments explicitly confirm H.E.J. Cowdrey's recent claim for the importance of Leo IX to Gregory VII as the exemplar of a reforming pope.[30]

At the same time, Bruno's memories bear witness to the fact that, although Gregory may have had a list of textual *desiderata*, he was not prepared to impose the 'life of Leo IX project' on any specific person. To be sure, Bruno's vivid recollection of Gregory's steely gaze falling upon him indicates that Gregory was not adverse to using subtler forms of persuasion to find 'volunteers' for his literary projects. Yet, the fact that Gregory was remembered to have rebuked the curia only in general and to have issued his command to write the 'life' *in commune* suggests that Gregory may have actively refrained from taking actions that might create a coercive intellectual atmosphere within the curia.

The specific language that Bruno used in his account of Gregory's explicit request for a papal *vita*, like Peter Damian's formulation of Hildebrand's earlier request for a canon collection, also cautions against drawing overly radical and static distinctions between the ecclesiologies of Gregory and those of his cardinals. The interests of the bishop of Rome and those of the Roman church were certainly not always in opposition; indeed, of all pontiffs, Leo IX had probably done most to make of the cardinalate a body of international importance and prestige.[31] Likewise, in his effort to stimulate action of some kind among his curia, Gregory VII may well have been prepared to recast his projects in terms acceptable to the cardinalate.[32] Far from seeking to use Leo IX's life as a narrow spotlight, which illuminated the pope but left the rest of the *ecclesia Romana* in darkness, Gregory is portrayed by Bruno as desiring instead a papal memorial that would shed a warm glow over the Roman church as a whole.[33] Bruno's narrative thereby calls into question the inherent tension so often assumed to exist between the supposedly papal ecclesiology of Gregory himself and the more ecclesial perspective of cardinals like Deusdedit.

For the historian of the Gregorian curia, however, the most important aspect of these reminiscences is perhaps Bruno's own profound apathy concerning the memory of the great reforming pope. By his own admission, prior to Pope Leo IX's ominous appearance in an episcopal colleague's dreams, he had never desired to write a life of the great pope and, indeed, very little active interest in

---

[30] Cowdrey, 25–6; 685–6. Cowdrey does not cite Bruno's explicit evidence for Gregory VII's devotion to Leo IX's cult.

[31] On which, see S. Kuttner, 'Cardinalis: The History of a Canonical Concept', *Traditio*, 3 (1945), 129–214, at 172–8.

[32] Bruno of Segni may, of course, have been adjusting the words of the dead Gregory VII to suit his own perspective or that of his fellow cardinals on the proper relationship between pope and Roman Church. Without further evidence, however, this question cannot be decided.

[33] *Libellus de simoniacis*, c. 3, 548 ll. 36–8: 'Qui [Gregorius papa] cum nobis audientibus aliquando de ipso loqueretur, coepit nos increpare et me precipue, ut michi uidebatur, siquidem in me oculos intentos habebat, quia beati Leonis facta scilentio (sic) perire pateremur, et quod ea non scriberemus quae Romanae aecclesiae ad gloriam et multis audientibus forent ad humilitatis exemplum.'

Leo IX himself. Far from being a *diligens imitator*[34] or *indefessus cooperator*[35] of Gregory VII like his near contemporary Anselm of Lucca, who was remembered to have zealously undertaken the various literary missions that Gregory enjoined upon him,[36] Bruno remained unmoved (at least to literary action) by the tales of Leo's sanctity evoked in Gregory's oft-repeated stories of the pope's exploits and resolutely idle before the pope's own direct and steely gaze and angrily earnest entreaties. Likewise, he let fall silent, in the highly charged ideological atmosphere of the late 1070s and 1080s, the liturgical commemoration of Leo IX that had apparently already been established in Segni when he had arrived as bishop in 1079. To be sure, he admitted to having sinned in this act of negligence; but this admission came only after over a decade of seemingly unrepentant neglect. Even when Bruno did write, he protested that he did so under compulsion and took every opportunity afforded by the ambiguities in the oneiric injunction to write less, not more, about this hero of reform.[37]

Why is Bruno's negligence and apathy significant? Does it signal the presence of a latent hostility within the curia to papal ambitions and initiatives, like that which some scholars have seen manifested in the '*conventus*' of 1082?[38] On the whole, it does not. To be sure, Bruno's lack of enthusiasm for papal hagiography now seems of a piece with his general lack of specific interest in the pope's position in his strongly ecclesiological exegesis.[39] Yet the real meaning of Bruno's sustained and, it should be remembered, papally recognized disinterest in the 'Leo IX project' lies in what it indicates about the actual intellectual atmosphere within Gregory VII's entourage. Although Pope Gregory was undoubtedly pleased by kindred spirits (or devoted followers) like Anselm of Lucca who took up his ideas and ran with them, Bruno's testimony cautions against assuming that Gregory VII demanded or expected intellectual conformity be the norm or that he viewed his curia as salaried propagandists, expected to write what they were told. That Bruno noted in passing that Pope Gregory never actually ordered any single person in the curia to undertake and complete the project in an effort to get it done stands as a counterweight to the evidence for clerical conformity offered by the schismatic cardinals and the prefatory

---

[34] See n. 8 above.

[35] Sigebert of Gembloux, *Liber de Scriptoribus Ecclesiasticis*, c. 161, *P.L.*, clx, col. 585A.

[36] See n. 8 above.

[37] See *Libellus de simoniacis*, c. 9, p. 553 ll. 25–45, where Bruno described his allegorical rationale, developed in conjunction with the clergy of Segni, for writing so brief an account of Pope Leo. In this context, Bruno's determination that Pope Leo did not claim that the bishop of Segni 'owed' him anything stands as an implicit claim to the legitimacy of his earlier decision not to write.

[38] See n. 14 above, especially the views of Robinson cited there.

[39] On which, see W. North, 'In the Shadows', 169–76, 363–6. It is as well not to overgeneralize Bruno's position. At one point in the life of Leo IX, Bruno implied that he was planning to compose a life of Gregory VII: 'Hic est enim Gregorius septimus papa, cuius prudentiam, constantiam et fortitudinem, cuius pugnas et labores enarrare alterius temporis et operis est.' (*Libellus de simoniacis*, c. 2, 548 ll. 13–14).

inscription in the Barberini MS. of Anselm's canonical collection.[40] Gregory's curia emerges from Bruno's text, in other words, as an intellectual milieu to which the pope did, in fact, turn for ideological and literary support of his reform agenda. Yet it was also one in which a range of individual perspectives, abilities, and interests was recognized and permitted. The simultaneous presence of Bruno's open antipathy (or at least apathy) for papal polemical projects and his unflagging loyalty to Gregory and his curial colleagues, in short, permits the historian to extend into the intellectual and literary sphere the conclusions recently reached by H.E.J. Cowdrey on Gregory's relations with the curia more generally: it was a rapport marked by flexibility and tolerance of difference and a high degree of personal loyalty to the pope.[41]

In sharp contrast to his apathy in the face of Gregory VII's desire for a written, perhaps polemical, monument to Pope Leo IX's memory, Bruno responded warmly when besieged by the requests of his curial brethren, and by Peter Damian's nephew, the cardinal deacon Damianus, in particular, for an exposition of that sweetest and happiest of Biblical books: the book of the prophet Isaiah.[42] Once again, time passed before Bruno fulfilled their urgent entreaties. Yet in this case, it was the press of pastoral business rather than lack of interest itself that slowed progress. For once trapped in Rome by Henry IV's seige of the city and immured within the Castel Sant'Angelo with his curial colleagues, Bruno happily embarked upon, not a life of Leo (which might be seen as the more pressing literary commission under the circumstances) but the oft-requested exegesis of the prophetic book:

And there [in the Castel Sant'Angelo] since I was very much at leisure and free from all worldly business, and since the venerable abbot Damian, one of the seven deacons of the sacred palace, had asked me, I trusted in Christ and, after working on it from Christmas through Easter, I finished it.[43]

When provided by King Henry IV with an unscheduled four-month sabbatical leave from his episcopal duties, Bruno thus chose to spend it not on polemic but on pastoral exegesis, that is to say, meeting the needs and desires of his local clerical community for Biblical edification and inspiration through commentary. His completion of the massive commentary[44] in just four brief months signals the congeniality of this literary undertaking to both his sensibilities and training.

Faced with such starkly contrasting responses to curial demands for new

---

[40] See above, pp. 5–6.

[41] Cowdrey, 321–9, esp. 325, where Cowdrey notes that inaction was also a frequently adopted strategy of the pope himself in his dealings with the Roman clergy.

[42] *S. Bruno di Segni*, 8: 'Rogatus multocies a fratribus meis, quatinus Ysaiae prophete librum eis exponerem, qui tante dulcedinis tante suavitatis tanteque iucunditatis est.'

[43] Ibid. This is not to say that elements of polemic, references to reform themes, or commentary on the contemporary struggle with the emperor do not find a place in the commentary (see I.S. Robinson, 'Political Allegory', 72–6), but it is important to recognize the larger spiritual/pastoral thrust of the project as a whole.

[44] *Commentarium in Isaiam*, ed. A. Amelli, Spicilegium Casinense, 3 (Montecassino, 1897).

texts, it would be easy to conclude that Bruno simply rejected the more global ideas and approach to reform envisioned by Gregory VII and typically embodied in polemic and canon law and contented himself instead with the traditional and introspective literary enterprise of Biblical exegesis. Yet the presence of curial colleagues demanding commentaries suggests, to the contrary, that neither Bruno nor Biblical exegesis was seen by contemporaries as marginal to the intellectual life of the curia. Indeed, the fact that Bruno's many exegetical commentaries frequently originated in the demands of his curial colleagues – his commentary on Isaiah was only the first of many examples – requires a sustained reconsideration of the principal intellectual ideals and objectives operative within Gregory's curia. To be sure, asserting the primacy of the Roman church and bishop within Christendom and advancing the reform policies on simony, clerical marriage, and lay investiture were crucial activities. Yet it is also important to keep in mind that these measures were understood by many, including Gregory himself, as the means to the greater end of improving the quality of the clergy and, by extension, the pastoral care of the Christian people.[45] When seen in this context, it is Gregory's own desire for works specifically intended to promote the authority of the Roman church that comes to seem a narrow and introverted endeavor, albeit an understandable and necessary one, as Peter Damian had learned in Milan long before. Bruno, in contrast, preferred even at the outset of his episcopate to spend what free time he had on providing his colleagues and his own clergy with scriptural exegesis, the lifeblood of good preaching and the inspiration for good living.

It is within this broader context of curial interest in improving clerical education and thereby promoting the pastoral care of the laity that the canonical collection known as the *Breviarium* compiled by Bruno's contemporary and colleague Atto, cardinal priest of San Marco and member of Gregory's curia,[46] attains its full significance. Far from having in mind the global audience that Hildebrand intended for Damian's collection of authorities, Atto had a more limited, local purpose in assembling his collection: to remedy, if only a little, the egregious ignorance and incompetence of his clergy in matters essential to the successful performance of their pastoral responsibilities. Thus, he remarks:

I know, most beloved brothers, that there are two reasons for your ignorance. One is that the unhealthiness of the location [Rome] does not allow strangers to live here who could teach you. The second is that poverty does not let you depart for other places where you

---

[45] This point has been recently made by Cowdrey, 511. On the wider connections between clerical reform, papal reform, and the renewal of Christian life, see J. Laudage, *Priesterbild und Reformpapsttum im 11. Jahrhundert*, Beihefte zum Archiv für Kulturgeschichte, 22 (Cologne–Vienna, 1984); for the role of exegesis in clerical reform, see W. North, 'In the Shadows of Reform', 181–306.

[46] On Atto and his *Breviarium* (preserved in MS. Vat. lat. 586 fols. 91r–124r), see L. Kéry, *Canonical Collections of the Early Middle Ages (ca. 400–1140): A Bibliographical Guide to the Manuscripts and Literature*, History of Medieval Canon Law, 1 (Washington, DC, 1999), 233–4 with further literature. Atto was also one of the participants at the 'conventus' of 1082, and it is at the end of the MS. of his *Breviarium* (fol. 125v) that the report of the assembly is preserved.

could learn. As a result of such causes, it happened that an apocryphal Roman penitential was contrived, in an unlearned style, so that those who do not know the authentic canons and do not know letters rely on these fables. And so with such confidence they lay hold of the sacerdotal office for which they are not fit and as blind leaders of the blind, they and their followers fall into the ditch. . . . And therefore, because such confusion has arisen, and since you do not know what to reject and what to keep from among these things, I was urged by you to gather from the sacred canons a kind of breviary which would be pertinent for giving penances and settling cases.[47]

Placed, significantly, immediately following a contemporary copy of Gregory the Great's *Pastoral Rule*, Atto's *Breviarium* had pastoral care, not papal primacy, at its heart, just as did Bruno's exegesis.

The vivid portraits of apathy and activity within Gregory VII's curia offered by Bruno's works challenge scholars to move beyond models that characterize the Gregorian curia as either ideologically homogenous or riven by discord. Instead these texts argue for the existence of a much more complex, shifting, and subtle intellectual milieu at the curia, a milieu in which differences in intellectual and literary ability, inclination, and ideological emphasis were recognized and could coexist, provided that there remained a fundamental loyalty to Gregory VII himself. Bruno's texts also bear witness to contemporary perceptions of the curia's role as a key literary milieu within the wider reform movement and to Gregory VII's own significant attempts to shape its agenda. At the same time, Bruno's testimony clearly indicates that polemic and canon law on behalf of the authority of pope or Roman church were but two dimensions of a much more multi-faceted understanding of the needs and aims of ecclesiastical reform, an understanding rooted ultimately in the demands of pastoral care.[48]

---

[47] Ed. A. Mai, in *Scriptorum veterum nova collectio e vaticanis codicibus edita*, vi (Rome, 1832), 60.

[48] I am currently working on a complete study of the significance of Bruno's *Life of Leo IX* and *Libellus de simoniacis* in the context of Urban II's pontificate.

7b

Principled Passion or Ironic Detachment?
The Gregorian Reform as Experienced
by Guibert of Nogent

Jay Rubenstein

In his chatty, introspective, and occasionally haunting memoirs, written in 1115, Guibert of Nogent frequently touches on the theme of church reform. Guibert's opinions about reform, however, have not received the attention they merit, either from students of Guibert's life or from historians of reform. Possibly his opinions have seemed too obvious. Guibert usually comes across clearly as an impassioned, if not bigoted, advocate of Gregorian ideals. According to John Benton, Guibert 'was a reformer at heart,' differing from Gregory VII only in the obscurity of his office and in the cowardice of his convictions.[1] For Benton, Guibert's reformist passions dovetail with his neuroses, his obsession with the creation of a church purified of any secular – in fact, sexual – influence. Georges Duby finds in Guibert's hatred of sex evidence of his acceptance of the church's broader attempt in the eleventh and twelfth centuries to control marriage.[2] R.I. Moore, in a perceptive character analysis of Guibert, hears in Guibert's condemnations of simony one of the monk's most prominent character flaws: his insistence that the corruption of the church and world serves only to confirm in him a belief in his own purity.[3] All of these analyses grow out of what seems to me a faulty assumption: that Guibert was a reformer, that he was committed to Gregorian goals, or else that he believed Gregorian ideals remotely attainable. His relationship to the reform movement was, I will suggest, an ambivalent one. He found the goals of reform – the enforcement of clerical celibacy and, in particular, the eradication of simony – neither exhilarating nor compelling but at best profoundly troubling.

This statement seems at first untenable, for Guibert filled his memoirs, or *Monodies*, with numerous sobering lessons about the deadly influences of sex and money on the religious life. Guibert notes with distaste, for example, that Bishop Enguerrand of Laon, upon assuming his office, gave King Philip I an enormous number of gifts – an act of simony which his successors had all been

---

[1] John Benton, *Self and Society in Medieval France* (Toronto, 1970), 24.
[2] Georges Duby, *The Knight, the Lady, and the Priest*, trans. Barbara Bray (Chicago, 1983), 152.
[3] R.I. Moore, 'Guibert of Nogent and his World', *Studies in Medieval History presented to R.H.C. Davis*, ed. Henry Mayr-Harting and R.I. Moore (London, 1985), 115–17.

forced to follow.[4] Bishop Gaudry, the colorful villain of Book Three of the *Mon-odies*, similarly attains office through money's influence. According to Guibert, clerics were misled into supporting his candidacy by the hope of getting rich.[5] On a simpler level Guibert tells the story of a monk who had hidden away a little stolen cash and was struck dead as a result. The effects of the tainted silver did not end there. A servant of the monk hid the same money in a child's crib, exposing the infant to attack from a group of demons disguised as wild dogs.[6]

These stories and others like them do reveal a mind sensitive to problems associated with money, but they do not necessarily indicate a principled adherence to the Gregorian reform. Enguerrand's simony is a problem for Guibert not because he handles money but mainly because he places the financial well-being of his church in jeopardy. Gaudry, similarly, is not a simoniac in that he is out to bribe the king to obtain office. He instead buys the loyalty of fellow clerics. Finally, the monk in the story above committed no simony at all, which is to say he did not pay money for ecclesiastical office. He oversaw a road-building project and kept the leftover funds for himself, thus depriving his church of its revenue. For Guibert the abbot, the lesson in these stories is not how secular leaders and secular influence can corrupt the church; it is more simply not to put your church's finances at risk. For Guibert the moralist, the lesson in these stories is how the emotion greed can overwhelm the soul's rational faculties. We see these moralizing tendencies also in Guibert's discussion of Manasses, the simoniac archbishop of Reims. Gregory VII deposed Manasses in 1080, as Guibert reports. The key issues from a Roman perspective were Manasses's disobedience to Gregory VII and to his legate Hugh of Die. But in Guibert's analysis simony and disobedience to the papal will would count as only minor examples of his 'shameless and stupid behavior' – behavior which reached its climax when he attempted to rob his church of its treasure by force of arms. The local people, lay and clerical, finally drove him forcibly from the city.[7] Again for Guibert the key point is not an act of simony but rather how a mind overwhelmed by greed can put its church's finances and treasury in jeopardy.

When Guibert does discuss the policies and politics of reform, his seemingly clear and direct opinions upon inspection sound a little more equivocal. In his crusade chronicle, written in 1108, he remarks with apparent disbelief on how the German people have been in a state of continuous rebellion against the pope, preferring perpetual excommunication to obedience. In the same passage he tells of a debate between himself and an archdeacon of the church of Mainz. The archdeacon apparently described the French and their king as indolent because they had recently allowed Pope Paschal II to travel unmolested about their kingdom. Guibert responded with a spirited defense of the Frankish people,

---

4   Guibert of Nogent, *Monodies*, iii, 3, 272–4.
5   Guibert, *Monodies*, iii, 4, 280–2.
6   Guibert, *Monodies*, i, 26, 200–6.
7   Guibert, *Monodies*, i, 11, 62–4. On the relations of Manasses to the reform papacy, see H.E.J. Cowdrey, *Gregory VII, 1073–1085* (Oxford, 1999), 375–88.

pointing explicitly to their role in the crusade. 'If they had not been present there restraining by their lively wits and unfailing strength the barbarity of foreign peoples from all about, there certainly would have been little enough help from you German lot, whose name was barely heard there!'[8] Whether Guibert bothered to defend Paschal II with similar vigor he does not say. This was the same Paschal II whom historians remember for having offered to surrender to Henry V all *regalia* held by German bishops and to transform these bishops from wealthy magnates into simple pastors.[9] This was also the same Paschal II whose court Guibert had attended and spoke at during the pope's visit to France in 1107. Guibert, however, did not remember Paschal as a reform idealist. On the contrary, money flowed freely at the papal court. Cardinals prowled around the papal throne eagerly seeking out bribes. The pope himself in Guibert's account comes off as a sort of amiable dunce, manipulated by his advisors and not really concerned with getting to the substance of the question before him: whether the rich but corrupt Gaudry should be confirmed as bishop of Laon.[10] It is worth noting that Guibert himself was carrying twenty pounds of silver as bribe money at the time and does not even pause to blush over the fact. Again, it is not money's polluted touch that raises Guibert's ire but rather the excessive greed that money inspires in those around him.

The outcome of Guibert's time at the papal court reveals further that, for him, corruption within the church did not confine itself to material money. After Guibert has successfully argued Gaudry's case – whether he actually bribed any of the cardinals he does not say – the pope's men sent to Guibert an emissary named Peter, a Cluniac monk. Peter informed Guibert that because Paschal II had now given support to Gaudry, the pope expected in turn to receive appropriate support from the new bishop. Paschal was probably hoping for assistance in his ongoing political struggles that had grown out of the issue of reform. 'And so honey coats the lid of a poisoned cup!' Guibert exclaims. 'For what could be better that to obey the commands of the pope? And what could be worse than to pay men for what is a blessing of God?'[11] What Guibert describes here is an ordinary exchange of political favors. Whether money was involved, the consecration of a bishop has grown out of a political transaction, one that differs hardly at all from an exchange involving money. Paschal II accepted a corrupt man as bishop in return for his help in rooting out corruption. Political blackmail and ecclesiastical purity join together in an ironic, if not perverse, alliance.

Guibert treats one other prominent figure from the reform movement directly in his *Monodies*, Abbot Desiderius of Montecassino. Desiderius, of course, was

---

8   Guibert, *Dei gesta per Francos*, ed. R.B.C. Huygens, *Corpus Christianorum Continuatio Medievalis* 127A (Turnholt, 1996), 108–9.
9   Uta-Renate Blumenthal, *The Investiture Controversy: Church and Monarchy from the Ninth to the Twelfth Century* (Philadelphia, 1988), 167–71.
10 Guibert, *Monodies*, iii, 4, 288–92.
11 'Ecce mel illitum per ora viosi pocduli. Quid enim melius quam papae obtemperare praeceptis? Quis pejus quam pro indulta Dei gratia hominibus?'; *Monodies*, iii, 4, 292.

Gregory VII's eventual successor as Pope Victor III, and as H.E.J. Cowdrey has demonstrated, Desiderius and his church were among the reform papacy's most notable partners during the eleventh century.[12] So what does Guibert tell us about Desiderius? According to a rumor picked up from a Montecassino monk, Desiderius purchased the papacy through money stolen from St Benedict. His foul heart caused him to collapse during his ordination. St Benedict later visited him in a dream and attacked him for robbing his church in order to gain higher office – the worst sin again is not the introduction of money into ecclesiastical affairs but doing harm to one's church. The dream left Desiderius so shaken that he abandoned the papacy, returned to Montecassino, and eventually resumed his old abbacy a year later.[13] The story is so defamatory and inflammatory that Guibert's first monastic editor, Luc d'Achery, seems deliberately to have omitted it from his first edition of Guibert's complete works.[14] The story is also hopelessly garbled. According to Cowdrey, the election of Desiderius as pope is 'one of the most obscure subjects in the history of the medieval papacy.'[15] Still, we can safely say that Guibert's source badly mangled the details. In fact, Desiderius was elected reluctantly as pope in 1086, he did not fully accept the results of his election until 1087, and he died four months later, as pope, while staying at his monastery. Guibert gives no indication that he was aware of Desiderius's connection to Gregory VII. What this story in particular tells us about Guibert's attitude towards reform, therefore, is thus by no means clear. The Montecassino monk, on the other hand, almost certainly did know his church's recent history and Desiderius's place within it. The story then at least suggests that Guibert was not the only person who delighted in repeating malicious gossip and in pointing out the hypocrisy of the righteous men who had set out to purify ecclesiastical practice.

Individual reformers thus do not come off well when Guibert writes about them. What about the reform as a whole? Guibert refers to it in the abstract for the first time in his *Monodies* when he describes how, during his childhood, his family had attempted to procure for him ecclesiastical office. At that time, Guibert writes, the papacy had inaugurated a new campaign to enforce clerical celibacy, a campaign carried out by, to use Guibert's language, a mob of zealots. They are driven by a rage, *rabies*, which burns, *aestuabat*, within them.[16] These

---

[12] H.E.J. Cowdrey, *The Age of Abbot Desiderius* (Oxford, 1983), 71–88.

[13] Guibert, *Monodies*, iii, 19, 456–8.

[14] The first edition of Guibert's complete works was edited by Luc d'Achery, *Venerabilis Guiberti abbatis B. Mariae de Novigento opera omnia* (Paris, 1651). The anecdote about Desiderius is one of four that d'Achery omitted.

[15] Cowdrey, *Abbot Desiderius*, 177. More generally on the circumstances of his election as Victor III and the events of his papacy, 185–213.

[16] My translation here is stronger than that adopted by either Archambault or Labande, but seems to me fully justified by the Latin: 'Erat, ea tempestate, nova super uxoratis presbyteris apostolicae sedis invectio; unde et vulgi clericos zelantis tanta adversus eos rabies aestuabat'; *Monodies*, i, 7, 42–4. 'There was at this time a new decree from the Apostolic See against married priests; as a result such a maddess burned against these people among a mob zealous for its clergy.' *Vulgus* for Guibert almost always carries extremely negative connotations. Labande translates: 'Il en

reformers – lay and ecclesiastical – are slaves to irrational passions comparable to the ones that made their simoniacal counterparts helplessly pant over money. Guibert does, in this passage, roundly criticize his family for their attempt to buy a position for him. It would be difficult, however, to build a case for Guibert having a reformist agenda around that criticism. To tell the story in more detail: one of Guibert's cousins, a man of boundless sexual appetite, used his influence over the lord of a castle to force a priest out of office, in order that young Guibert might be inserted into the man's place. The priest immediately gained sympathy, Guibert says, from an audience sensitive to the appearances of simony – which in this case was obviously the correct conclusion for reform-minded churchmen to draw. What makes the issue more complicated is the justification used for driving this priest from office: he was married.[17] In other words, Guibert's family risked a charge of simony in order to enforce celibacy. The priest and his supporters, on the other hand, sacrificed celibacy in order to stamp out simony.

This story is notably the only time when Guibert discusses what must have been the most common form of nicolaism in the eleventh century. That is to say, the priest has one wife. Sexually polluted characters tend otherwise to be monsters. Consider, for example, the monk who sacrifices some sperm to the devil in order to learn the powers of black magic, takes a nun as a lover, and eventually disguises her as a dog in order to hide the affair from one of his brethren.[18] The priest in the earlier story, however, has an otherwise ordinary marriage. He doesn't try to hide the fact, and from all appearances, his parishioners are not terribly upset about the relationship either. The priest even attempts a compromise with his persecutors – he offers to give up the performance of the Eucharist provided he can continue to hold his office and perform his other duties. Guibert's party refuses the compromise, and the priest responds not only by resuming his performance of the mass, but also by pronouncing an excommunication against Guibert's mother. The force of this gesture causes Guibert's party to withdraw their petition, and apparently the married priest continued to carry out all the duties expected of him, burned by reform but no less determined to hold his office and to serve his followers. The actions of Guibert's family, on the other hand, indicate that reform was not an ideal. It was a political weapon wielded as a matter of convenience and one based on a moral apparatus that Guibert and the world at large found unfamiliar and uncomfortable.

Guibert's early life brought him into direct contact with the reformers' agenda on one other occasion – the deposition of Guy, bishop of Beauvais. Guibert describes Guy, before his deposition, as a good and generous bishop. Among his praiseworthy deeds Guy had actually laid the foundation stone for the church of

---

résulta qu'un peuple passionnément attaché à son clergé s'échauffa de rage contre ces gens.' Archambault: 'some zealots began railing against these clerics'; p. 21.
[17] Guibert, *Monodies*, i, 7, 46.
[18] This story takes up most of *Monodies*, i, 26.

Saint-Quentin, the original church of the canon lawyer and reform theorist Ivo of Chartres.[19] Guy was of noble birth and endowed with great courtliness or *curialitas*, a word to which, in this case, Guibert does not seem to have attached negative connotations. Guy was also a friend of Guibert's family. When Guibert's mother pondered the adoption of a more formal religious life, it was Guy who provided her with food and shelter on his estates, allowing her time to search her conscience before setting up a hermitage next to Saint-Germer de Fly. But in spite of all his generosity, upbringing, and abilities, Guy still had his career destroyed by a charge of simony – a charge brought against him, Guibert says, by some of the very men who had benefited most from his patronage. He was condemned *in absentia* and stripped of his office. 'Out of terror,' he abandoned Beauvais and joined Cluny.[20] Guibert does not comment whether the charge of simony was true. The moral of the story is not about money. It is rather that Guy, a good man, was destroyed by radical reformers, men whom Guibert has described, in the context of their campaign against nicolaism, as rabid zealots. If there is a villain in this piece, it is not the simoniac.

We can evaluate Guibert's attitude towards the reform movement with the most precision if we examine how it affected his own career, that is to say, how it colored his election as abbot of Nogent. Guibert is vague about most of the mechanics of the process, but the one detail which he states with absolute clarity is its purity. There could be, he writes, no hint of simony. He had neither paid money for his office, nor had any of his relatives exerted influence on his behalf. He had never heard of Nogent, and the monks had based their decision entirely upon his reputation as a teacher and upon the quality 'of the few things I had written.'[21]

We do have reason to doubt these claims. For one thing, to describe Guibert's scholarly output as meagre at the time of his election is generous. In 1104 he would still have been refining his *Moral Commentary on Genesis*, a text he had begun around 1085 and didn't finish until around 1115. He had long since completed a book called his 'Little Treatise on Virginity,' but apparently he did not circulate it until around 1118. He would not have begun his chronicle of the First Crusade, the *Dei gesta per Francos*, let alone have circulated it among a wider audience.[22] Also, while Guibert himself may not have known the monks at Nogent, he does seem to have had relatives in the area. He mentions in his *Monodies* a certain ineffectual nobleman named Ranier who had married one of Guibert's cousins. It was, in the year 1112, a recent marriage, which leaves open

---

[19] On Ivo as a reformer, see Blumenthal, *Investiture Controversy*, 163–4.

[20] Guibert describes Guy's career at *Monodies*, i, 14, 100. See also Olivier Guyotjeanin, *Episcopus et comes: affirmation et declin de la seigneurie episcopal au nord du royaume de France* (Geneva, 1987), 70–2.

[21] 'Paucarum igitur quas attigeram literarum, et docentis, ut dicebatur exterius litura personae, electores meos effecerat caecutientes et lippos'; Guibert, *Monodies*, i, 19, 166.

[22] On the dating of these texts, see R.B.C. Huygens, *La tradition manuscrite de Guibert de Nogent* (Steenbrugis, in Abbatia S. Petri, 1991), 12–13, and 55; and Huygens's introduction to the *Dei gesta per Francos*, 51–6.

the possibility that she had come to the Laonois in the years after Guibert's election and perhaps as a result of it. On the other hand, Guibert relates how, during the communal riot of 1112, she was able, disguised as a nun, to reach her own family's house (as opposed to her husband's family's house) after less than a day's journey on foot.[23] Some sort of pressure from this end of Guibert's fragile patronage network is an explanation far more likely than any scholarly reputation his thin literary output might have gained him.

Still, Guibert maintains emphatically that his election was one untainted by corruption.

Whether this election happed with God's disapproval or mere tolerance, I don't know. But this one thing I can say without hesitation, that it did not happen with my knowledge or because of my ambition, or due to the the influence of any particular faction of my relatives.

He then wonders, a little mysteriously, whether this was a good thing, that no one in the area knew him, and suggests that readers can judge for themselves based on the narrative of his abbacy which will follow.[24] Unfortunately, at this point the *Monodies* are textually flawed – which is to say that Guibert refers his readers to anecdotes which the book does not in fact contain.[25] In spite of the fact that the *Monodies* do lack this information, they provide us with enough evidence to answer Guibert's question – whether the purity of his election was indeed a good and useful thing – or at least to see what conclusion Guibert himself expected us to draw.

Sometime around 1100, Guibert writes, he began to feel a renewed ambition for office, something that had not troubled him since childhood. By the year 1100 an ecclesiastical promotion must have seemed long overdue for a forty-year-old monk of his background and abilities. He was, he reminds us, of good birth, handsome by worldly standards, and, of course, endowed with 'a little bit of knowledge.'[26] His acquaintances and friends, his *necessarii* as he calls them, began to encourage him to use these advantages in order to bring about his own advancement. And as had happened once before, Guibert's family exercised its political influence to obtain for him appropriate office. Their efforts were not entirely without result. Guibert describes himself as entering something like a job fare, albeit a vicious one.

---

[23] Guibert mentions his cousin and her recent marriage at the end of *Monodies*, iii, 7, 336, and names her husband at the start of *Monodies*, iii, 8, 338. The story of her daring escape from the riots appears in the middle of *Monodies*, iii, 9, 350.

[24] 'Electio autem utrum Deo nolente an tolerante fuerit nescio; hoc unum secure pronuncio, quia neque meo ambitu, neque me conscio, aut meorum factione parentum procurata sit mei illa quaesitio; et istac quidem res bene utcumque processit, illac vero, quod scilicet a nemine eorum cognoscebar, nec quempiam eorum noveram, non utiliter forsitan, non integre quod quod secutura lecturus attendat'; *Monodies*, ii, 3, 234. Labande describes the text as *douteux* here, though I see no clear justification for doing so.

[25] At a later point, in fact, Guibert states that he actually has elsewhere in the text described the exile from his monastery; *Monodies*, ii, 4, 242.

[26] Guibert discusses his desire for higher office and his qualifications in *Monodies*, i, 19, 158.

Many praised me – some in order to discover the quality of my character so that they might turn over information to those who wrongly envied me, some thinking that they pleased me by pretending to honor me and saying that my advancement would be to their advantage. These people all desired only their own advantage through my promotion.[27]

Even at the time Guibert recognized these activities as a violation of accepted moral standards but nonetheless went along with them enthusiastically. 'You know, Jesus,' he confesses, 'that not by my own instinct, but rather because of the sin that controlled me, I ordered one who was procuring me such things to do quickly whatever he was doing.' The words deliberately echo Christ's commandment to Judas at the Last Supper. 'What you are doing, do quickly.'[28] As Guibert fretted more and more about the propriety of his job search, he began to pray for purity – that his advancement would occur only through divine judgment and not through any sort of 'carnal procurement.' He even started to feel ashamed when he heard others talking about how his family worked for his benefit, while others reached office 'with God alone the sole cause.'[29]

But then, abruptly, the campaign ended.

Eventually God – who did not want me deceived any longer – inspired my advocates [*procuratoribus*] to leave the area [*commigrarent*] for the sake of their souls' salvation. The monks who had been counting upon my election were forced to turn their attention elsewhere.[30]

It is an unusual passage, one that implies more than it says. Guibert's hopes for election failed not because he proved inadequate or because his patrons could not find a receptive audience. On the contrary, at least one group of monks left the negotiations frustrated and disappointed that they had not obtained his services and, presumably, his family's money. The only reason that Guibert failed was because his supporters left the Beauvaisis. Why they did is not at all clear. Benton suggests, though Guibert's terminology does not demand it, that they went to Jerusalem.[31] If so, it is surprising that Guibert is not more specific, in light of his interest in the Holy Land. But the details of his relatives' sudden 'migration for the sake of their souls' remain shrouded in obscurity. After Guibert's advocates abandoned his cause, and their homeland, Guibert himself enjoyed a time of contemplative peace, but it lasted only a few months, because the monks of the church of Nogent unexpectedly elected him abbot.[32] Since Guibert took office on 18 December, 1104, his advocates must have given up his cause and their cause earlier that same year.

Let us reiterate what we do know about Guibert's election. For an indefinite

---

[27] Guibert, *Monodies*, i, 17, 158–60.

[28] Guibert, *Monodies*, i, 19, 160.

[29] Guibert, *Monodies*, i, 19, 162.

[30] 'Tandem Deo me diutius nolente deludi, procuratoribus meis inspiravit, ut pro suis animabus salvandis alias commigrarent, et quarundam abbatiarum monachis, qui eisdem super mea electione innitebantur, necesse fuit ut aliorsum diverterent'; *Monodies*, i, 19, 162–4.

[31] Benton, *Self and Society*, 99 n. 13.

[32] 'Vix paucis mensibus talia pregustaveram'; Guibert, *Monodies*, i, 19, 164.

period Guibert expected to obtain a higher office, probably an abbacy, through
the help of his family and through some other unidentified advocates. The campaign on behalf of Guibert lasted perhaps as long as three years. It continued
long enough for Guibert to become actively involved, to meet several people
who took an interest in his case, to grow disillusioned with the process, and to
feel relieved when it all apparently collapsed. We know that the effort nearly
succeeded, but that in 1104 the *procuratores* for Guibert abandoned not only
their quest for his promotion but also their own homeland. They may have gone
to Jerusalem, but we can only be sure that they left Beauvais.

It is probably no accident that this campaign coincides almost exactly with a
major political and ecclesiastical conflict centered around the bishopric of
Beauvais.[33] Between 1100 and 1104 two candidates claimed the episcopacy.
The canons of Beauvais, with the approval of the burghers, had elected Etienne
de Garlande as bishop. Etienne was an archdeacon at Paris and a member of one
of the most important families at the royal court. In 1108 he would attain the
office of royal chancellor, which he would hold until 1127 and again from 1132
to 1137.[34] But in 1100, because of his election as bishop, he had incurred the
hostility of Ivo of Chartres.[35] Ivo, as noted, had come from Beauvais, and he
wished to protect his former community at Saint-Quentin from this 'illiterate
man, a gambler, a womanizer, his name already stained by public adultery.'[36] In
Etienne's place Ivo had, with the help of the papacy, inserted into the bishopric
Galon, abbot of Ivo's former church at Beauvais. The episcopal see remained in
dispute until 1104. At that time Galon was elected bishop of Paris and the two
parties settled on a compromise candidate, Geoffrey, a subdeacon at Orléans.
Etienne de Garlande, along with his brothers, fell afoul of the king and joined
the castle of Montlhéry in a rebellion.[37] The years of Etienne's push to become
bishop of Beauvais thus corresponded exactly to the years of Guibert's push to
attain the abbacy that he felt he richly deserved.

Guibert's candidature for ecclesiastical office almost certainly did not have
an existence independent of these larger political events. Rather, his
procuratores were probably among the local men who supported Etienne de
Garlande's election against the reformist candidate of Ivo of Chartres. And in
fact one of the few identifiable members of Guibert's family is on record as a
Garlande supporter. For in the midst of the controversy over the election, the
clergy of Beauvais wrote a letter to Bishop Lambert of Arras, requesting his
assistance for them and for their candidate, Etienne de Garlande, against those

---

33 For a detailed summary of this affair, see Guyotjeanin, *Episcopus et comes*, 75–8.

34 On Etienne Garlande, see J. Dufour, *Recueil des Actes de Louis VI, roi de France, 1108–1137*,
iii (Paris, 1893), 38–9. Also, Robert-Henri Bautier, 'Paris au temps d'Abélard', *Abélard et son
temps, actes du colloque international organisé a l'occasion du 9e centenaire de la naissance de
Pierre Abélard* (Paris, 1981), 58–61.

35 See Ivo's letters nos. 87, 89, 144, 260, 263–65, in *P.L.*, clxii.

36 Ivo of Chartres, quoted by Dufour, *Recueil des Actes de Louis VI*, 39.

37 On the Garlandes at this time, see Suger, *Vita Ludovici Grossi*, ed. H. Waquet (Paris, 1964),
§ 8.

who had wrongly attacked the man's character. The letter is co-written by Hugh the deacon and by the subdeacons Roger and Lisiard, and this same Lisiard was Guibert's uncle.[38] The clergy of Beauvais describe Etienne as a 'capable and honest man, elected by the will and the common counsel of both clergy and people, removed from any stain of simony.'[39]

We cannot really sort the truth from these competing propaganda campaigns. As events would prove, Etienne de Garlande was one of the half dozen most capable politicians of his age. Outside of Abbot Suger of Saint-Denis, no one did more than he to shape royal politics in the first half of the twelfth century. And undoubtedly Etienne would not have balked at handing out a little money to secure his own election. For a reformer such as Ivo, Etienne's predisposition to simony by itself would have justified the other charges of womanizing and gambling. For the clergy and people of Beauvais, on the other hand, Garlande probably looked like a good catch, a well-connected man who knew how to get things done, not all that different from their old bishop Guy, who had thrown around family money and who had been brought down by a reformist cabal on charges of simony.

To return to the question of Guibert's own career, we can observe that his political ambitions burned anew when there existed a vacancy in the bishopric of Beauvais. At least one member of Guibert's family, in his capacity as archdeacon, campaigned for Etienne de Garlande to obtain the bishopric. The same Etienne enjoyed strong local support, which included second-tier nobility like Guibert's clan. Guibert's prospects for advancement probably depended on Etienne's success in claiming the bishopric. The election at Beauvais, however, turned into a protracted struggle involving the royal court, Ivo of Chartres, and the papacy. Guibert eventually grew disillusioned with the process. Perhaps he suffered a genuine moral crisis inspired by a growing discomfort with simony, or maybe he just lost interest in an exceedingly convoluted affair. Whatever the case, he withdrew from active participation in the the simoniacal comings and goings even as his family pressed ahead with his cause. Then, in 1104, the Garlande family fell from royal favor, a compromise candidate became bishop, and Guibert's family and all his supporters 'left the area for the sake of their souls' salvation.' According to Olivier Guoyotjeannin, the battle for the bishopric ended with neither victor nor vanquished.[40] The above reading, however, suggests that the collapse of Etienne de Garlande's campaign dragged down with it several of the local aristocracy. The small base of support Guibert had enjoyed had disappeared entirely by 1104. And, almost unfathomably, immediately after

---

[38] Guibert mentions Lisiard as his uncle at the end of *Monodies*, i, 26, during one final anecdote about the devil.

[39] 'domnum Stephanum Parisienem archidiaconum, utilem et honestum virum, cleri et populi pari voluntate et concordi consilio, remota omni simoniaca pravitate, in dominum et episcopum elegimus'; printed as *Ep.* 35 in *Epistolae Lamberti Atrebatensis episcopi*, printed in *Recueil des Historiens des Gaules et de la France*, xv, 178–207.

[40] 'La crise de 1100–1104 e'était achevée sans vainqueur ni vaincu'; Guoyotjeannin, *Episcopus et comes*, 78.

his network had collapsed, he actually did achieve office. Even if he did have connections around Laon, his election must have seemed to him no less miraculous and remarkably free from corruption, at least in comparison with what might have been.

These circumstances, then, were the ones that allowed Guibert to qualify his election as remarkably pure. But he raises another question. Was the purity a good thing? Monastic figures, of course, routinely expressed dread at the prospect of holding higher office. Guibert's old teacher, Anselm of Bec, upon being named archbishop of Canterbury, is said to have had his fist prised open and a pastoral staff forced into his hand.[41] Anselm's old master, Lanfranc of Bec, contemplated retirement from Canterbury in the first letter he wrote after his election.[42] At the other end of the spectrum and later in the twelfth century, Henry II expressed shock when the newly elected Abbot Samson of Bury St Edmund's accepted his office without complaint. 'By God's eyes,' the king had cried in disbelief, 'this man considers himself worthy to take charge of the abbey!'[43] But for Guibert it is not an issue of humility. He raises instead a question wholly appropriate to the age of reform: Is it useful for a monk to be elected by a community he does not know through a process free from secular influence? Put another way, are the ideals of the Gregorian reform beneficial, or even practical?

The obvious answer would be 'yes.' But as R.I. Moore notes, Guibert blames his difficulties as abbot on the fact that he and his new monks did not really know each other, in Moore's words, 'characteristically feeling himself punished even for his virtue.'[44] But Guibert does more than engage in self-indulgent grumbling. Instead, or at least additionally, he encourages his readers to think seriously about the problems raised by church reform and directs them towards a conclusion that might have seemed too dangerous to state explicitly: free elections are not necessarily a good thing. Sometimes political connections and political deal-making might actually prove salutary for the health of a church and for the success of an abbacy. Unfortunately, we cannot fully evaluate this proposition since we know so little about the early years of Guibert's own abbacy. The only event that he describes in detail is the sermon which he gave upon assuming office, a long meditation on why effective ecclesiastical leadership is impossible and why leaders themselves are doomed to failure.[45] Admittedly, Guibert lacked, in modern parlance, 'good people skills,' but even he surely would not have given such an uncompromising prophecy of failure on his first day at a new job. It is likely instead to have been the sermon that, in

---

41 Eadmer describes these events in the *Historia novorum*, ed. M. Rule (RS; London, 1884), 31–7. See also R. W. Southern, *Saint Anselm: a Portrait in a Landscape*, 186–94, and Sally Vaughn, *Anselm of Bec and Robert of Meulan* (Berkeley and Los Angeles, 1987), 125–35.

42 Lanfranc, *Epistolae*, ed. H. Clover and M. Gibson (Oxford, 1979), 32.

43 Jocelin of Brakelond, *Chronicle of Bury St. Edmunds*, ed. and trans. H.E. Butler (Oxford, 1949), 23.

44 Moore, 'Guibert and his World', 116.

45 The sermon appears in *Monodies*, ii, 3, 238–42.

retrospect, he felt he ought to have given, an apology for faults already committed rather than a forecast of things to come.

So what exactly did go wrong? Again, we can't say. We do know, from two passing reference in the *Monodies*, that at some point in the early years of Guibert's tenure he had to abandon Nogent to return to his old church at Fly for several months. The one fact about the incident which the current state of the *Monodies* allows us to know is that the monks of Nogent were dissatisfied with his governance. Guibert seems to have believed – and Bishop Gaudry of Laon encouraged him in these thoughts – that an archdeacon at Laon named Gautier had stirred up dissent against him, presumably among his monks but perhaps in the wider ecclesiastical community. Gaudry later told Guibert that the archdeacon had tried to turn the bishop himself against Guibert, too.[46] A charter dated 1108 which refers to Guibert's abbacy in the pluperfect tense would suggest that he had left his church in that year and was not expected to return.[47] Since Gaudry became bishop in 1107, the crisis must have developed quickly upon his assumption of the episcopal see. Gautier the archdeacon had himself been a candidate for the vacant bishopric.[48] It is possible that Guibert had crossed him during the maneuvers for power during the election, or at least had failed to support him adequately. Whatever the case, Guibert left his monastery in a disordered state, with a significant part of the community turned against him.

We cannot be more specific about why the community drove him from office, but Guibert's job cannot have been helped by the memory of his predecessor, Godfrey, who had left Nogent to become bishop of Amiens. Guibert is notably disdainful in the *Monodies* of Godfrey – Moore describes him as 'particularly feline' when discussing his predecessor.[49] And Guibert's frequent innuendo about his predecessor, as others have noted, was almost certainly unjustified.[50] Godfrey had left Nogent with a reputation not only for efficient administration (for he had saved the church from financial ruin and recovered its agricultural surroundings from the depredations of bandits) but even for saintliness. Indeed we know Godfrey best from a hagiography written about him by Nicholas of Soissons.[51] But if Godfrey was a successful abbot, he owed his success not only to a dynamic personality and an aura of sanctity, but also to the political connections he enjoyed. Nicholas tells us that Godfrey's parents had lived near Soissons and had endowed Nogent generously from their own estates. At a slightly later date such generosity would have reeked of simony and would

---

[46] Guibert refers to Gautier's role in the context of a conversation he had shared years later with Bishop Gaudry; *Monodies*, iii, 7, 322.

[47] The charter is preserved in the Nogent cartulary, copied in Bibliotèque Nationale MS. *lat.* 17775, pp. 193–4, and printed by d'Achery, p. 625.

[48] Guibert, *Monodies*, iii, 4, 282.

[49] Moore, 'Guibert and His World', 114.

[50] See Labande's note in his edition of the *Monodies*, 232 n. 1.

[51] Nicholas of Soissons, *Vita S. Godfredi, Acta Sanctorum*, Nov., iii, 905–44.

have offended more refined minds, such as Guibert's.[32] In Godfrey's case, however, family wealth and connections were not problematic but simply useful. Nicholas tells us, for example, how during a time of war in the Vermandois and around Soissons and Laon, Godfrey was the only man able to travel safely, without fear of reprisal from any of the leaders.[53] Having as a predecessor a well-connected, effective abbot who enjoyed a reputation for sanctity and who had had a ready supply of cash to hand could have done Guibert no good, either in controlling his monks or in dealing with the nobility and the other dangers, such as the bandits who lurked in the woods just beyond the monastery's walls.[54] Such was the reward for the purity of his election – Guibert had no base of support among the locals to draw upon. 'Whether this process was a good thing or perhaps not wholly advantageous – that no one there knew me and that I knew none of them – let the reader take note of what follows.' The *Monodies*, even in their current state, with almost no information on the early years of his abbacy, allow us to see that Guibert anticipates an answer in the negative.

What then can we learn from this experience of reform, both in terms of Guibert and in terms of the reform movement in France? France is, of course, one of the few places where the reform agenda is seen to have advanced in a relatively orderly fashion. As Cowdrey observes in his recent biography of Gregory VII, in France, unlike Germany, the pope could and did proceed with moderation. He responded to specific persons and situations, and his goals remained pastoral rather than ideological, aimed at creating peace rather than fomenting division.[55] None of Guibert's experiences undermines this position. His sensitivity to issues of clerical celibacy and especially to simony also demonstrates how quickly Gregorian ideals had taken hold in France. But the goals of reform were not ones that Guibert understood clearly or that he accepted. Simony was not an issue of freeing the church from secular influence or from the corrupting influence of money so much as it was a financial necessity: simony costs churches valuable assets. Not paying for office, or at least not paying too much for office, was for Guibert a question of sound financial management, as his frequent stories about the dangers of money so vividly illustrate. Guibert obviously believed in celibacy. But experience had taught him that at least some married priests were no worse than many of the celibate. As for the broader goal of freeing ecclesiastical elections from secular influence, Guibert accepted it in principle. That is to say, he understood its moral soundness. His

52 Godfrey's parents were from the *pagus Suessionicus* and were *secundum saeculi dignitatem ingenuii*; Nicholas, *Vita S. Godfredi*, i, 1.

53 Nicholas, *Vita S. Godfredi*, i, 15.

54 At *Monodies*, ii, 2, 228, Guibert comments on how generous nobles used to be during Godfrey's time as abbot, indicating what a successful fundraiser he was. In the same place he also writes that Godfrey knew how to adapt his exterior to his audience and adds, 'In actione forasticarum causarum, in quibus addiscendis non minimamoperam dederat eis', 228–30.

55 Cowdrey writes, 'At all times, but especially during the years of special concern [1077–1080], Gregory's approach to French persons and problems was, in general, moderate and restrained'; *Gregory VII*, 419, and more generally 398–418.

attempt to apply it to his own life around 1100 triggered within him a profound moral crisis. But Guibert also recognized the case against reform – that there was a perfectly good reason to involve secular powers in elections. Abbots and bishops had to deal with castellans, counts, and dukes. It would be a good idea if the elected leader knew with whom he was dealing when he started the job. Simony was, after all, as Guibert would write in another treatise, the least of sins.[56]

What Guibert gives us, effectively, is an anecdotal version of the sort of polemic characteristic of imperialist writers like Sigebert of Gembloux. Sigebert, in his *Apologia contra eos qui calumpniantur missas coniugatorum sacerdotum*, does not question the high moral goals set by church reformers. He does question the logic, and the orthodoxy, which leads reformers to take extreme positions against married priests. All priests are flawed and unworthy. If the sacraments of married priests are not valid because carnal sin has polluted the priests' hands, then no sacrament is valid.[57] But above all Sigebert attacks the needless divisiveness and impossible moral dilemmas which the reformers' agenda has created. Attempts to purify Christianity, he argues, have led to dissension, argument, and outright warfare between clerics and laymen, where there ought to be only peace.[58] However honorable the reformers' goals, the practical effects of their work were only destructive. Simony and nicolaism, 'these least of sins,' had become labels, used to destroy the careers of men both worthy and unworthy of pastoral office.

Guibert is no polemicist on the issue of reform. He could treat the topic only indirectly and ambivalently. He does so one final time at the end of his *Monodies*. There, out of all chronological sequence, he recalls a childhood crisis. When he had been under the care of his mother and his tutor, before all of them had relocated to Saint-Germer de Fly, he had suffered a life-threatening fever.

---

[56] The context is a discussion of the Eucharist in Guibert's famous relic treatise, *De pigneribus sanctorum*, ed. R.B.C. Huygens, *CCCM*, 127 (Turnholt, 1993), 79–175. If a priest has paid for office, when he is ordained, he receives no blessing from the priest. These sins – paying for office – he describes as *haec minima*. 'Si haec ad sacrificii divini comparationem perminima ob unius peccati immanitatem et detrahuntur et dantur et divinae pro gratia suscipientium censurae mutantur, in illo sacrosancto misterio a damnatis iustus nemo discernitur?'; *De pigneribus*, ii, 121.
[57] Printed in Erwin Frauenknecht, *Die Verteidigung der Priesterehe in den Reformzeit*, M.G.H., *Studien und Texte*, 16 (Hanover, 1997), 217–38. This is the theme of much of the text. To take one example: 'Nos neque ita diligentes sumus, ut sacerdotes indignos hoc modo abhorrendos et quae per eos ministrantur sacramenta polluta esse in orum verbis intelligere possimus, vel permissam, immo iniunctam laicis in eorum contumelias et supplicia licentiam, seu malunt obedientiam, approbare valeamus'; Sigebert, *Apologia*, 231. My thanks to William North for the reference to this text.
[58] Such is the note on which Sigebert concludes his polemic. Referring to Micah 2:8, *Eos qui transibant simpliciter convertistis in bellum*, he writes, 'Quod quam vere de istic dicatur, non tam verbo quam miserabili dissensioniset contentionis, blasphemiae et contemptus laicorum in clericos bello cotidie edocemur'; *Apologia*, 238. See also I.S. Robinson, *Authority and Resistance in the Investiture Contest: the Polemical Literature of the Late Eleventh Century* (Manchester and New York, 1978), 175–83.

Adjoining his family's castle was a church dedicated to Saints Léger and Maclou. As was the deplorable custom in those days, Guibert admits, the church pertained directly to his mother instead of to a cleric, and his mother kept an oil lamp burning on the altar constantly. When the fever worsened, Guibert's mother sent him, along with his tutor and her personal chaplain, to keep a vigil and to pray to Saint Léger for help. The night passed quietly enough, until suddenly, while Guibert slept, the power of God visited the little church. The ground shook, chests seemed to leap from the floor and to struggle against their very locks, and it sounded as if hammers and iron rods were striking every inch of the building. By morning, as we might expect, the fever had broken. This story is the last one Guibert tells us about himself in his memoirs, the final image he wishes to leave us with. He lets us know here at the end of his book that the world where he had grown up existed no longer. In those old days it was the deplorable custom for lay people to hold churches.[59] In newly reformed Europe, by implication, such was no longer the case. But the irony behind this claim of victory is unmistakable. In those misguided days and in that polluted church, Guibert had experienced directly the power of God. It was a sensation he knew all too infrequently later in life, as doubts and uncertainties began more and more to gnaw at him in a world newly moral and reformed.

[59] 'Iuxta pravitatem', the Latin reads; *Monodies*, iii, 20, 464.

Monks and Mediocrities in the Shadow of Thomas Becket: Peter of Blois on Episcopal Duty

John D. Cotts

When four of Henry II's knights murdered Thomas Becket at Canterbury in 1170, they granted church reformers a superficially unambiguous illustration of royal brutality and created an instant exemplar of all that could be noble in a bishop. There was little public discussion, at least in ecclesiastical circles, about what manner of man Becket had been through the course of his long dispute with the English monarch.[1] He had died for the liberty of the church and thwarted Henry's attempts to control it. In historiographical treatments of the 1170s and 1180s, however, the seemingly straightforward implications of the martyrdom give way to uncertainties that shroud the long-term effects of the dispute on both the English church and Henry II's administration.[2] Moreover, while Becket had presented a clear ideal for episcopal behavior, none of his three immediate successors emulated his aggressive interference with royal ambitions. His death marked an identifiable consummation of radical traditions of church reform stretching back to the first half of the eleventh century, so the supporters of less than radical bishops in the post-1170 period had a formidable task ahead of them, that is, to employ prevailing conceptions of episcopal duty to portray positively those who displayed their devotion to the church less spectacularly than the Canterbury martyr.

Indeed, relatively few writers of the late twelfth century praised Becket's immediate successors at Canterbury – Richard of Dover, Baldwin of Ford, and Hubert Walter – for exemplary episcopal conduct. All three encountered criticism for their lack of learning, administrative incompetence, acquiescence to royal policy, or hostile relations with the cathedral chapter of Christ Church. If these archbishops provided less than stellar examples of reforming zeal, many in

---

[1] Becket's hagiographers, however, did disagree about Becket's character earlier in life. See Michael Staunton, 'Thomas Becket's Conversion,' *A.N.S.*, 21 (1998), 193–211.

[2] For general accounts of the ecclesiastical history of this period, see Henry Mayr-Harting, 'Henry II and the Papacy, 1170–1189'; Raymonde Foreville, *L'église et la royauté en Angleterre sous Henri II Plantagenet (1154–1189)* (Paris, 1943), esp. 327–564; W.L. Warren, *Henry II* (Berkeley, 1973); C.R. Cheney, *From Becket to Langton: English Church Government, 1170–1213* (Manchester, 1956); David Walker, 'Crown and Episcopacy under the Normans and Angevins,' *A.N.S.*, 5 (1982), 221–33.

the church nevertheless looked to these men as leaders of the Anglo-Norman episcopacy, and perhaps as many depended on them for preferment in the hierarchy. Prominent among such clergy was Peter of Blois, who by the summer of 1174 had crossed the Channel from Rouen, where he had served Archbishop Rotrou as a letter writer, to join the archiepiscopal household of the newly consecrated Archbishop Richard. Peter, now a middle-aged ecclesiastic who had studied in Tours, Paris, and Bologna, would spend the next twenty-five years writing to, for, and about the highest-ranking clerics of the Anglo-Norman world, as well as prominent members of the papal curia.[3] His position in the Canterbury circle throughout the 1170s and 80s, along with his continuing quest to find institutionally appropriate ideals for clerical conduct, render his writings a uniquely valuable source for considering how clerics formulated ideals of episcopal duty after Becket and for examining how the controversies within the church conditioned their reception of the precepts of the reform movement. While scholarship has traditionally explored the aftermath of the Becket affair in light of developments in canon law or Henry II's continued ability to control the Anglo-Norman episcopate, I here propose to use Peter of Blois' letters and treatises to explore how ideals of bishops and clerics were constructed in the last three decades of the twelfth century. In a broad ecclesiological sense, using an approach that takes into account the development of conceptions of the clergy leading up to the Fourth Lateran Council of 1215, we can argue that Peter reveals the ambiguities and contradictions inherent in the position of bishops at a crucial point in the church's institutional development. Genuinely troubled by these ambiguities, Peter articulated his views of church power and episcopal duty through a precarious synthesis of the rhetoric of reform and traditional ideals of sacerdotal obligations.

Detached in many respects from the scholarship of ecclesiological developments in western Europe, the historiography of the Becket controversy remains fragmented and a bit inconsistent, in part because so little regarding the motivations and the principles of the prominent players can be stated with any certainty. W.L. Warren, in a brilliant exercise in historiographical character development, argued that the conflict is ultimately most easily comprehensible as a clash of its two foremost personalities rather than as an irreconcilable difference of theological ideals.[4] In such a reading the jurisdictional issues that legal

---

[3] On the life of Peter of Blois, see R.W. Southern, 'Peter of Blois: A Twelfth-Century Humanist,' *Medieval Humanism and Other Studies* (Oxford, 1970), 105–34, and a more recent treatment by the same scholar in his *Scholastic Humanism and the Unification of Europe. Volume II: The Heroic Age* (Oxford, 2001), 178–218. There is still no modern edition of Peter's writings, but information on the problems with the manuscript tradition can be found in the appendix to Southern's 1970 article as well as in Lena Wahlgren, *The Letter Collections of Peter of Blois: Studies in the Manuscript Tradition*, Studia Graeca et Latina Gothoburgensis, 58 (Goteborg, 1993); cf. Southern, 'Towards an Edition of Peter of Blois' Letters,' *E.H.R.*, 110 (1995), 925–37. References in the present study are to the edition of Peter's works in *P.L.*, ccvii.

[4] Warren, 517: 'Yet it was the manner of Becket's opposition rather than its ideological content which caused the implacable hostility of the king. . . . For [Henry], the conflict remained, as it had

historians have detected in the controversy take second place to personal politics, though admittedly this sort of politics stemmed at least in part from the centralizing ambitions of the Angevin monarchy. Charles Duggan, among others who have examined the canonical implications of the controversy, claimed that, personality conflicts notwithstanding, Becket viewed his differences with Henry through the lens of solid theological and legal ideas, which were far more significant to him than personal animosity toward his king and former friend.[5] Many members of the English episcopacy indeed saw the conflict in terms of ideals that could not be compromised, but the political manifestations of their attitudes often played out in labyrinthine fashion.[6] When speaking of the English clergy, we are hard pressed to identify unbreakable alliances based on clear political or theological positions; the associations we can identify seem to defy classification by ideological rubric. Becket, for instance, could count 'Gregorians' such as Gilbert Foliot among his most bitter critics and occasionally may have offended clerics more by coarseness than by his ideals, while even sympathetic colleagues, among them John of Salisbury and Bartholomew of Exeter, were not always unambiguously supportive.[7] The history of the English episcopacy both before and after the 1172 settlement with the king at Avranches plays itself out through shifting alliances and alternating periods of unanimity and splintering, without political 'parties' identifiable by their adherence to a particular theory. While the language of ecclesiastical liberty, so dear to reformers from Gregory VII to Innocent III, pervades the correspondence surrounding the dispute, and some bishops appear as unequivocal enemies of the church's freedom, most of the ecclesiastical actors in the drama agreed over basic principles and displayed an almost uniform desire for compromise. Peter of Blois, who inhabits the rough edges of animosity engendered by the dispute, did not write for any sort of party and so places the conflict in the soul of the men who received his letters (monks, clerks, and prelates alike) rather than between adherents of competing views of church power.

The ambiguities and contradictions of the Becket controversy persisted into

begun, a conflict of personalities set on a collision course from which neither could retreat without an unthinkable loss of prestige.'

5   Charles Duggan, 'The Becket Dispute and the Criminous Clerks,' *Bulletin of the Institute of Historical Research*, 35 (1962), 131.

6   For a particular example of these complicated relationships that affirms the importance of canonical and political ideals to the individuals involved, see Anne Duggan, 'John of Salisbury and Thomas Becket,' *The World of John of Salisbury*, ed. Michael Wilks, Studies in Church History, Subsidia, 3 (Oxford, 1984), 427–38.

7   On Gilbert's ideas on church and state, see Adrian Morey and C.N.L. Brooke, *Gilbert Foliot and his Letters* (Cambridge, 1965), esp. 174–87; for Becket's periodic alienation of the episcopacy see, in addition to Warren: Frank Barlow, *Thomas Becket* (Berkeley, 1986), esp. 109–16, 165, 186; David Knowles, *The Epsicopal Colleagues of Archbishop Thomas Becket* (Cambridge, 1951); Carolyn P. Schriber, *The Dilemma of Arnulf of Lisieux* (Bloomington, 1990), 105–8. See also J.W. Alexander, 'The Becket Controversy in Recent Historiography,' *Journal of British Studies*, 9 (1970), 67.

the 1170s and beyond, and Peter's writings bear witness to them. His own relationship to the various figures of the dispute is often unclear, as he had associated and corresponded with both friends and enemies of the archbishop in the final years before the murder. On several occasions he invoked the martyr's memory as a glorious defender of the church, but during the same period, in his position as secretary to the next archbishop, he wrote a letter, discussed below, that effectively contradicted Becket's all-important position concerning punishment of criminous clerks. For close to twenty years Peter loyally served Archbishop Thomas's first three successors as they attempted to come to terms with his legacy. Meanwhile, as Henry II attempted to mitigate the damage of the humiliations consequent to the murder, the English church followed the contemporary ecclesiastical currents emanating from a rapidly centralizing Roman curia. It is thus within a context of increased papal jurisdiction, systematic collection of decretals and general interest in canon law, as well as relative archiepiscopal co-operation with the Angevin monarchy, that Peter articulated his ideas on episcopal obligations. He took stock of these ecclesiastical trends and developed a complicated notion of what it meant to be a cleric. While the reform movement provided Peter with some of his vocabulary for discussing Becket and the role of bishops in the world, his construction of the ideal bishop carries him through varied and sometimes conflicting ideological traditions.

While Peter himself played no major role in the actual disputes between Becket and Henry II, the fallout from Becket's anger affected him indirectly in the late 1160s, by which time he had acquired the patronage of Reginald of Salisbury, the son of Bishop Jocelin of Salisbury. Father and son alike incurred the wrath of the archbishop, and Peter trod carefully, writing letters in defense of Reginald while simultaneously praising Becket's heroic struggle in a letter of comfort to John of Salisbury.[8] After the murder Peter still seems to have played the ends off the center, and for modern readers this results in rather perplexing rhetoric. In a letter that contains a famous description of Henry II, for example, he praises Becket as a martyr while insisting that the king is innocent or, irrespective of his guilt, canonically absolved.[9] This convergence of agendas, so prominent in much of Peter's writing, results in the glorification of an ecclesiastical martyr in the total absence of a royal antagonist. Nor did Peter fail to recognize the value of Becket's memory for political purposes, as when he used it to justify Archbishop Baldwin's long-running dispute with the monks of Christ

---

[8] Letters to, on behalf of, and in defense of Reginald include letters (hereafter abbreviated as *Ep.*) 24, 30, 58, 59, 61, 85, and 163; the letter to Jocelin is *Ep.* 51. On the complicated relationship between Reginald and Peter, see Lena Wahlgren, 'Peter of Blois and the Later Career of Reginald of FitzJocelin,' *E.H.R.*, 111 (1996), 1202–15.

[9] *Ep.*, 66, *P.L.*, ccvii, 195–210.

Church in the 1180s.[10] Peter clearly found in the martyr's legacy a versatile adornment to his rhetorical program.

Following Henry II's penance and the resolution of the Becket dispute at Avranches in 1172, Peter became the secretary and ultimately chancellor of the new archbishop, Richard of Dover, who was elected in 1173. Henry filled four episcopal vacancies that year, and of the newly elected only Richard did not come from the circle of royal *curiales*.[11] The king had made clear that Richard, although not his first choice, was an acceptable candidate, and he fit in well with the tradition of monk-bishops at Canterbury that had been broken only by Thomas Becket's appointment.[12] Richard's consecration, delayed until the vehement objections of the younger Henry had been dealt with, did not take place until 1174.[13] The new archbishop had large shoes to fill, and there were many who wished that they remain empty, for no one was prepared for another decade of strife between *regnum* and *sacerdotium*. This gentle Benedictine seems to have been regarded as at best a mediocrity and at worst dangerously acquiescent to royal whim. Gerald of Wales even remarked that Richard's tenure threatened to deprive the church of all Becket had gained.[14] Still, Peter served Richard loyally and defended his character, sharing with his new master deference to royal authority and caution when framing controversial issues. In his correspondence to, for, and in defense of Richard we find prescriptions for episcopal service and church–state relations ideally suited to the time when the English church had exhausted itself through years of struggle, but when the principles of clerical reform remained current in ecclesiastical discussions.

Richard had little in common with his predecessor, and inevitably his reputation suffered for it. He certainly recoiled from Becket's antagonistic approach to church–state relations, as illustrated by his treatment of the matter of criminous clerks, one of the issues championed by Becket that remained to be dealt with during his rule. Between Becket's fervent claims that clerics ought to be tried in clerical, rather than secular, courts and Henry's insistence on the prerogative of the secular courts to judge clerks who committed crimes lay the rhetorical and legal battlefield Richard had to traverse.[15] For Thomas, as for John of Salisbury

---

[10] On the dispute see the dated but remarkably engaging account in William Stubbs, *Historical Introductions to the Rolls Series* (London, 1902), 366–438. A modern treatment is found in Margaret Gibson, 'Normans and Angevins, 1070–1220,' *A History of Canterbury Cathedral*, ed. Patrick Collinson et al. (Oxford, 1995), 66–7.

[11] The others were Richard of Ilchester (elected to the see of Winchester), Geoffrey Ridel (Ely), and Reginald of Salisbury (Bath). For Richard of Ilchester, see Charles Duggan, 'Richard of Ilchester, Royal Servant and Bishop.' For Reginald see above note 8. For Geoffrey Ridel see Cheney, *From Becket to Langton*, 22–3, 27–8.

[12] Foreville, 374–9; Warren, 536.

[13] R.W. Eyton, *Court, Household, and Itinerary of King Henry II* (London, 1878), 178.

[14] Gerald of Wales, *Speculum ecclesiae* 2.25, ed. J.S. Brewer (R.S., 21.3, London, 1873), 76.

[15] The royal position is asserted in *Constitutions of Clarendon*, Article 3, in *E.H.D.*, ii, 719.

and radical reformers like Herbert of Bosham, at issue was the principle of clerical immunity, and he would not budge.[16] Richard saw the matter differently and
framed it in terms of proper jurisdiction within a symbiotic church–state relationship, as we know from a letter that Peter wrote in the archbishop's name.
This letter, addressed to the three bishops who had risen to the bench from the
royal household in 1173, deftly but obliquely approaches the question from an
angle favorable to the king, leaving no question that Becket's position was too
extreme. Peter and Richard addressed the communication to three bishops, formerly members of the royal household, who had been far from friendly to
Becket.[17] The letter's *narratio* refers not to 'criminous clerks' as such but to
those, not specifically clerics or laymen, who kill clerics:

In the English Church there survives a custom, pernicious to all and altogether damnable,
which, unless your careful attention should remove it, will increase to the detriment of the
whole clergy. If a Jew or the most vile of laymen is killed, the murderer is at once
sentenced to the punishment of death. If anyone, however, kills a priest or cleric of greater
or lesser or standing, the church must be content with excommunication alone, and not
seek out the aid of the earthly sword.[18]

Peter avoids explicit mention of the crucial and much-debated jurisdictional
issues in play; he simply makes the altogether acceptable point that priest-killers
should be vigorously pursued and punished. His language, moreover, reveals the
popular belief, advanced by Becket and his followers, that local custom ought to
bow to church law, but here the reference to murderers of clergy is doubly
charged, since the most famous murdered priest of the age was indeed the martyred archbishop himself.[19] As the letter proceeds, we discern an obvious
discomfort with Becket's views on the efficacy of ecclesiastical courts:

---

[16] The reforming principles of Archbishop Thomas and his circle are well outlined in Beryl
Smalley, *The Becket Conflict and the Schools: A Study of Intellectuals in Politics* (Oxford, 1973),
passim.

[17] It is probably not coincidental that these are the promoted *curiales* referred to in note 11.

[18]   In Ecclesia Anglicana damnosa omnibus, et omnino damnanda consuetudo invaluit, quae
       nisi per industriam vestram fuerit omnino sublata de medio, in enorme dispendium
       vehemente excrescet. Si Judaeus aut laicorum vilisisimus occiditur, statim supplicio
       mortis addicitur interfector; si quis vero sacerdotem vel clericum minoris aut majoris
       status occiderit, ecclesia sola excommunicatione contenta, aut, ut verius loquar,
       contempta, materialis opem gladii non requiret
Ep., 73, *P.L.*, ccvii, 225. Cf. Peter's reference to the swift punishment given to the murderers of
the wife of Aaron the Jew (of Lincoln) in *Canon Episcopalis, P.L.*, ccvii, 1110. For the evidence
that this sort of criticism was directed at Becket himself for protecting thieves and murderers in
clerical orders, see Barlow, *Thomas Becket*, 299 n. 39.

[19] On the related debates over custom and jurisdiction see Barlow, *Thomas Becket*, 100–5;
Duggan, 'The Becket Dispute and the Criminous Clerks'; Smalley, *Becket Conflict*, esp. 127–33,
149–51, 161–2. Maitland lucidly introduces the key problems in Frederick Pollock and Frederic
William Maitland, *History of English Law Before the Time of Edward I* (2nd edn., 2 vols.,
Cambridge, 1968), i, 449–56.

But we deserve these things [the lenient punishment of priest-killers] and worse, because we usurp another's jurisdiction, which is in no way ours, as a result of our rash ambition. You may recall that we have read these words in the corpus of decretals, as well as the epistle to the Romans. There are great crimes that should be judged by the judges of the world rather than the rulers and judges of the church . . . Let the church exercise its own jurisdiction first, and if this does not suffice, let the secular sword compensate for the shortcoming.[20]

The underlying assumption is that in attempting to extend ecclesiastical jurisdiction to those who kill clerics, Becket's program threatens to denude the church of its ability to defend itself. Peter, then, portrays the church as the victim of violence that excommunication alone cannot discourage. Although he never explicitly refers to criminous clerks, he shows clear frustration with the purely ecclesiastical censures to which they were subject, and he unquestionably has Becket in mind when he uses the martyr's own formula for prohibiting the prosecution of clerks in lay and ecclesiastical courts: *bis in id ipsum*.[21] In cases concerning capital offenses, Peter sees a single judgment with no double jeopardy. By way of articulating this idea, Peter enters into one of the very few uses of Two Swords imagery in his letter collection:

Let it not be said that anyone would in this way be punished twice for the same crime, for something is not repeated if it is begun by one and finished by another. There are two swords which implore reciprocal aid of each other, and so each in turn they impart to themselves different strengths, the priesthood to kings, and the kingship to priests . . . Therefore, rendering to Caesar what is Caesar's and what is God's to God, according to the petition of the Lord King, we relinquish to him the punishment of such transgressions.[22]

The church, through its bishops, fulfills its proper role by granting absolution to the killers so they are properly prepared to receive their just punishment – a single punishment carried out by complementary powers.

This letter cannot have pleased everyone in the English church. Its argument, blatantly anti-Becket but soundly rooted in Gelasian tradition, is not at all inconsistent with the pronouncements of Anglo-Norman decretal collections from the

---

20 Sed his et deterioribus digni sumus, qui jurisdictionem alienam, et nobis omnino indebitam ambitione temeraria usurpamus. Nam in corpore decretorum, et in Epistola ad Romanos haec verba nos legisse meminimus. Sunt quaedam enormia flagitia, quae potius per mundi judices, quam per rectores et judices Ecclesiarum judicantur . . . Ecclesia jursidictionem suam prius exerceat; et si illa non sufficit, ejus imperfectum suppleat gladius saecularis   *Ep.*, 73, *P.L.*, ccvii, 225–6.

21 Warrren points out this parallel, *Henry II*, 480. Becket's statement is found in *MTB*, 7:563.

22 nec dicatur quod aliquis puniatur propter hoc bis in id ipsum; nec enim videtur quo ab uno incipitur, et ab altero consummatur. Duo sunt gladii, qui mutuum a se mendicant auxilium, atque ad invicem sibi vires impartiuntur alternas, sacerdotium regibus, et sacerdotibus regnum . . . Reddentes igitur Deo quae Dei sunt, et Caesari quae sunt Caesaris, iuxta petitionem domini regis, ei tantorum vindictam excessuum relinquamus

Ep., 73, 227.

1160s. It does, however, run against the grain of post-1170 decretals.[23] Peter refers in passing to the *corpus decretorum,* but in general his argument is more theological (in a very general sense) than canonical. Richard of Dover, himself an accomplished canon lawyer, must have been aware of the legal issues at play, but Peter does not address them.[24] He was, of course, skirting a legal minefield. Even today, scholars debate the extent to which Becket's position conformed to canon law, and Richard M. Fraher has argued that the decretal collections fully backed Becket's position only after 1170.[25] As the literary mouthpiece of Becket's successor, Peter of Blois skips the crucial aspects of the canonical difficulty and turns to a vision of harmony between the two spheres dependent on a peace-loving bishop, while tacitly objecting to Becket's extreme position on clerical immunity. Though he refers to neither Becket nor criminous clerks *per se,* his brief discussion of the need for secular punishment brings to light the problems of jurisdiction central to the Becket dispute. The solution presented in the letter, an idealized espousal of co-operation between two swords, floats on a surface that hides a current of canonical ambiguities and represents a spirit of compromise that inspired hostile criticism towards Archbishop Richard.

And Richard had a multitude of other public relations difficulties. He incurred a rebuke from Alexander III because he allowed episcopal elections to take place in the royal chapter, and he appears in a decidedly negative light in Gerald of Wales's *Speculum ecclesiae,* which attacks the archbishop as a prime example of why monks ought not to be bishops.[26] According to a letter Peter wrote to Richard, the *curiales* of Henry II, hardly the most edifying examples of clerical conduct, engage in daily rants about the primate's ineffectiveness:

Where is your lord? Where is he hiding? Where does he sleep? To what end does this sluggish man sleep? Rise, o sleeper, and awake from the dead. The hour is here for him to wake from sleep and to watch over the flock entrusted to him, and to be mindful of what sort of predecessor he had. Did he accept the grace of God in vain, in order to destroy the grace given to him, as well as the glory of his predecessor? . . . Your archbishop found the church in a great state, but he has forsaken it and cast it down. His faint-heartedness has destroyed the privileges of the church of Canterbury, which the glorious martyr adorned with his own blood and confirmed as an eternal witness with his death and the effusion of blood

---

[23] Warren, 540; C. Duggan, 'The Becket Dispute and the Criminous Clerks,' 23–4.

[24] For Richard as a canonist, see Charles Duggan, *Twelfth-Century Decretal Collections and their Importance in English History* (London, 1963).

[25] Richard M. Fraher, 'The Becket Dispute and Two Decretist Traditions: The Bolognese Masters Revisited and Some New Anglo-Norman Texts,' *J.M.H.,* 4 (1978), 347–68; Edward M. Peters, 'The Archbishop and the Hedgehog,' *Law, Church, and Society in the Twelfth Century: Essays in Honor of Stephan Kuttner,* ed. Kenneth Pennington and Robert Somerville (Philadelphia, 1977), 167–84.

[26] *Regesta Pontificum Romanorum,* ed. P. Jaffé, 2nd edn. by G. Wattenbach et al. (2 vols., Leipzig, 1885–8), no. 14312; Gerald of Wales, *Speculum ecclesiae,* ii, 25, ed. J.S. Brewer (R.S., 21.3, London, 1873), 76; Warren, 553.

from his head, and he has returned it into the humiliation of its former servitude, when it had risen to freedom.[27]

The *communis opinio* among the whispers at court holds that Richard does not defend the Church from its enemies and thus supports Gerald of Wales's assessment. Peter claims that he has responded to the detractors by portraying Richard as a good monk, thoughtful and kind, if relatively passive. The clerics at court, Peter suggests to Richard, want a new Becket, an activist bishop who will fight for the church's freedom. Nothing Peter says is good enough for his adversaries. If he protests that Richard has done nothing wrong, they reply that 'it is not enough to do no evil, unless he strikes out to do good'.[28] If he praises Richard's building program at Canterbury, which included parks, these are dismissed as detrimental to the cloisters, whose walls steadily crumble.[29] Peter concludes with an exhortation for Richard to look to his ministry and avoid the impending ignominy. What he provides, however, is less an exhortation to reform than an exposition of the complexities of ecclesiastical politics in Becket's shadow. The new archbishop has impossible expectations to fill, a monarch to appease, and a chorus of critics who will not stop defaming him.

This letter reveals as much about Peter's situation as about Richard's. Here as elsewhere Peter presents himself as a concerned adviser, a mediator between his master and the court. Although many criticized Richard for letting the church be trampled by *laici*, Peter does not frame his discussion as a simple conflict between *regnum* and *sacerdotium*, reflecting, perhaps, his conception of the Two Swords as complementary. *Libertas ecclesiae*, in Peter's eyes, coexists with royal co-operation, and he occasionally flirts with outright acquiescence to royal interference in affairs of the church. Concerns of power and the image of the church mingle in Peter's appraisal of courtly opinion, while the rhetorical debris left in Becket's wake obstructs his attempts to turn Richard into an ideal bishop. Despite the desire for compromise pervading the church in the early 1170s, Peter continually runs into opponents whose polemic recalls the ideal of Becket as an aggressive opponent of royal authority.

---

27   ubi est dominus tuus? ubi latitat? ubi dormit? usquequo piger dormit? exsurgat qui dormit, et exsurgat a mortuis. Et jam hora esset a somno surgere, et vigilare super comissum sibi gregem, attendere, qualem habuit decessorem. Nunquid Dei gratiam accepit in vacuum, ut gratiam sibi datam, et gloriam sui decessoris evacuet? . . . reperit, inquiunt, archiepiscopus tuus Ecclesiam in optimo statu, ipse vero destituit, et dejecit. Cantuariensis Ecclesiaie dignitates, quas gloriosus martyr rubricaverat sanguine suo, et quasi testamentum aeternum morte et cerebri effusione firmaverat, pusillanimatas eius evacuavit, eamque reduxit in antiquae servitutis opprobrium, quae se in gratiam plenae libertatis erexerat
Ep., 5, *P.L.*, ccvii, 13–14.

28   'Non sufficit, inquiunt, tantae praelationis homini, non facere malum, nisi adjiciat facere bonum': *Ep.*, 5, *P.L.*, ccvii, 14.

29   'quae gloria est, inquiunt, quod vivaria construit, quod claudit feras indagine, si clerici imprecantur, si in omnem dissolutionem religiosorum claustrorum ostia relaxantur?': *Ep.*, 5, *P.L.*, ccvii, 15. Cf. Michael Markowski, 'Peter of Blois, Writer and Reformer' (Ph.D. diss., Syracuse University, 1988), 237–8.

In the letter discussed above, Peter implies that Richard had enemies at the papal curia, and a piece addressed to Cardinal Albert of Morra, the future Gregory VIII, confirms this. Here he sets himself the task of representing Richard as an ideal bishop despite his co-operation with the king and his perceived laxity in matters of the church's liberty. Avoiding any mention of Thomas Becket, Peter shows Richard to be an ideal monk and hence an ideal bishop. His humility and mildness become virtues: 'He was not a dominator of the clergy but a model for his flock among the people, guarding his vessel in holiness, and not allowing his consecrated lips to speak vanities.'[30] From an account of Richard's monastic virtues Peter passes on to his priestly virtues, and in his effort to make his subject as saintly and meek as possible, allows the conventional descriptions of monastic passivity to lead him off track, so that he overlooks or de-emphasizes some of Richard's finest qualities. Like Job and the Apostles Peter and Andrew, he is a *simplex*, from a fishing boat rather than the forum of Justinian.[31] At this point, to highlight Richard's holy *simplicitas*, Peter draws on a dichotomy that may not be entirely relevant to the case at hand by opposing Richard to those who study the law and to *sapientia mundi* in general. Although the archbishop was a learned canonist, Peter portrays him as almost simple-minded:

If my lord judges humbly, if he does not understand lofty matters, if he does not walk with great and marvelous things above him, if he is ignorant of the precedents of the old law, he is nonetheless learned in the law of God. In this, which is wisdom from on high, he walks upon the paths of justice, decreeing nothing in the decision of cases that he does not grant to common audience and public notice, for he pronounces his justice as a light, and his judgment as the midday sun.[32]

Peter hints here at the traditional notion of *indocta sapientia* to place Richard in the company of simple, unlearned saints, and in so doing he significantly understates the archbishop's actual attainments as a jurist. Rhetorically, however, the strategy is sound, accepting the criticisms of Richard as mild and inactive, and turning his perceived faults into virtues by way of a monastic ideal. Peter then exposes what he takes to be the true reasons for criticism of the archbishop. Richard's critics are upset, so Peter claims, that he does not confiscate the goods of paupers and does not give church property to hunters. In fact, he argues, Richard's problems have arisen because he fixes his mind on the work of God

---

[30] 'nec fuit dominator in clero, sed forma gregis in populo, vas suum in sanctificatione custodiens, et labia consecrata ad vaniloquia non relaxans': *Ep.*, 38, *P.L.*, ccvii, 117.

[31] 'sane Christus Jesus Petrum, et Andream, et alios, per quos operatus est salutem in medio terrae, non de foro Justiniani, sed de simplicitate piscatoria legitur assumpsisse': Ibid.

[32] si dominus meus humiliter sentit, si alta non sapit, si non ambulat in in magnis et mirabilibus supra se, si praestigia versuti juris ignorat, eruditus tamen in lege Domini, et in ea, quae desursum est sapientia, ambulat super semitas justitiae, nihil in causarum decisionibus statuens, quod in commune auditorium, et publicam hominum notitiam non deducit. Educit enim quasi lumen justitiam suam, et judicium suum tamquam meridiem
                                                            Ep., 38, *P.L.*, ccvii, 118.

without regard for glory, despite Peter's warnings that he look out for his reputa tion.[33] Peter concludes by warning Albert of the schemes of gossips who conspire against Richard and by requesting continued assistance with Richard's *negotia*. Richard, the docile monk, appears in stark contrast to the rapacious, worldly ecclesiastics who care not about the more basic, and hence more impor- tant, obligations of a bishop.

Elsewhere in Peter's writings the defense of Richard hinges on a positive assessment of *lenitas*, that is, his 'softness' or 'gentleness.' Apparently Richard's detractors used this same word in its pejorative connotation. Peter not only turns this quality into a virtue, but makes it the prerequisite to improved relations between *regnum* and *sacerdotium*:

My friend, there are two sorts of mildness. There is necessary mildness and dissolute mild- ness . . . You wish, as all those who share your foolishness wish, that my lord out of some insanity would dissolve the pact between *regnum* and *sacerdotium* . . . and so destroy the peace. But this mildness makes *regnum* and *sacerdotium* one; hence he obtained by his kindness what he could never wrench from princes through threats or violence.[34]

A mild, conciliatory bishop brings greater harmony to the world. Richard (along with Peter) reacts to the tumult of the 1160s by turning away from Becket's con- frontational stance. Peter's writings recall the ideal, expressed by writers such as Peter Damian and Bernard of Clairvaux, of a diarchy in which church and state in fact become one.[35] The pastor, then, is not a litigator or an overly severe critic, but a gentle sage. Peter describes Richard as the ideal leader outlined in Gregory the Great's *Pastoral Care*, and Bernard of Clairvaux's *De con- sideratione*, often using similar language.

Peter had to defend Richard's character as he repeatedly had to defend his own. Richard seems to have had a deep-seated aversion to conflict, which may account for the relatively small number of attacks on him in the letter collection of his monastic chapter, famously hostile to archbishops.[36] His conciliatory atti- tude toward the *regnum* exposed him to criticism, which Peter tried to avert through appeals to an ideal that had not been applicable to Becket. In Richard he saw a bishop who could not be described as a heroic martyr or the sort who was

---

33 'ipsum saepe monui, ut esset propitius famae suae, et donis obstrueret os loquentium iniqua, et erat ejus responsio: Si talibus, dicebat, placerem, Christi servus non essem': *Ep.*, 38, *P.L.*, ccvii, 118.

34   amice, est lenitas, et est lenitas. Est lenitas necessaria, et lenitas dissolute. . . . Velles, vellentque omnes, qui tecum desipiunt, quod dominus meus ex quolibet motu animi inter regnum et sacerdotium foedus, pacemque dissolveret. . . . Haec lenitas regnum et sacerdotium facit unum; unde haec sua benignitate obtinet, quod nunquam per minas aut violentias a principibus extorqueret   *Ep.*, 100, *P.L.*, ccvii, 309.

35 *Ep.*, 100, 310.

36 The *Epistolae Cantuarienses* refer to Richard only rarely, but the prologue to that collection clearly contrasts his humble piety with what was perceived as his successor's rapaciousness. See W. Stubbs, ed., *Chronicles and Memorials of Richard I, Volume I: Epistolae Cantuarienses* (R.S., 21.2, London, 1865), 2.

admired for administrative acumen.[37] He fulfilled his duty by helping widows and orphans, not by resisting the king or displaying administrative prowess.

In 1184, upon the death of Richard of Dover, Baldwin of Ford, then bishop of Worcester, was translated to the see of Canterbury. Peter apparently had a close relationship with the new archbishop, though he did not retain the title of *cancellarius*. In general, Peter treats Baldwin, a Cistercian, much as he had treated his Benedictine predecessor, focusing on his qualities as a monk.[38] Peter's admiration for Citeaux, which he articulates several times in his later letters, may have roots in his association with Baldwin. In letter 96, a request for prayers as he assumes the prelacy, Baldwin enters his new office humbly and timidly, unsure whether he can look after his own salvation, let alone that of a province.[39] This hand seems a bit overplayed, since Baldwin had already led the abbey of Ford as well as the see of Worcester, but it emphasizes the role that Baldwin's monastic experience will play in his episcopal career. As in the case of Richard of Dover, Peter's collection associates Baldwin's vision of episcopal service with his monastic spirituality. The beginnings of the dispute with Christ Church, a later letter relates, stem from the lax discipline effective in the cathedral chapter, which offended Baldwin's Cistercian sensibilities.[40] Again, as with Richard, Peter ignores Baldwin's proficiency in canon law. Later, after he died on crusade at Acre in 1191, Peter would eulogize Baldwin to the secular canons of Beverley as the paragon of monastic virtue as well as a martyr, and goes on to impart nearly angelic qualities to Baldwin, implying that he was too good for the world.[41] This may have been intended to excuse some of Baldwin's failures, just as Peter attributed Richard's inactivity to his Christian gentleness. Once again, monastic ideals help mitigate the perception of episcopal laxity.

As a prominent member of the Canterbury *curia*, Peter, a secular cleric through and through, found himself with the rhetorical task of turning monks into ideal bishops. Bernard of Clairvaux's *De consideratione* had recognized this difficulty, but Peter wrote from a politically less secure position than Bernard, and had to deal with the memory of Becket and those who waved the Canterbury martyr's bloody shirt when attacking his successors. Peter does not try to turn either of his employers into another Becket. Instead he focuses on their obvious virtues, sometimes overstates their faults, and ultimately arrives at a kind of synthesis of monastic and clerical ideals, just before the emergence of the radical Franciscan and Dominican models for the apostolic life and leader-

---

[37] See Constance Brittain Bouchard, *Spirituality and Administration: The Role of the Bishop in Twelfth-Century Auxerre* (Cambridge, MA, 1979).

[38] *Ep.*, 82, *P.L.*, ccvii, 252–5; *Ep.*, 96, *P.L.*, ccvii, 302–4. The *argumenta* in the *P.L.* incorrectly state that these letters were written in the name of Richard of Dover.

[39] *Ep.*, 96, 303.

[40] *The Later Letters of Peter of Blois*, ed. Elizabeth Revell, Auctores Britannici Medii Aevi, 13 (London, 1993), no. 10, p. 58.

[41] *Ep.*, 27, *P.L.*, ccvii, 93–6.

ship.[42] Peter's own anxieties are never far from the surface of his defense of Richard and Baldwin, for he too found himself trapped between the ideal of Becket and a more prudent course.

Peter did not play a prominent role in the archiepiscopal household of Baldwin's successor, Hubert Walter, but in the mid-1190s he seems to have thrown in his lot with Walter of Coutances, archbishop of Rouen.[43] Like Hubert but unlike Thomas Becket and many others, Walter of Coutances did not shed his secular duties and title of justiciar when he became a prelate. As a patron and perhaps an employer, Walter presented Peter with a figure vastly different from Richard of Dover or Baldwin of Ford. Toward the end of his career, probably around 1196–7, Peter channeled his views on episcopal duty into a treatise longer than most of his letters, variously titled *Canon episcopalis* or *De institutione episcopi*, that he dedicated to John of Coutances, Walter's nephew.[44] John, as Peter himself makes clear in the tract, was a royal *curialis* himself who knew his uncle's business well, and Peter wrote him the tract on the occasion of his election to the see of Worcester. The treatise provides a non-systematic but effective attempt to integrate the fundamental clerical virtues that he valued with the bishop's role in the world, and it depicts an ideal bishop of far greater charisma and authority than the one that appears in his letters about Richard and Baldwin. The *Canon episcopalis* represents both several years of development in Peter's conception of episcopal duty, as well as a synthesis of several strands of thought on right behavior and church–state relations. Once again Peter draws on his exposure to diverse ideological currents to connect ideals of monastic provenance with traditional notions of pastoral care, and so he creates a prescriptive work suited to the period.

The piece is remarkable in that it manages to emerge from embarrassing sycophantery in the opening lines to end with some of Peter's most compelling prose. Along the way, he takes note of the important models and anti-types of the ideal bishop, beginning with praise of Walter of Coutances, John's own uncle. His panegyric for Walter hinges primarily on an adaptation of a description, common in the Middle Ages, of the attributes of a Christian leader, similar to one employed by Bernard of Clairvaux in his *De consideratione*:

If you wish to imitate [your uncle] faithfully, you will be in composed in your manners, liberal, courteous, gentle, prudent in giving advice, forceful in your actions, careful in

---

[42] The clearest account of this transformation is still Herbert Grundmann's *Religious Movements of the Middle Ages*, trans. Steven Rowan (Notre Dame, IN, 1995), 31–67.

[43] On Walter, see Peter A. Poggioli, 'From Politician to Prelate: The Career of Walter of Coutances, Archbishop of Rouen, 1184–1207' (Ph.D. diss., Johns Hopkins University, 1984).

[44] The *Canon episcopalis* appears in the manuscripts among the letters. It has been published as a distinct tract since the 16th century, presumably because in his *Invectiva in depravatorem* Peter refers to it by this name in a list of his works. *P.L.*, ccvii, 1115.

giving orders, modest in your speech, fearful when your fortunes are good, confident in adversity, calm in the midst of those who quarrel, peaceful in the presence of those who hate peace, profuse in alms-giving, moderate in zeal but fervid in mercy, neither anxious nor indifferent in the acquittal of household business, circumspect towards all things.[45]

Peter urges this English bishop to adapt the same habits and virtues that are described in a passage of *De consideratione* concerned with the men that Pope Eugenius III ought to admit to the papal curia.[46] In the *Canon episcopalis*, Peter does not equate the perfect bishop with the perfect monk as explicitly as Bernard does, and in fact not so much as he himself did in his defense of Richard of Dover. While he certainly had great admiration for Cistercian and other monastic ideals, his use of the list of episcopal virtues favored by Bernard of Clairvaux need not lead to the conclusion that he consciously set out to 'monasticize' the ideals for the episcopal office. These ideals had been a fundamental part of his education and were easily applicable to the pastoral responsibilities of the secular clergy.[47]

The ideal bishop of the *Canon episcopalis* edifies his flock by projecting his personal charisma onto his subjects through preaching and his own conduct: 'Edify others not only by word, but by deed and example . . . Edify your subjects with respect to their appearance, countenance, bearing, attire and gait.'[48] The phrase *docere verbo et exemplo*, crucial to what Caroline Bynum has identified as the distinctive spirituality of regular canons, was indeed commonly used in Victorine and Cistercian writings, but Peter employs it here in a specifically episcopal context.[49] According to writers who invoked this formulation, a bishop needs to stand out before his people through the quality of his own life, and he needs to use his exceptional virtue for edification, not for profit. Peter's use of the expression likely recalls not so much regular canonical spirituality as

---

[45]	si velitis fideliter imitari, eritis ad mores compositus, liberalis, affabilis, mansuetus, in consiliis providus, in agendo strenuus, in jubendo discretus, in loquendo modestus, timidus in prosperitate, in adversitate securus, mitis inter dyscolos, cum eis qui oderunt pacem pacificus, effusus in eleemosynis, in zelo temperans, in misericordia fervens, in rei familiaris dispensatione nec anxius, nec supinus, circumspectus ad omnia

Canon episcopalis, *P.L.*, ccvii, 1099.

[46] Bernard of Clairvaux, *De consideratione*, 4.4.12, in *S. Bernardi Opera Omnia*, ed. J. Leclercq, C.H. Talbot, and H.M. Rochais (7 vols., Rome, 1957–74), iii, 457.

[47] On Bernard, see Hayden White, 'The Gregorian Ideal and Saint Bernard of Clairvaux,' *Journal of the History of Ideas*, 21 (1960), 321–48. Cf. Elizabeth T. Kennan, 'The *De consideratione* and the Papacy in the mid-Twelfth Century: A Review of the Scholarship,' *Traditio*, 28 (1964), 73–115.

[48] 'Aedificat alios non solum verbo, sed opere et exemplo. . . . aedifices subditos in vultu, aspectu, gestu, habitu, et incessu': *Canon episcopalis*, 1102.

[49] See Bynum, 'The Spirituality of Regular Canons in the Twelfth Century,' *Jesus as Mother: Studies in the Spirituality of the High Middle Ages* (Berkeley, 1982), 22–58; *Docere Verbo et Exemplo: An Aspect of Twelfth-Century Spirituality*, Harvard Theological Studies, 13 (Missoula, MT, 1978). For an example of the phrase in Cistercian writing, see Martha G. Newman, *The Boundaries of Charity: Cistercian Culture and Ecclesiastical Reform, 1098–1180* (Stanford, 1996), 164–5.

the tradition of charismatic episcopal leadership that has been studied with par
ticular reference to early cathedral schools.[50] Beneath Peter's conventional cata-
logues of virtues, then, lies a complex interplay of several traditions.

The first half of the tract thus presents a series of dichotomies governing
proper and improper behavior in a prelate, leading ultimately to a distinction
between the worldly and the spiritual. As noted above, Peter of Blois, like Peter
Damian and Bernard, conceived of government as a dyarchic co-operation of
church and state. Here Peter of Blois stresses the distinctions, rather than any
symbiotic relationship, between the two spheres. The bishop is a *minister non
dominus*, with *officium pastoris non baronis*.[51] The dilemma of the courtly
cleric, so crucial throughout his letters, again commands Peter's attention.[52]

John of Coutances, the recipient of this tract, had experienced secular administration first-hand, but Peter warns rather than rebukes. Peter never fully
resolves the contradictions between ideal and reality – they stand uncomfortably
against each other. One of Bernard's recent translators has shrewdly remarked
that the abbot's great achievement in the *De consideratione* was to write of the
pope's duties in terms that recognized the paradox without attempting to deny
the inherent contradictions of the office.[53] The situation of a curial bishop is different from that of the pope, but Peter still formulates his advice in a way that
takes into account the bishop's situation as a possible royal servant and thus as a
self-contradicting entity. According to decrees of various councils, holding
royal office while a bishop was damnable – even the passionately Henrician
curialis Geoffrey Ridel, as noted above, resigned the chancellorship upon taking
an episcopal see.[54] Peter could not get around such decrees and precedents
cleanly, but he does manage to focus on the obligation of a bishop close to the
centers of power to use his position for the benefit of his flock:

It behooves a soul to be free of secular concerns if it is consecrated to the obedience of holy
servitude. You were dedicated to great things – do not be occupied by the most negligible.
Minuscule and vile are whatever things pertain to the business of the world, and not to the
profit of souls. If you should have secular affairs to deal with, as the Apostle says, bring
those who are most contemptible among you to judgment (I Cor. 6). If, however, the case
of a pauper should come to you, judge the paupers in justice, and beseech in equity for the

[50] C. Stephen Jaeger, *The Envy of Angels: Cathedral Schools and Social Ideals in Medieval
Europe, 950–1200* (Philadephia, 1994), 76–8.
[51] *Canon episcopalis*, 1103, 1105.
[52] For Peter as a courtier see C. Stephen Jaeger, 'Courtliness and Social Change,' *Cultures of
Power: Lordship, Status, and Process in Twelfth-Century Europe*, ed. Thomas N. Bisson (Phila-
delphia, 1995), 287–309; Rolf Köhn, '*Militia curialis*: Die Kritik der geistlichen Hofdienst bei
Peter von Blois und in lateinischen Literatur des 9 – 12 Jahrhunderts,' *Soziale Ordnungen im
Selbstverständnis des Mittelalters*, ed. Albert Zimmerman (Berlin, 1996), 227–57; John D. Cotts,
'The Critique of the Secular Clergy in Peter of Blois and Nigellus de Longchamps,' *H.S.J.* (forthcoming).
[53] Elizabeth T. Kennan, 'Introduction,' *Five Books on Consideration: Advice to a Pope*, trans.
John D. Anderson and Elizabeth T. Keenan, The Works of Bernard of Clairvaux, 13 (Kalamazoo,
1976), 16.
[54] See above, note 11.

harmony of the earth (Isaiah 11). Pass judgment for those suffering injury, procure peace for the lowly, obedience for rebels, quiet for cloisters, order for monasteries, discipline for the clergy.[55]

This passage suggests that Peter allows for a bishop involved in *negotia* to maintain his position so long as he secures justice for his people by acting as a shield for the oppressed and an enforcer of ecclesiastical order. Again, Peter never quite resolves the contradictions; perhaps he realized it would be impossible to do so.

Consequently, he modifies some of his earlier exhortations to close church–state relations, warning that the church should avoid, in certain cases, excessive co-operation with the royal authority, and it should not tacitly assent to things it cannot rightfully perform itself. Once again repeating the sentiments of countless church councils, he inveighs against churchmen who, following the example of Pilate, wash their hands of judgments of blood that they had a part in bringing about:

It arouses heavenly anger, brings to many the danger of eternal damnation, that certain princes of the church and elders of the people, who cannot pass judgments of blood, nevertheless carry them out by discussing and debating them, and they think themselves free from fault, because while they decree the judgment of death or severing of limbs, they simply absent themselves from the pronouncement and execution of the sentence. What can be more pernicious than this deception? Is it acceptable to discuss and delimit what it is not acceptable to pronounce? . . . You are the prelate for souls, not for bodies, and a prelate has nothing in common with Pilate. You are the *vilicus* of Christ, and the vicar of Peter; nor ought you to answer for the jurisdiction entrusted to you to Caesar, but to Christ. Certain men, when they usurp responsibility for things of this world submit themselves to the chains of the court.[56]

The distinction between the values of *regnum* and *sacerdotium* is clearly defined even as Peter shows that the two are intermingled in practice. For Peter, as for

---

[55] Vacuum a saecularibus opportet esse animum, divinae servitutis obsequio consecratum. Magnis addictus es, noli minimis occupari. Minima et vilia sunt, quaecumque ad saeculi quaestus, et non ad lucra pertinent animarum. Saecularia negotia si habueritis, dicit Apostolus, eos qui contemptibiles sunt inter vos, constituite ad judicandum. Si autem ad te intraverit causa pauperis, causa pupilli et viduae, judica in iustitia pauperes, et argue in aequitate pro mansuetis terrae. Fac judicium injuriam patientibus, procura humilibus pacem, rebellibus obedientiam, claustris quietem, ordinem monasteriis, clericis disciplinam   *Canon episcopalis*, P.L., ccvii, 1105.

[56] Illud coelestam exasperat iram, et plerisque discrimen aeternae damnationis accumulat, quod quidem pincipes sacerdotum et seniores populi, licet non dictent judicia sanguinis, eadem tamen tractant disputando et disceptando de illis, seque ideo immunes a culpa reputant, quod mortis aut truncationis membrorum judicium decernentes, a pronuntiatione duntaxat et exsecutione poenalis sententiae se absentant. Sed quid hac simulatione perniciosus est? Nunquid discutere et definire licitum est, quod pronuntiare non licet? . . . Animabus prelatus es, non corporibus, nihil praelato commune est cum Pilato. Christi villicus es, et vicarius Petri; nec te respondere oportet Caesari de comissa tibi jurisdicione, sed Christo. Quidam tamen per usurpatas saeculi administrationes se vinculo curiali obnoxiant   *Canon episcopalis*, 1109–10.

many reformers, mere deference to technical distinctions in legal procedure did not in itself create a pure and independent clergy. It will not do for a prelate to attempt, at least in the matter of judgments of blood, to participate in *saecularia negotia* innocently by quibbling over words. The story of Pilate washing his hands of the crucifixion of Christ (Matt. 27), which he carried out for the scribes and Pharisees who could not legally put a man to death, is presented as an example of a pernicious co-operation between church and state. Having denounced such co-operation, Peter moves on to set the church against the state, urging bishops to resist those contemporary laws that are unjust, concluding his list of abominations with an attack on the royal hunting laws which take into account only the 'immunity of beasts' and not the welfare of the populace:

This is said to be no less absurd and to be detested: that the immunity of churches is destroyed and the dignity of holy orders trampled underfoot, when certain princes of the world think only about the immunity of their beasts, and as men groan under the anguish of slavery, stags, roebucks, gazelles and hares exult in the right of total freedom. They freely feed off the gardens and crops of the poor, and no one dares fence them out; for today the hateful law condemns men not only for the poaching of animals but for the simple suspicion of poaching them. The members which nature created for the propagation of humankind are severed, their eyes are put out, even their feet or hands may be cut off, and man, who was created in the image of God, is horribly deformed – a grave disgrace to his creator. The lord king did not make these laws, but found them established . . . it would be much to the benefit of his salvation if he, by your urging, either sought to repeal them or in some way moderate them.[57]

With magnificent prose Peter urges John to urge the king (again by imparting wisdom as an adviser) to reform customs that harm ordinary Christians. Peter again shows his audience a bishop who speaks with the voice of moderation and intercedes for his flock. While the dangers of a rapacious administration are only implied in much of Peter's writing on clerical court service, here the coercive power of the rising monarchy appears in all its brutality. Playing on traditional clerical uneasiness with mutilation and other harsh punishments, Peter makes clear the essential position of the bishop in the life of church and state. As the tract nears its conclusion, he continues to delineate explicitly the proper way for a bishop to situate himself in relation to the secular authority:

[57]   Illud nihilominus absurdum detestandumque dicitur, quod effracta ecclesiarum immunitate et dignitate sacri ordinis conculcata, quidam principes terrae de sola immunitate cogitant ferarum, et, hominibus gementibus inter serviles angarias, cervi, capreoli, damae et lepores privilegio summae libertatis exsultant. Pauperum segetes et hortos impune depascunt, nec est qui eos arcere praesumaat; lex enim funesta homines hodie, non solum de captione ferarum, sed de simplici captionis suspicione condemnat. Succiduntur membra, quae in causam humanae propagationis natura creavit, effodiuntur oculi, pedes etiam manusque truncantur, et homo qui ad imaginem et similitudinem Dei creatus est, in sui Creatoris contumeliam horribiliter deformatur. Hanc quidem et alias odibiles Deo leges dominus rex non instituit, sed institutas invenit . . . ita domino regi cederent in praemium salutis aeternae, si eas, hortatu vestro, aut omnino delere studeret, aut ex parte aliqua tempararet   *Canon episcopalis*, 1110.

You are placed among the princes of the people, among the conscript fathers, into whose hands are given swords for doing satisfaction for the nations. Rise therefore, man of God, rise from adversity, girding yourself for mighty deeds. Soften the blows of the church . . . With the sword of preaching unsheathed, ride forth to carry out episcopal justice, according to the duty incumbent upon your order.[58]

Ultimately the *Canon episcopalis* presents as its ideal a bishop who intervenes in the government and does not stand aloof from it. Peter thus suggests a solution to the dilemma of the curialist bishop, but the ideals and accepted theories available to him do not allow him to articulate it as explicitly as one might like. The *Canon* allows the bishop to operate in curial circles by endowing him with a subversive apostolic quality. By introducing this potential for subversion into his tract, Peter declares that a bishop who truly leaves the court is in essence abandoning his flock, while too many contemporary bishops, opting for the other extreme, conspire with the royal powers to fleece it. The tract grandly summarizes Peter's ideas on the relationship between *regnum* and *sacerdotium*. He recognizes essentially one church, a dyarchy with two spheres that ought to be distinct, but he finds that in the rough and tumble world of the royal court, whence are issued judgments of blood and military orders, the bishop finds his true calling. He can use the defining mark of the cleric, wisdom, as well as Christ's compassion, to attack unjust laws and restrain violent monarchs. Peter combines the traditional role of the literate cleric with more novel ideas such as the quest for an apostolic life of hardship and suffering, and so he hints at a major shift in Christian ecclesiology that would be finally realized with the advent of Francis and Dominic.

The English episcopacy in the late twelfth century included a diverse assortment of men and hence could be described and exhorted using an almost boundless range of models. The Becket controversy brought into spectacular relief the image of the bishop who resisted royal authority and made himself a martyr for the church. Not everyone approved of Becket's example when he lived, but few could resist the growth of his cult and his elevation to the status of emblem for ecclesiastical liberty. Though he never reached the episcopal bench himself, Peter of Blois was subject to the same pressures as the men whom he served and counted on for patronage. Perhaps because of his personal experience with the archbishops of Canterbury, Peter constructs his model for episcopal duty differently from other clerical commentators. Unlike Gerald of Wales and Walter Map, for instance, he felt that monks made good bishops; his ideas are outlined in a group of context-specific pieces, and not in a general satire on the higher

---

[58] positus es inter principes populorum, inter patres conscriptos, quibus dati sunt gladii in manibus eorum ad faciendam vindictam in nationibus. Exsurge igitur, homo Dei, ex adverso ascende, ad opus fortitudinis te accingens: succurre plagae Ecclesiae. . . . Evaginato linguae gladio, in exsecutionem episcopalis justitiae, juxta formam quae tuae professioni annexa est, circumcurre   *Canon episcopalis,* 1111.

clergy.[59] His own enthusiasm for the new monastic orders and his exposure to the writings of Bernard of Clairvaux also conditioned his ideal. He felt the force of the Becket controversy, as his letters to various figures involved in the dispute show, but only later in life does he advocate anything resembling an antagonistic posture towards the secular power. Thus, we can trace a certain development in Peter's theories of episcopal duty away from the extreme advocacy of deference to kings displayed in his early letters. Peter's thought synthesizes a great number of strands from a number of traditions, and he is equally comfortable with ideas of monastic, patristic, and regular canonical provenance. This great *compilator*, a compiler of ideologies as well as of phrases and literary allusions, balances a number of streams of sometimes contradictory political theology in order to find a place for the bishop in the world, and he founds this synthesis on an appeal to the most basic obligations of the pastor to teach and advise.[60]

---

[59] Walter Map, *De nugis curialium*, trans. M.R. James, rev. C.N.L. Brooke and R.A.B. Mynors (Oxford, 1983), 84–117. For Gerald, see above, note 14.

[60] The term *compilator* was apparently leveled against Peter as an insult during his lifetime. He defends himself tenaciously in *Ep.*, 92, *P.L.*, ccvii, 289–91.

8

The *Casus Regis* Reconsidered

J.C. Holt

The *casus regis* may be simply stated: suppose a man has several sons, and suppose that at his death an elder son is already dead but himself leaves a son. Who takes precedence in the inheritance, the grandson in the senior line or a junior surviving son? Is the grandson to succeed to all that his father would have inherited had he survived, thereby representing his father's claim? Or does the younger son inherit on the ground that a son is nearer to the father than a grandson? Is it to be the representative claimant or the cadet? In 1199 John succeeded to the throne of England as a cadet and by the bequest of his elder brother, Richard Lionheart. Arthur, duke of Brittany, the son of John's defunct elder brother, Geoffrey of Brittany, was seen as the representative claimant, both before and even more after his death in 1202.

The argument began much earlier. The elements were debated in Glanvill and were known in the court of Henry II. I dealt with these matters in my first discussion of the cause and I shall not repeat them.[1] Likewise, I shall not say much about the royal succession, the dispute between John and Arthur, because I have dealt with this in a paper in a recent issue of *Nottingham Medieval Studies*;[2] except perhaps for two matters with which we can begin.

First, there seems to be no documentary evidence that Arthur ever laid claim to the throne of England. That he did depends almost entirely on a retrospective fiction of Roger Wendover (the alleged encounter between Arthur and John after Arthur's defeat and capture at Mirebeau), and Roger was very good at inventing that sort of thing. The legend of Arthur's seal ran 'duke of Brittany, count of Anjou, and earl of Richmond'; in July 1202 King Philip of France also threw in 'duke of Aquitaine', but this was prospective. There was, however, no mention of England – how could there be? Philip was not lord of England. So at this stage, the doubts about the succession to the crown were engendered on the Anglo-Norman, not the Franco-Breton side. And the doubts, once engendered, persisted.

---

1 'The *Casus Regis*: The Law and Politics of Succession in the Plantagenet Dominions', *Law in Medieval Life and Thought*, ed. Edward B. King and Susan J. Ridyard, Sewanee Mediaeval Studies, 5 (Sewanee, TN, 1990), 21–42; reprinted in J.C. Holt, *Colonial England, 1066–1215* (London, 1997), 307–26, to which all subsequent references are made.
2 'King John and Arthur of Brittany', *Nottingham Medieval Studies*, 44 (2000), 82–103.

Secondly, Arthur's fate was a matter of deliberation, discussed and perhaps determined, though by no more than a nod and a wink, at John's Easter court at Rouen and Molyneux in 1203.[3] Now Geoffrey fitz Peter, the justiciar of England, appeared at Molyneux on 2 April, the day before Arthur 'went missing'. This was only the second occasion in the reign on which he paid a flying visit to Normandy (the first occurring at the outbreak of the war with Philip the previous Easter). So something was up and that, almost certainly, was what to do about Arthur. Both John and Geoffrey were consummate planners and plotters. In 1199 Geoffrey had aided John to the throne; in return John confirmed Geoffrey in the lands of the Mandeville earldom of Essex and granted him the title of earl. John succeeded as a cadet; Geoffrey as a representative in right of his wife, Beatrice de Say, who had died in 1197. Henceforth Geoffrey and John were bound together like Siamese twins. What a mess!

John now needed Geoffrey to concur in Arthur's fate. It would take the bite out of the *casus regis* issue if one representative heir could be brought to condemn another in the interest of the cadet. Was John so subtle? He may have been. The consequence, at least, was brutally clear. To pursue one line of argument for his own succession and allow the opposite for his justiciar was to defuse the whole issue, or so John imagined. There would be no law in the matter; each case would be settled *ad hoc*. Arthur's was. So much for John.

Did Geoffrey need John? There is the clearest evidence that he did. It has become almost mandatory to regard Geoffrey as the prime example of men 'raised from the dust', a knight who rose to become master by marriage of the honour of Mandeville, then chief justiciar of England, and finally earl of Essex.[4] Maybe. However, Geoffrey now held his lands by what became known as courtesy of England; his wife being dead, he was lucky to have her children, who, in turn, succeeded him. So he was far from secure in the early years of the reign of John. When he came to Normandy at John's summons at Easter 1203 he was probably already pledged to the crusade. He had second thoughts about it. Application was made to the highest authority and on 7 July 1205 Pope Innocent granted an indulgence. The pope reviewed the terms of the submission which had been made by Geoffrey, or on his behalf: England was at war with France, so the king and magnates would not let him leave England because his presence in the country was essential; the king and magnates of France likewise would not allow him to travel through their land, so that the fulfilment of his vows was impossible. Moreover, he had heirs, little boys (*parvulos*), with the most powerful enemies who were striving in every way to disinherit them, who had already occupied a great part of the boys' inheritance, and who would easily seize the rest in their father's absence. And then a plea perhaps for the pope's own ear: Geoffrey had founded a monastery of the Gilbertine order in the inheritance of his sons, and this, according to the law of the province of England, could not

3 See Holt, 'King John and Arthur', 91–2.
4 See, most recently, R.V. Turner, *Men Raised from the Dust* (Philadelphia, 1988), 35–70.

stand if his sons were deprived of their inheritance.[5] This referred to the priory of Shouldam. Very moving! And Geoffrey would know all about such matters because of his own maltreatment, as an upstart newcomer, of the Mandeville foundation of Walden.[6] So Geoffrey needed John all right, and in this case he was duly supported by a royal letter to the pope: 'his presence is so necessary to us and our land that we cannot possibly do without him'.[7]

So John and Geoffrey were interlocked, and note the complications. Geoffrey, as I have said, held by courtesy of England; it was his sons' interests which he pleaded in his letter to the pope, appearing both as a father and a benign custodian. John, too, brought complications. He was not an immediate cadet successor to Henry II; Richard had intervened; so John played for all he was worth that he was successor to Richard (rather than Henry), an argument strengthened by Richard's deathbed bequest of the realm to him, not to Arthur. Richard who had recognized Arthur in 1190, recognized John in 1199; if anyone kicked the law of succession around to suit political interests it was Richard; he seems the least consistent of them all.

But was it law? Are we entitled to say that Richard, or anyone else, was inconsistent? Or was it simply an issue to be debated by justices and exploited by litigants? If so, who knew about it, paid attention to it? And how far down the social scale? The debate, if that is what it was, ran back at least as far as Glanvill and was continued in the Norman law books. Was it anything more than a fine point of law for judges to mull before the fire over their evening wine? That is the question this article seeks to investigate. It will proceed with case-studies, starting at the top with the great noble families and ending with the litigating freeman. And it will show, I hope, that the common man speaking through the juries was the more likely to settle on the representative heir. The logic of primogeniture scarcely permitted any other solution although, as we shall see, it certainly allowed exceptions.

So let us turn to the Mandevilles, who have been much discussed by Warren Hollister and Ralph Turner, not to mention Round.[8] The earlier history of their misfortunes is well known so let us begin rather with the misfortunes of the Says, namely with the cadet claimants. It is beyond any reasonable doubt that

[5] *P.L.*, ccxv, 746; *The Letters of Pope Innocent III (1198–1216) concerning England and Wales*, ed. C.R. Cheney and Mary G. Cheney (Oxford, 1967), nos. 633, 660, which do not include reference to 'the custom of the province of England'; the phrase reads like a papal rendering of 'the custom of the realm of England', which would be Geoffrey's original wording. I am obliged to Professor Jane Sayers for bringing this letter to my attention. I know of no other reference to the 'law' which Geoffrey fitz Peter advanced.

[6] *The Book of the Foundation of Walden Monastery*, ed. Diana Greenway and Leslie Watkiss (Oxford Medieval Texts, 1999), 152–60.

[7] *Foedera*, I. i. 91.

[8] C. Warren Hollister, 'The Misfortunes of the Mandevilles', *History*, 58 (1973), 18–28; J.H. Round, *Geoffrey de Mandeville* (London, 1892); Ralph Turner, 'The Mandeville Inheritance, 1189–1236: its Legal, Political, and Social Context', *H.S.J.*, 1 (1989), 147–72, which is marred by its reliance on the extracts of the Walden Chronicle in *Monasticon Anglicanum*.

they were intended as the appropriate successors to the Mandeville estates, recognized as such by William, the third earl of Essex, by his sister Beatrice who married William de Say, the originator of the Say claim, and by the monks of the family house, the priory and later abbey of Walden. But this side of the family tended always to land themselves in the soup. In 1189 Henry II died; so did Earl William de Mandeville. Beatrice the heiress was faced by a new king, Richard Lionheart, ravenous for money. She was now of great age – she had borne at least two sons to her husband, who had died in 1144. She made no move to claim the inheritance for herself, which would have been beyond challenge. Instead she sent her son Geoffrey, accompanied by the prior of Walden and the chief men of the barony, not to claim it for her but to claim the succession for himself. In effect she sought a *dimisit se* without appearing in person to renounce her title, and without apparently paying any relief or rendering the homage which would have legalized that title. This was critical. The *dimisit se* was a very 'feudal' procedure whereby a tenant went to the lord's court accompanied by the proposed heir. He resigned his homage to the lord who then took the homage of the heir and conveyed the inheritance. The procedure was formal and public. Beatrice ignored all this. She was a grand old lady according to the Walden chronicler, but one very much in a hurry – indeed in too great a hurry. By contrast the claim of the representative contestant, Geoffrey fitz Peter, was simple; he made it in right of his wife, daughter of William de Say, Beatrice's elder son, who had died in 1177. But Geoffrey de Say won, his case supported as it was by men of influence. But it is not surprising that he had to face the enormous fine of 7000m. for his succession. It was not just a relief; it was also a payment for recognition of a *dimisit se* which had been carried out in a most irregular fashion. Hence Geoffrey de Say paid for three things: relief for the Mandeville succession, a *dimisit se* or the equivalent to meet Beatrice's wishes, and the irregularity of that *dimisit*.[9] Fitz Peter's subsequent proffer, by contrast was just 3000m. The circumstances which I have described do much to explain the disparity between the two.

Geoffrey de Say held the barony for a very short period. Earl William de Mandeville died on 14 November 1189.[10] Geoffrey's claim was approved by King Richard sometime between 25 November and 5 December. Seisin came a little later, after he had provided sureties of payment. However he was unable to meet the terms and surrendered the barony to the 'justiciar', William de Longchamp. Longchamp reverted to Geoffrey fitz Peter's bid and installed him in the succession, this around midsummer 1190; this was confirmed by charter of King Richard dated 23 January 1191 at Messina.[11] So Geoffrey de Say was in charge for eight months at most, during which he seems to have installed his son, also called Geoffrey, in part of the barony. What formal procedure he used

[9]   *Foundation of Walden*, 86–9; Holt, *Colonial England*, 313–15.
[10] *Foundation of Walden*, 84–5.
[11] *Foundation of Walden*, xxix, 88, 104.

is now impossible to determine; there is no evidence of a *dimisit se*; but by some means he achieved a substitution.[12] In the sessions of the curia coming from the interregnum of 1199 William de Mora countered an assize of *mort d'ancestor* concerning 12 acres and a messuage in Thorley by presenting a charter of Earl William (de Mandeville), which he called Geoffrey son of Geoffrey to warrant.[13] This can be no other than Geoffrey de Say junior. In a similar assize, entered a few entries later on the roll, concerning 8 acres in Gilston, William son of Godfrey called Geoffrey son of Geoffrey to warrant as the heir of Earl William de Mandeville.[14] Thorley and Gilston were both members of the great Mandeville manor of Sawbridgeworth, which had a rocky history going back to the reign of Henry I;[15] it was not securely restored to the family until the early years of Henry II.[16] By then a considerable portion (74 librates), perhaps as much as half, had been enfeoffed to Warin and Henry fitz Gerald in 1144. The other portion, perhaps the other half, we can see originating in Geoffrey senior's arrangements for his son in 1190. This came to be known as Saybury.[17] It was the establishment of Saybury which led to the fears expressed by Geoffrey fitz Peter in the papal indulgence of 1205. He really had 'enemies' who had moved in on the estate and done so by a legal manoeuvre which would be difficult to challenge without dragging the whole question of his title back into court. He was hamstrung and at risk, and he knew it. He and his son, Geoffrey, who took the name de Mandeville, were saved by the Says. Geoffrey senior transferred his right to Geoffrey junior before King John; even so in 1213–14 both sued, the senior appointing the junior as his attorney, and they sued for the whole honour of Mandeville including a number of named manors. This left Geoffrey de Mandeville with an easy reply: much of the honour of Earl William was lacking to him, including Sawbridgeworth and Edmonton which Geoffrey de Say himself held. The Says, he held, were seeking more than he had; he went *sine die*; the Says were allowed to seek another writ but were in mercy.[18] They had shown themselves to be legally illiterate. They never recovered their loss of

---

12 For the tactic see S.F.C. Milsom, *The Legal Framework of English Feudalism*, Cambridge Studies in English Legal History (1976), 146–53.

13 *Rotuli Curiae Regis*, ed. Francis Palgrave (2 vols., Rec. Com., 1835), i, 328. The printed text should be corrected to 'et vocat inde ad warantum Gaufr. fil. Gaufr. ... S... qui debet ei terram illam warantizare quia in carta continetur quod idem Comes et heredes sui debent ei terram waran . . . et heredibus suis contra omnes homines' (P.R.O., KB26/11). Palgrave gave this roll an uncertain date – see his Table of Contents; but entries on 324, 325 establish that it comes from the interregnum.

14 *Rotuli Curiae Regis*, i, 333–4. Once more the text should be corrected to 'Quam terram Willelmus filius Godefr' tenet et Willelmus filius Godfr' venit et vocat inde ad warantum Gaufridum filium Gaufridi heredem scilicet Willelmi Comitis de Mandevile' (P.R.O., KB26/11).

15 C. Warren Hollister, 'The Misfortunes of the Mandevilles', *History*, 58 (1973), 18–28; R.H.C. Davis, 'Geoffrey de Mandeville reconsidered', *E.H.R.*, 79 (1964), 299–307.

16 J.H. Round, *Geoffrey de Mandeville* (London, 1892), 235–6. I by-pass the earlier grants of Matilda and Stephen.

17 *V.C.H. Hertfordshire*, iii, 335–7.

18 *Cur. Reg. R.*, vi, 270; vii, 110–11.

balance. Sundry members of the family sued on into the reign of Henry III, but the estate, admittedly sadly diminished, passed from Earl Geoffrey to his brother William, then to their sister and then through her to the Bohuns. The case came to a formal conclusion in a final concord in 1284.[19] Throughout my narrative, you will note, no one stated the principles of the *casus regis*. Geoffrey de Say, whether father or son, claimed as the nearest and lawful heir. So also did fitz Peter and the Mandevilles. And that was that.

The intrusion of the *dimisit se* is illustrated yet again, and more critically, in the case of the de Briouzes, to which I now turn. The outline is well known. William III de Briouze died in exile in France in 1211 after being one of King John's favourite courtiers and most loyal supporters. His wife Matilda died of starvation in a royal prison, most probably Windsor, along with William IV de Briouze, the eldest son, in 1210. They all knew too much, and Matilda talked too much, about the death of Arthur, duke of Brittany. The Briouze estates were enormous: their patrimony, the baronies of Bramber and Knepp in Sussex, half of Barnstaple and of Totnes in Devon, and then in Wales, Radnor, Brecon, Builth, Abergavenny, and Gower, to which had been added the three royal castles of Gwent (Skenfrith, White Castle, and Llantilio), and finally in Ireland, the lordships of Limerick and Thomond. Some of these were recent acquisitions of John's reign: Totnes, the Three Castles, and Limerick. One, Thomond, was little more than speculative, and there, as in Limerick, the Briouzes were largely absentees. So title was varied and in some cases debatable. To understand what happened we must first get a grip on the calamity which befell the Briouzes. The father of the family, William III escaped to France in 1208 to die in exile at Corbeuil in August 1211; his main contribution was to give King Philip of France details of the end of Arthur of Brittany. His wife Matilda, who was probably John's main target, escaped to Scotland from the siege of Carrickfergus in 1210 along with her eldest son William IV and his children, but they were taken by Duncan of Carrick and handed over to King John. The subsequent death of mother and son obscures the fact that the grandchildren survived. The eldest of these was John; once in his majority, he was to become the representative claimant. Meanwhile the cadets had their day. The first was Giles, bishop of Hereford, brother of William IV. In May 1215 he fined in 9000m. for the whole inheritance and repeated his offer in October. A month later he died. But he and his brother Reginald, the next in line, were already in close collusion with Llewelyn ap Jorwerth, prince of Gwynedd, who was sweeping away English power in south and central Wales. At Giles of Hereford's death Reginald seized all the Welsh properties of their house.[20] In November 1213 King John tried desperately to remedy matters by offering Reginald the same settlement which had

[19] *Feet of Fines for Essex*, ed. R.E.G. Kirk (Essex Archeological Society, 1899–1928), ii, 136.
[20] *Brut y Tywysogyon, Peniarth MS 20 version*, ed. and trans. Thomas Jones, Board of Celtic Studies, University of Wales, History and Law Series, 11 (1952), 90–91. See also J.E. Lloyd, *History of Wales* (2 vols., London, 1911), ii, 644–5.

been agreed with Giles, but Reginald was securely tied to the Welsh: he married a daughter of Llewelyn in 1215. Agreement was not reached until March or June 1217, when Reginald finally came to the peace on the terms which Giles had accepted, but with the important exclusion of the fine which Giles had offered. Letters of seisin covering all the Briouze estates, including Bramber, followed and Reginald was fully acknowledged in the succession, a ringing victory for the Briouze policy of playing both ends, i.e. English and Welsh against the middle, namely themselves.[21] But he was not fully in control. Worse still, John de Briouze, son of William IV, was released from custody in January 1218 and soon began legal action concerning all the Briouze estates.[22]

It is sometimes stated that the *casus regis* stood in the way of John's claims.[23] No one said so at the time. More important, no one, least of all the regent, wanted to do anything to upset the fragile peace which had just been concluded with Reginald. So John de Briouze soldiered, or rather litigated on, first before the eyre in Sussex, then before the justices at Westminster. It is important to recognize that he did not claim as a representative; he claimed as heir to his father who, he said had been put in seisin by King John consequent on a *dimisit se* by his grandfather. This must have taken place sometime before 1208 when relations between William III de Briouze and the king broke down. It is vital to our understanding of all the subsequent legal actions. Now the *dimisit se* by William III does not appear in any contemporary record prior to his disgrace. It is, however, recorded in an account of the Briouze family preserved in a seventeenth-century extract from the lost cartulary of Neath Abbey now in the Dodsworth manuscripts.[24] Here William III is stated to have devised the whole of the Briouze lands on William IV.[25] The cartulary has the procedure correct; it uses the term *dimisit*, states that it was done *de licentia domini regis*, and adds that the king took homage from William IV. But the account is garbled: it presents King John's grant of Gower to William III as a reward for William's capture of Arthur at Mirebeau and as compensation for the lands he had devised. This would place the *dimisit* before the date of the Gower charter, 24 February 1203;[26] that William III devised all his baronies before that date is improbable. But at some point before 1208 he devised Bramber and probably Bramber and Knepp alone.

The argument was indefeasible. In stating the case before the justices of the bench in Michaelmas 1219, John claimed Bramber as heir not only to his grandfather but also to his father who died seized of the demesnes, homages, reliefs, services, and tenancies for which King John took the homage *ipsius Willelmi*

[21] *Cal. Pat. 1216–1225*, 72–4, 103, 109–10; *Rot. Litt. Claus.*, i, 312, 318b. Letters of restoration were also issued for the Irish estates (*Patent Rolls*, 72, 112–13, 132, 263).

[22] *Cur. Reg. R.*, viii, 10–11; *Rot. Litt. Claus.*, i, 405b.

[23] Lloyd, *History of Wales*, ii, 658n.; D.A. Carpenter, *Minority of Henry III* (London, 1990), 246.

[24] Oxford, Bodleian Library, Dodsworth MS. 20, fols. 76–77, printed by F.R. Lewis in *Bulletin of Celtic Studies*, 9 (1939), 149–55.

[25] Ibid., 151.

[26] G.T. Clark, *Carta . . . de Glamorgancia*, iii, 254.

junioris (William IV).[27] This was never contradicted by his opponents or rejected by the court. The claim was renewed in the same terms in Michaelmas 1220,[28] and confirmed in the final transfer of the barony to John at Easter 1227.[29] But it was restricted to Bramber and Knepp; so too was the claim for dower launched by Matilda de Clare, widow of William IV.[30]

But Reginald de Braose had already queered the pitch. First he argued that John was under age;[31] and then, in Michaelmas 1220, that he no longer held in Bramber.[32] He had in fact pulled a fast one; he had executed a *dimisit se* in favour of his eldest son, William IVC, on 7 August 1218; this disgraceful tactic was carried out *teste comite*, that is before William Marshal.[33] It delayed and complicated young John's action. In the end the parties came to concord but it was not finally executed until Easter 1226, when John in effect had to buy the honour at a price of £252 – this to compensate Reginald and William IVC for the damage which John was alleged to have done through invading the property. John was in seisin before 1228, but details of the agreement were still being tidied up in Hilary 1230.[34] Not a pleasant family, the Briouzes! And, with one exception, that was all John was able to achieve. His claim to the Welsh lands flickered out; Reginald was too strongly established and his loyalty was too valuable to the council. Hubert de Burgh likewise retained the Three Castles. John made no claim to Totnes and there is some indication that William III had made another *dimisit se* to establish Reginald there as early as 1207. John entered a *prece partium* against Henry de Tracy to Barnstaple in 1224 but that also faded away. He entered no challenge to the Irish lands which came into Reginald's hands in 1217. Only in the case of Gower did he enjoy success and that not by legal action but by the same political route which had been followed by William III and Reginald. Reginald's settlement with the regency in 1218 left Llewelyn high and dry and indeed increasingly irate. It did not stop his rapid expansion into central, west, and south Wales. In 1220 he transferred Gower to John with the hand of his last daughter, Margaret. Just as the Briouzes had made a speciality of playing the Welsh against the English, so Llewelyn was now in a position to play one Briouze against another, both of them his sons-in-law. There was poetic justice in that. The Briouzes were a nasty lot, especially to the Welsh. When William IVC, Reginald's son, was caught *in flagrante delicto* with Llewelyn's wife (Joan, bastard daughter of King John), he was hanged from a tree amidst a crowd of jeering Welshmen.

The rough justice of the Marches and the nervousness of the Minority government confronted by the energetic expansion of Welsh rule led by

27 *Cur. Reg. R.*, viii, 10–11.
28 *Cur. Reg. R.*, ix, 306–7.
29 *Cur. Reg. R.*, xiii, 133.
30 *Cur. Reg. R.*, viii, 11.
31 *Cur. Reg. R.*, viii, 11.
32 *Cur. Reg. R.*, ix, 306–7.
33 *Cal. Pat. 1216–1225*, 165.
34 *Cur. Reg. R.*, viii, 754, 1425, 1583; xiii, 2585.

Llewelyn left little room for the judicious arguments of the *casus regis*. John must have been aware of it; he claimed Bramber as heir of his father, all the other lands as heir to his grandfather, but beyond that it played no part in this bruising family quarrel. The *dimisit se*, on the other hand was given full play in both the senior and cadet line.

Now it was possible to conduct these matters in quite a different manner. I turn now to the Quencys, and here I shall have to summarize a great deal of complex genealogical argument and also bring in some matters of diplomatic. We are concerned here with the progeny of Saer de Quency who became earl of Winchester in 1208. He had a son, Robert de Quency, husband of Hawise of Chester, by whom he had a daughter, Margaret. So in order of generations we have Saer, Robert, Margaret. Saer also had a cadet son, Roger. Robert, the elder son, died in 1217 and sometime between then and his departure for the crusade in 1219 Saer made provision for the succession of the younger son; Roger was recognized as heir during Saer's lifetime.[35] This was a provident move because Saer died before the walls of Damietta later in 1219. Roger succeeded; at this time Margaret, Robert's daughter, cannot have been more than fourteen at most. It is a classic case in which at a time of risk, a young female representative was bypassed in the interest of an older cadet and more broadly of keeping the family property within the male line. It was done without question or trouble of any kind. Margaret did not suffer. In 1231 Earl Ranulf of Chester resigned the earldom of Lincoln to his daughter Hawise, and she passed it to her daughter, Margaret, who carried it to her husband John de Lacy in 1232. After two further husbands she ended her days a widow, a highly respected countess of Lincoln and a correspondent of Grossetete.

This was the generally accepted view until it was challenged, first by Sidney Painter and then by Geoffrey Barraclough. Painter failed to consider the *casus regis* pattern of succession and therefore dismissed the marriage between Robert de Quency and Hawise of Chester as 'absolutely impossible' on the ground that the child of that marriage (Margaret) did not inherit; he then concocted a non-existent Robert, brother of Saer, as husband of Hawise of Chester and buttressed all this with a false pedigree chart – a good example of how one error leads to others.[36] Then Barraclough, following and relying on Painter, had to confront a charter, namely a grant by Saer de Quency, earl of Winchester, to his newly married son, Robert and his wife Hawise, of lands in England and Lothian amounting to one hundred librates.[37] This was matched by a similar grant from Ranulf, earl of Chester. Saer's grant only survives in copies; Ranulf's is an original charter. The two are apparently inconsistent. Saer was created earl of Winchester in 1207; his charter must therefore be dated 1207 or later. Earl

---

35 See, for example, *Liber cartarum prioratus Sancti Andree in Scotia* (Bannatyne Club, Edinburgh, 1842), 255–6.

36 S. Painter, 'The House of Quency, 1136–64', *Medievalia e Humanistica* 11 (1960), 3–9.

37 *The Charters of the Anglo-Norman Earls of Chester, c.1071–1237* (Record Society of Lancashire and Cheshire, cxxvi, 1988), 306.

Ranulf's charter must be placed *c.* 1200 and not later than 1202, chiefly because of the attestations. Yet the attestations of Saer's and Ranulf's are identical. Therefore, concluded Barraclough, the charter of Saer must be dismissed as a forgery. Barraclough was perhaps in a rush or engaged on other matters such as China and World History; this may excuse him, but not his editor. At all events Barraclough got Saer's charter from the text printed in Ormerod's *History of Cheshire*[38] and did not pursue the manuscript evidence. In fact there is not just one charter of Saer's but two, both made in favour of Robert, his son and heir. Both are accompanied by drawings of Saer's fourth seal with the arms of fitz Walter impaled (probably as an indication of brotherhood in arms) and with the title of earl on the counterseal: SECRETUM COMITIS WINTONIE.[39] Now the notion of one forged charter is acceptable, but the notion of two, each with a correct drawing of an authentic seal, each in a different hand, beggars belief. Moreover there are differences between the two charters which are highly significant; one concerns the English lands granted and follows the diplomatic of English law; the other concerns the lands in Lothian and has slight diplomatic variants probably to meet the requirements of the Scottish courts. The two documents are genuine enough, so how to reconcile them with Earl Ranulf of Chester's charter? The obvious explanation is that they are *renovatio(s)* (or should I say *renovationes*) preserving the attestations of an earlier grant of *c.* 1202, reissued in 1207 to assert Saer's new dignity as earl and to give the same enhanced dignity to the marriage portion. The difficulty in understanding the Quency arrangements lies not in the original arrangements but in the modern commentaries, which now have to be rejected. It was a perfectly normal, and in the end amicable, arrangement in favour of the cadet, made for obvious reasons. No one objected to or challenged the arrangement.

I come now to the Percys, a family which was perhaps the most litigious of all. The contention between the main parties ran on for more than thirty years from 1204 to 1234 and later. The courts must have been heartily sick of the Percys and their reiterated disputes. Yet these yield the clearest statement of all of an argument in favour of the representative heir. In the Yorkshire eyre of 1219 Richard de Percy sought a ploughland in Wansford (E. Riding, Yorks), claiming it to be his right and inheritance, whereof his grandfather William was seized in the time of king Henry the father; from William the right in that land descended to Agnes his daughter, mother of Richard, and from Agnes to Richard as to her son and heir. The tenant, Richard of Halley, put himself on the grand assize and sought recognition whether he had the greater right of holding

---

[38] G. Ormerod, *The History of the County Palatine and City of Chester* (3 vols., London, 1882), i, 28.

[39] B.L., Lansdowne MS. 203, fol. 14v; P.R.O., DL 42/2 (Great Coucher of the Duchy of Lancaster), fol. 481v. The second of these has no drawing of the seal, but it is preserved in an English summary in B.L., MS. Cotton, Julius cvii, fol. 190r. For the complications of the Quincy arms see *Complete Peerage*, xii, pt. 2, Appendix I, 29–31; my numeration follows J.H. Stevenson and M. Wood, *Scottish Heraldic Seals* (3 vols., Glasgow, 1940), iii, 550–51.

that land of Richard or the same Richard of holding it in demesne. So far so good, but note: this is not an ordinary plea recorded in an ordinary fashion; it is entered on the memoranda roll of the justices where it is not included among the standard entries of cases referred to Westminster. And it continues not with a pleading but with a draft judgement.

But since Richard had an elder brother, namely William (*recte* Henry) father of William de Percy, and no land could descend to the same Richard by hereditary right from the aforesaid William his grandfather, but rather to his elder brother and his heirs, it is adjudged that the assize does not lie.

Now this entry was entered by itself on the dorse at the end of the entries headed *loquendum d*e in a scruffy hand not otherwise apparent anywhere on the roll. Who made the entry? Not one of the usual clerks; probably not a clerk at all, for the entry trod on serious matters; perhaps one of the justices, Martin Pattishall, say, feeling a bit squiffy after a good meal.

This is the only instance in all the Percy cases in which the root of the matter was touched. Why then were they at loggerheads? The answer is that they brought it on themselves. When William de Percy died in 1175 his lands were divided between his two daughters, Maud, who married William, earl of Warwick, and Agnes, who married Jocelin de Louvain.[40] Both died 1200–4 and both were widows. Maud had no heirs of the body. Agnes had two sons, the elder of whom, Henry, died in 1198 leaving a son, William, the representative in the story, who came into the custody of William Briwere and did not come of age until 1214. The younger son, Richard de Percy, who is the Percy of Magna Carta, was the cadet. Now there were many complications in the division of the lands between the two heiresses, but for the moment I will concentrate attention on the main division between the two parties. In 1200 William Briwerre acquired the custody and marriage of the heirs of Henry de Percy with the whole of their inheritance.[41] Then on 13 October 1204, both heiresses now being dead, the sheriff of Yorkshire was instructed that William was to have full seisin *tamquam custodi* of all the lands of the Earl of Warwick in Yorkshire, except for the fee held of the earl of Chester.[42] On the same days he was also ordered to give to Richard de Percy all the lands of his mother (Agnes) with the addition of the fees which Matilda, countess of Warwick held of the earl of Chester.[43] For the rest, the division of 1204 closely followed the lines agreed in 1175. William de Percy reached his majority before 1214 when he sued for his ancestral estates in Richard's possession. Unfortunately he included Guisburn, which he held already, and the case went *sine die*.[44] After the civil war following 1215 the two parties came together and the division of 1204/1175, was broadly agreed once

[40] *E.Y.C.*, xi, 85–9.
[41] *Rotuli Chartarum*, ed. T.D. Hardy (Rec. Com., 1837), 48b.
[42] *Rot. Litt. Claus.*, i, 11b.
[43] *Rot. Litt. Claus.*, i, 11b.
[44] *Cur. Reg. R.*, vii, 160.

again and was confirmed yet again in 1219.[45] By this time the abbots of St
Mary's York and Fountains had intervened to secure agreement. (I shall be
dealing with this elsewhere.) There was a further agreement in the *curia regis* in
1225, another in 1227–8, and a further one in 1234–5.[46] Not all the disputes had
been settled when Richard died without lawful issue in 1244, thus bringing
matters to a conclusion.

What were the issues? They had nothing to do with the principle of division
once that had been established in 1204. Most of the troubles arose because in
1175 the parties proceeded to divide manors and other interests. The abbey of
Whitby, for example, a Percy refoundation of the Conquest, was to be *in
communi*, and it may be that compromises could be reached there, but it was
wildly optimistic to imagine that the forests of Litton and Buckden with their
hunting rights could also be *in communi*, without it leading to serious disputes
and disturbances. And this is what happened. The main contendants tried to
resolve the difficulty in 1225 by allocating Littondale to Richard and
Langstrothdale to William, marking the boundary at the crest of the ridge
between the two. The crest is easy enough to follow for most of the way; then
and later it marked a parish boundary; but here and there, especially between the
townships of Halton and Litton, it broadens into an ill defined plateau dotted
with rocky outcrops and little lakelets. Here the crest becomes anyone's guess,
especially the guess of bailiffs and huntsmen drawing a line always in the interest of their masters. Then there were questions of pursuing quarry across this
boundary, of hounds and strays invading it, because how were they to know?
Was one forest to provide sanctuary for the other? Then there were problems of
impounding hounds in pursuit and beasts at pasture, and of chasing, beating, and
arresting trespassers.[47] It was a recipe for mayhem and mayhem is what it produced until a genealogical accident, the death of Richard de Percy without legitimate heirs, solved the problem.

It took much longer, indeed much much longer, to solve other problems. The
division of manors and services often attempted the impossible. Tenants challenged tenure and services, and the Percys did the same in reverse. The statement of the Percy pedigree and claims I have already mentioned arose from just
such a case. And how is a manor of settled economic structure to be divided?
Take the village of Linton in Craven a few miles down Wharfedale from the disputed forest areas. It is still a remarkable place, with very few houses later than
the seventeenth century, a small village green with a stream running down to the
Wharfe a mile away, a small eighteenth-century chapel, in the style of and possibly by Vanbrugh, in which you can still attend a service, with six almshouses
and an inn, the Fountaine Arms, named after the benefactor of the chapel and
almshouses. The village may show signs of an old division to an economic

---

[45] *E.Y.C.*, xi, 86–9.
[46] *Percy Cartulary*, 54–7; *Cur. Reg. R.*, xii, 1426; *Yorkshire Fines, 1218–31*, 108–11; *Yorkshire
Fines, 1232–46*, 12, *Cur. Reg. R.*, xv, 1125.
[47] *Percy Cartulary*, 54–5.

historian with his boots on, but I can detect nothing of it. Nevertheless it was divided, possibly along the line of the Wharfe, for the parish included Grassington and Hebden, nearly two miles downstream, both on the north bank of the river. Each half was enfeoffed differently and each went its own way with its own tenurial history. But what then about the church?, for Linton has a lovely little church standing isolated about a mile from the village centre on the banks of the Wharfe, so sited as to serve the needs of the whole parish; it has a little bit of Norman (the arches of the north aisle), but was largely rebuilt in decorated style, very simple with no fringes, then much restored. Now the first rector we hear of was one William who attested a charter of William of Threshfield, 1180–1200.[48] But on the next occasion on which we hear of rectors, in the middle years of the thirteenth century, there was not one but two, and as we progress into the fourteenth century we find that one was called 't'one' and the second 't'other', each attached to one of the medieties of the manor. As we find out more about 't'one' and 't'other' with the onflow of time, it is apparent that the two rectors each had his own stall in the chancel, sitting opposite each other; they took the service on alternate Sundays. And so it lasted into the sixteenth century, when in 1569 both medieties fell into the hands of the crown following the rebellion of the northern lords. The old manor was at last reunited but not the rectories. For Linton continued with 't'one' and 't'other' until 1866 when they were united by Order in Council and transferred first to the bishop of Ripon and then in 1895 to the dean and chapter. However the good people of Linton have maintained their ways. Instead of the usual two wardens the church has four, which have descended from the two medieties in which the manor was divided in 1175.[49]

There is yet another case of considerable interest, that of the constables of Richmond – not baronial, true, but with their thirteen fees held of the barony, clearly representing a rank of importance, Stenton's honorial baronage. At an early stage, probably in the reign of Henry I, this fee was divided between the descendants of Roald the Constable and the de Rollos family, probably as a result of descent through co-heiresses. It was not reunited until 1208 following de Rollos's siding with Philip Augustus after his reconquest of Normandy.[50] Thereafter it descended in the direct line until 1247, when Roald fitz Alan was dead, leaving a representative grandson and a cadet younger son, both confusingly named Roald.[51] This was the occasion, 20 July 1247, when Henry III instructed the chief lord, Peter of Savoy, resolutely to enfeoff the grandson.[52] Henry might direct, but it was not so simple up in Richmondshire or indeed at

48 *E.Y.C.*, xi, 328.
49 T.D. Whitaker, *The history and Antiquities of the Deanery of Craven* (London, 1805), 392–7. The story is summarized in the descriptive and illustrated guide to the church, J.E. Wright, *The parish church of St. Michael and All Angels, Linton in Craven* (no publisher, n.d.).
50 *E.Y.C.*, vi, 81–99.
51 *V.C.H. Yorks, North Riding*, i, 234.
52 *Close R. 1242–7*, 524; Holt, *Colonial England*, 326.

court. For Henry's instruction cloaked some devious operations. First, Roald had to promise a fine; the king acquitted him 500m. of this against Peter of Savoy.[53] If this was simply a relief it was in direct contravention of Magna Carta; more probably it was a relief combined with a recognition of his claim as representative grandson. In the same deed Roald resigned the manor of Aldeburgh to the king, saving the knights' fees which his grandfather had held on the day he died. The king then granted the manor to Peter of Savoy for the annual render of a barbed arrow – a highly expensive arrow![54] So Roald had to fend off both his chief lord and the king, or at least buy their support. This may well have helped him in dealing with the cadet claimant, his uncle. Here after five years, he reached a settlement on 13 December 1261 in a bipartite agreement with Roald, son of Roald and Matilda his wife, concluded before Wyschard de Carron, seneschal of lord Peter of Savoy, and many knights of the honour in the abbey of St Agatha the Virgin, near Richmond.[55] The uncle quitclaimed all the lands of Roald the constable saving annual renders totalling 15m. and 1lb pepper, and their tenancies in the manor of Hudswell. He and his wife renounced all claims and agreed to go at Roald's expense to the royal court and there conclude a cyrograph before the justices of the bench. In return Roald fitz Alan conceded, in addition to the annual rent charges and the rights in Hudswell, an annual render of robes. He also agreed that the arrangements should be supervised by the bailiff of Richmond.[56] The whole agreement smacks of tight honorial management. Nevertheless it is clear that the representative claimant, at the cost of large payments to his lord and ultimately the king had won the argument.

I have dealt at length with five cases. They share a common feature. In each one the *casus regis* type of argument was known, but it did little to settle the succession. This was determined by political influence (Mandeville), powerful external concerns (Briouze), family settlement (Quincy), long established division between heiresses (Percy), or an unholy alliance between the chief lord and the royal exchequer (constable of Richmond). These scarcely allowed the argument a free run. However, in one other case of a disputed barony there was such a free run, which despite King John's intervention on the side of the cadet, was settled in favour of the representative, in this case a female. This was the barony of Redbourne, Lincolnshire, disputed by the Crevequers. Their complicated pedigree was discussed by Round and Doris Stenton and the latter leads us through much of the legal action. Reginald de Crevequer acquired the barony through his wife Maud, but died sometime between 1166 and 1172. His son and heir was

---

[53] *Cal. Chart. R.*, i, 535.

[54] *Cal. Chart. R.*, i, 327.

[55] Here Christopher Brooke has kindly pointed out that this must refer to the abbey of Easby, the foundation of Roald the Constable, 1151.

[56] The two cyrographs survive in perfect condition, except for severely damaged or missing seals, in Westminster Abbey Muniments, 1434, for the charter of Roald and Matilda and 1409 for the deed of Roald fitz Alan.

already dead, so the barony went to the younger son Simon. He was dead by 1185; his son, Alexander, was then aged five, so the barony now went to Cecily, daughter of the eldest son. Married to Walter de Neville, she was widowed in 1196–8. In 1201 Alexander, now of age, sued, cleverly going for a *mort d'ancestor*, i.e. his father, Simon, rather than a writ of right. Cecily claimed that he and she were too close of kin for the assize, and when that failed that she was heiress of Maud, her grandmother, who had died seised. The court ordered an enquiry as to whether Maud or Simon had died seised. The result is not recorded but the justices would have discovered that each did. In the end Cecily made her case, it ended in an agreement whereby she retained the barony and Alexander held half a knight's fee by concord made between them when he claimed the whole barony. That was recorded in 1212, a satisfying conclusion to legal actions which ran intermittently for nearly half a century.[57]

Why satisfying? Satisfying, I think, because it represents the common sense solution. Some may have recalled King Alfred who succeeded at a time of crisis as a cadet. This solved the crisis, but it left his son, Edward the Elder, to face the heir of the representative; the result, a bloody civil war which ended only with the death of the claimant.[58] William of Malmesbury had known this.[59] So also did Roger Wendover, who copied it from John of Worcester.[60] They all accorded the claimant Aethelwold the title *Clito*, the Latin for Aetheling, but Wendover gave no hint at all that there might be a parallel between 900–2 and 1199. The analogy was lost, if indeed it had ever been discovered. The plain fact was that to ensure peace and order in a society committed to primogeniture, where bequest of land had not yet taken root, the only orderly procedure was for the property to descend in the senior line and for the cadets to accept second, or third place. Gradually, in the thirteenth century this truth was realized once King John's influence was out of the way.

We are left with some twenty cases, no more, because the genealogical situation which produced them was unusual.[61] A few, not many, concern considerable estates, a knight's fee or more, but the most striking feature is that the majority concern quite small parcels of land, a messuage, how big or valuable that was we can only guess, 7 oxgangs, 3 oxgangs and 64 acres, one oxgang, half an oxgang, one acre and a messuage, a widow's dower of unrecorded size or value, in a single village, and so on.[62] There is very little to show whether these were the litigants' total holding, in most cases probably not. But the

---

[57] The pedigree and the various legal actions are summarised in *Rotuli de Dominabus*, ed. J.H. Round (Pipe Roll Soc., 35, 1913), xxxiv–vi, and *The Earliest Lincolnshire Assize Rolls 1202–1209*, ed. Doris M. Stenton (Lincoln Record Society, 22, 1926), lxxx–lxxxii.

[58] For the most detailed account see Alfred Smyth, *King Alfred the Great* (Oxford, 1995), 401–17.

[59] I am indebted to John Gillingham for reminding me of William of Malmesbury, *G.R.*, i, 197–9.

[60] *Chronica Majora*, ed. H.R. Luard (6 vols., R.S., 1872–83), ii, 435–7.

[61] In order to avoid a clutter of footnotes, the cases are listed in the Appendix below, and reference is made to the cases by number.

[62] Nos. 15, 12, 3, 8, 7, 6.

claimants, whether cadet or representative, were often people of small importance, so small that they cannot be identified elsewhere. In one case the parties
were alleged to be villeins.[63] In two others it was noted of representative
demandants *pauper est*.[64] The arguments of the *casus regis* had filtered well
down the social scale. That is entirely consistent with the spread of literary
knowledge that there had been something fishy about King John's succession.
And this means that the jurors were also well acquainted with the issue, not just
with the facts of a particular case, their official role as the court saw it, but with
the issue in principle. To choose Chris Wykeham's terms, they gossiped, in the
tavern, over the evening fire and perhaps above all in the churchyard after
service. So a jury finds for the children of the older son, because they ought to
inherit, *sicut eis videtur*, a very remarkable finding because the inquiry had been
made on the order of the king and their names were recorded; they ran the risk of
attaint. Even more remarkable they stepped over the boundaries of the particular
to state a principle of succession.[65] One jury may have set the mark for others or
they may all have drawn on a common line of thought. In Wiltshire in 1203
there was a pair of cases in which the findings went to the representatives.[66] In
other actions the *dimisit se* played a part, especially where it was initiated in a
lord's court; this usually ended in favour of the representative.[67] Conversely, the
cadet sometimes called on the notion of the youngest member remaining in the
family house when all his sibs had fled, thus as the *astrarius*, calling on a line of
argument and a moral balance which drew more on the tale of Benjamin than on
any legal principle.[68] So there was a counter to the claim of the representative. In
some cases it proved convincing and was accepted by the court; in some cases it
was common sense, especially where the seniors had established themselves
without impinging over much upon the patrimony.

In this last part I have avoided statistics. I do not accept that it is legitimate to
base statistics on a cohort as small as twenty. There is also one final consideration on which I can do no more than make an assertive statement, or rather ask
a question. Is it likely that the record presents any where near the complete
picture? The records of the court give us only those cases which for one reason
or another, could not be settled without dispute within the family. Many more
would be settled quietly by family arrangements which never reached the courts.
Many more still would not require even that. In the records of the court families

---

[63] No. 9.

[64] Nos. 16, 19.

[65] No. 1.

[66] Nos. 7–8.

[67] Most notably, no. 11.

[68] The term *astrarius* appears only occasionally in *casus regis* type cases. See nos. 14, 16. A more
frequent claim was that a tenant had 'remained in the land' until the ancestor's death and awaited
(*expectavit*) the inheritance. See no. 6. I am grateful to Dr Paul Brand for letting me see his preliminary findings on the *astrarius* or hearth-child. There is very little overlap between his set and my
set for the *casus regis*. On the whole, his are later, but it is perhaps early to attempt to draw conclusions.

are almost always in dispute, especially in the type of case with which I have been dealing. Real life might be different. Consider this: in Michaelmas 1225 a jury, agreed between the parties, reported on the rightful tenure of 40 acres of land in Starston, Norfolk.[69] The story went back a long way. First Robert de Bosco held the land and used it to dower his wife, Mabilia. In the next generation the elder son, Gilbert, confirmed the grant of dower. Mabilia then gave the land to a second son, William, and after her death he continued to hold it with the kind permission of his brother Gilbert (*bene permisit*). Gilbert died and his son Robert continued the arrangement. Robert married Matilda, one of the parties in the later dispute, but William continued to hold the land for ten years after the marriage. He then fell into old age and put himself in the custody of his nephew Robert along with the land. So we have a peaceful family arrangement lasting for three generations. But when Robert died his wife Matilda entered upon the land – unjustly, so the jury reported. The decision was clear: the heirs of William were to have seisin and after some delay they got it. Matilda was in mercy. A common enough story, we may think, but for my present purposes the point of it is this: how should we know of these kindly family arrangements if in the third generation Robert's widow had not challenged them?

List of cases

Note: The defining element in a *casus regis* action is the existence of an elder child, now defunct, intervening between the decedent and the grandchild or his heirs. There are several cases where the existence of such a senior, or the date of his/her death, is not proven by the record and is therefore in doubt. These cases, some of which have been used by other scholars, are excluded. The list therefore provides a minimal list of certainties. I am indebted to Professor Milsom and Dr Paul Brand who have contributed to the list at various stages, some long ago.

In order to avoid encumbrance the references are usually to the main action where the argument or the pedigree is fully stated. In certain cases reference is also made to previous discussion in *Colonial England*. The list is arranged in chronological order; it ends at 1250 with *Curia Regis Roll*, xix, which was still in typescript when I completed work; I have been able to use it through the kindness of Dr David Crook of the Public Record Office.

References to Holt and Milsom are to J.C. Holt, *Colonial England, 1066–1215* (London, 1997); and to S.F.C. Milsom, *The Legal Framework of English Feudalism*, Cambridge Studies in Legal History (1976).

1. 1198–1200: *Vautort v Vautort* (*Rot. Curiae Regis*, ii, 189): demandant, heirs of representative, in custody of Hubert de Burgh: re land and advowson in Shepperton: jury find for demandant, with the statement that sons in the elder

---

[69] *Cur. Reg. R.*, 1075, further elaborated in 1077.

line are the heirs *ut eis videtur*. Annotated: *Notandum quod hec inquisicio facta fuit per preceptum domini Regis non per considerationem curie vel secundum consuetudinem regni* (Holt, *Colonial England*, 318–19; Milsom, 175–6n.).

2. 1199: *Lanvallei v le Bret* (*Cur. Reg. R.*, i, 72): demandant, cadet: re 5 hides in Abington, Cambs: tenant defends by alleging that demandant had elder brother who had sons who are the nearer heirs; demandant accepts this but alleges son of elder bro. conceded by charter in court of count of Brittany. Tenant goes *sine die*. (Milsom, 110n.)

3. 1199: *Bodenham v Travele* (*Rot. de Ob. et Fin.*, pp. 30–31, *Cur. Reg. R.* , i, 125): demandant, cadet: re 3 oxgangs and 64 acres in Bodenham, Heref.: fine for inquisition on pedigree made before John landed in England, 25 May 1199, but brought to king 29 May, i.e. two days after coronation: finding to be reported to the king. No result.

4. 1199–1205: *Daventry v Daventry* (*Rot. Curiae Regis*, ii, 134; *Cur. Reg. R.*, ii, 134): demandant, representative nephew: re 14 oxgangs and appurtenances in Daventry, Northants: demandant claims that his father, now dead, was in seisin as result of *dimisit se:* tenant countered that father died before grandfather who therefore died in seisin and to whom, as his son, he is *apparens heres* (Milsom, 147–8).

5. 1200, 1211: *Ros v Ros* (*Cur. Reg. R.*, i, 187; vi, 134–5): demandant, representative: re two knights' fees in Farningham, Kent: cadet tenant, third of four brothers, performed homage and paid relief to chief lord, but fined with custodian of representative, resigning claim in return for life tenancy and rent of 100/- p.a. Fourth brother later succeeded *per preceptum regis*, but representative countered with record of fine. Judgement for representative, 1211: cadet in mercy (Holt, *Colonial England*, 319–20).

6. 1201: *Sot v Walter nephew of Philip* (*Pleas before the King or his Justices*, ii, nos. 484, 528): demandant, representative: re one acre and a messuage in Helston, Cornwall: tenant claims that on death of Philip, his eldest brother he remained in the land as his heir and seeks view of court on whether he or Walter are the next heir. Adjourned *sine die* because judgement is pending by will of the king.

7. 1203: *Roger the clerk v Adam of Stawell* (*Cur. Reg. R.*, ii, 197–8, 293): demandant, cadet: re one oxgang in Ebbesborne, Wilts: *Mort d'ancestor* on Anger, bro. of Roger: Jury find that Anger did not hold in fee and had an elder bro., now dead, who has surviving sons and daughter who are nearest heirs: judgement for Adam, who is presumed one of these: Roger in mercy for false claim.

8. 1203: *Agatha and Agnes, ds. of Walter v Brichtmer Norensis and Robert the Englishman* (*Cur. Reg. R.*, ii, 98–9, 295): demandants, cadets: re half oxgang in 'Sumerfeld', Wilts: jurors find that Agatha and Agnes are not nearest heirs because they had an elder sister, who had a daughter, who still survives. Title of Brichtmer and Robert seems to derive from her. No judgement recorded.

9. 1204: *Sunniva v Reginald Basset* (*Pleas before the King or his Justices*, iii, 905, 959): cadet sister, seeking v lord: re one oxgang in Scagglethorpe, Yorks: lord counters that she had an elder bro. who had sons who have greater right: also claims that she, the dead bro. and elder bro. are his villeins.

10. 1214: *Danville v Danville* (*Cur. Reg. R.*, vii, 142–3; Milsom, p. 148): demandant, cadet: re advowson of church of Langton Matravers in Purbeck, Dorset: father sought bride for elder son in household of lord (earl of the Isle), who refused because succession uncertain: bride granted following *dimisit se* which ensured son's succession: later differences led to a return of half the holding to father: cadet claims father retained capital messuage and advowson and that he holds what his father held. Judgement: representative granddaughter and husband retain advowson.

11. 1214: *Dunmere v Dunmere* (*Cur. Reg. R.*, vii, 117–18): demandant, cadet: re one knight's fee in Penselwood, Som: sues *mort d'ancestor* on death of Agnes his mother: Agnes had executed *dimisit se* with chief lord in favour of grandson: assize stayed when demandant accepts that tenant was son of elder bro. and was seised of the land: demandant allowed an alternative action. None recorded (Holt, *Colonial England*, 320).

12. 1224: *Amundeville v Amundeville* (*Bracton's Note Book*, no. 230): demandant, representative: re 7 oxgangs in 'Wlfus', Rutland: demandant claims to hold whole fee of grandfather, and that tenant put in while he (demandant) was in custody of Thomas Basset. No result recorded.

13. 1224–5 *Richard son of Roger v Agnes d. of Brian* (*Cur. Reg. R.*, xi, 2033, *Bracton's Note Book*, ii, 689n.): demandant, representative: re 30 acres in Benfleet, Essex: he argues that right descended to him through eldest son. Tenant counts that eldest son 'non expectavit mortem patris' and that her father, Brian entered into the inheritance. Demandant then maintains that eldest son died on the morrow of the grandfather, thereby evading the *casus regis* argument. No result recorded.

14. 1234–9: *Hose v Hose* (*Cur. Reg. R.*, xv, 1409; xvi, 605, 959): demandant, representative niece: re three knights' fees in Harting, Sussex, and other lands: demandant argues that right descended to her father 'ut filio suo primogenito et heredi'; tenant counters that she had no claim because father died prior to grand-father; he claims as 'astrarius et qui expectavit hereditatem patris sui et fuit cum